Principles and Practices of Organizational Performance Excellence

Also available from ASQ Quality Press

The Quality Toolbox
Nancy R. Tague

Success Through Quality: Support Guide for the Journey to Continuous Improvement
Timothy J. Clark

Root Cause Analysis: A Tool for Total Quality Management
Paul F. Wilson, Larry D. Dell, and Gaylord F. Anderson

Mapping Work Processes
Dianne Galloway

Quality Quotes
Hélio Gomes

Let's Work Smarter, Not Harder: How to Engage Your Entire Organization
in the Execution of Change
Michael Caravatta

The Change Agents' Handbook: A Survival Guide for Quality Improvement Champions
David W. Hutton

Understanding and Applying Value-Added Assessment: Eliminating Business Process Waste
William E. Trischler

To request a complimentary catalog of ASQ Quality Press publications,
call 800-248-1946.

Principles and Practices of Organizational Performance Excellence

T.J. Cartin

ASQ Quality Press
Milwaukee, Wisconsin

Principles and Practices of Organizational Performance Excellence
Thomas J.Cartin

Cartin, T. J. (Thomas J.), 1924–
    Principles and practices of organizational performance
excellence / Thomas J. Cartin
      p.   cm.
    Includes index.
    ISBN 0-87389-428-6 (alk. paper)
    1. Total quality management. 2. Industrial management.
3. Industrial productivity—Management. I. Title.
HD62. 15. C3639 1999

658.4'--dc21   98-42726
                                                     CIP

10 9 8 7 6 5 4 3 2 1

ISBN 0-87389-428-6

Acquisitions Editor: Ken Zielske

Project Editor: Annemieke Koudstaal

Production Coordinator: Shawn Dohogne

ASQ Mission: The American Society for Quality advances individual and organizational performance excellence worldwide by providing opportunities for learning, quality improvement, and knowledge exchange.

Attention: Bookstores, Wholesalers, Schools and Corporations:

ASQ Quality Press books, videotapes, audiotapes, and software are available at quantity discounts with bulk purchases for business, educational, or instructional use. For information, please contact ASQ Quality Press at 800-248-1946, or write to ASQ Quality Press, P.O. Box 3005, Milwaukee, WI 53201-3005.

To place orders or to request a free copy of the ASQ Quality Press Publications Catalog, including ASQ membership information, call 800-248-1946. Visit our web site at http://www.asq.org.

Printed in the United States of America

  Printed on acid-free paper

American Society for Quality

ASQ

Quality Press
611 East Wisconsin Avenue
Milwaukee, Wisconsin 53202
Call toll free 800-248-1946
http://www.asq.org
http://standardsgroup.asq.org

Dedication
To my wife who has supported all my writing efforts.

Contents

List of Figures

Preface

QUALITY, PRODUCTIVITY, AND MANAGEMENT

Organization success today and for the foreseeable future depends on the views and actions of management. One recurrent management action in the leading U.S. international companies has been to implement some form of improvements for quality and productivity, and with them the adoption of continuous improvement and customer satisfaction as the organization's operating focus. It is well exemplified by a quote by the CEO of Corning Company, in their 1997 annual report:

> Contributing to profitability is our relentless focus on continuous improvement in our manufacturing operation. This effort is fueled by a Manufacturing Effectiveness Council that crosses all organization boundaries and uses goal sharing incentive programs for all employees, innovative auditing processes, and internal and external benchmarking to drive results. Factory gross margins have risen seven percentage points over the past four years, largely as a result of these activities.

That paragraph is a bird's eye view of what this book is all about; it also reflects the results of an organization's following the modern road map to improvement.

Modern management is under constant pressure from shareholders and the financial community to improve performance in both the short and long run. Companies adopting a customer-focused and continuous improvement policy have been able to meet that relentless pressure—even with the often conflicting short- and long-term objectives. It isn't easy because their is no quick solution. It requires management knowledge and skills that are fundamentally different from the traditional style. Success today requires a much greater leadership component in "managing."

A systematic approach is a transformation of the workplace, being driven by the transformation of competitive objectives in the marketplace. However, in spite of the evidence, many managers appear to be unconvinced that a systematic, improvement-focused management is necessary and pays large dividends.

Quite a few organizations say they have tried the new way to manage and it didn't work very well. However, since thousands of organizations have been successful, it is likely that those who failed didn't do it properly. More specifically, management didn't understand what the change would entail and likely didn't want to make the personal commitment required. It was a failure of management—not the principles involved. Frequently management tried to use pieces of the methodology and couldn't make it

Custom

work. It wanted quick results. The June 1998 issue of the AS magazine *Quality Progress* contained an article describing the results of a survey to identify the main causes of total quality management (TQM) implementation failures. (The major component of organization improvement methodologies is TQM in some form.) Sixty-five percent of the managers responding said that failure was due to the fact that meeting improvement objectives was not tied to management compensation. Managers, like everyone, respond to the real reward payoffs. Any other stated management objectives become ambiguous, if not hypocritical, to employees. A systematic, continuous approach to quality and quality improvement is the only effective option.

This book is an evolution from the author's *Principles and Practices of TQM.* The technique *called* TQM has become less attractive to management because it is considered too narrow and parochial. Also, TQM did not emphasize financial measures, which reduced management interest. As a result, organizations have invented their own names, such as the popular one, Six Sigma. Two elements in particular discussed in *Principles and Practices,* have become more attractive as management objectives in satisfying the customer and in becoming more competitive—a systematic focus on both quality and productivity. These focusses are the emphasis of this book, but TQM principles and practices are still the foundation of system improvements.

Over the nine years since the writing of *Principles and Practices,* a few new tools and techniques have been developed (process mapping and total productive maintenance), as well as the implementation of international standards and quality/performance awards worldwide. These subjects are discussed.

Principles and Practices of Organizational Performance Excellence is still presented in two parts, with new and updated material as well as more examples and study questions to stimulate deeper understanding and insights.

Part I, chapter 1, is a discussion of quality fundamentals. The material is the foundation for developing the principles and practices in subsequent chapters. Chapter 2 emphasizes the critical role of management commitment and leadership in organization change. Chapter 3 expands the coverage in *Principles and Practices* of managing through employee empowerment, which is the way to tap the knowledge and commitment of employees.

Chapter 4 describes the relationships that must be developed to achieve the desired goal of customer satisfaction. Chapter 5 discusses the factors involved in organization planning and the role of quality in that activity. Chapter 6 identifies the relationship and need for a systems approach in process improvement. It also discusses the basis for reengineering.

Supplier management is a major element in quality and productivity improvement, and chapter 7 has been expanded to include partnerships and strategic alliances. Chapter 8, quality costs, covers the fundamentals of the most basic organization measurement, cost.

Study questions follow each chapter. The five chapters in Part II contain the basics of the key quality improvement tools and techniques. The new material includes international quality standards (ISO) and an overview of the essentials in quality and improvement awards, national and international.

Finally, a glossary of terms has been added to aid in communicating the language of improvement. Appendices included are Deming's 14 points for managing. Following this is a list of Internet Web Sites on the subject of quality.

PART I

Chapter 1

Quality and Productivity Fundamentals

- **The History, Evolution, and Essential Elements of Quality**
- **Quality and the Marketplace**
  Limitations
- **Quality and Society**
- **Quality and Productivity**
- **Definitions of Quality**
  Total Quality Management
- **Common Terms**
- **Variation and Statistical Control**
  Process and Quality Improvement
  Process Variation and Statistical Control
  Variation Measures
  Process Dynamics
  Variation and Statistical Thinking
  Variation Basics
  Control
  Statistical Control
- **Trends in Quality Management**
- **References**

THE HISTORY, EVOLUTION, AND ESSENTIAL ELEMENTS OF QUALITY

The 1990s have been a period of rapid, even revolutionary change for organizations worldwide and a challenging period for management and employees. From a historical perspective, the rate of change reflected in such fundamental political and business market factors as the sudden end to the "Cold War," the development of a world economy and competition in worldwide markets, and new technologies and information systems is difficult to fully comprehend. When so many factors change so rapidly, management and organizations have little time to plan their responses. They are too busy just coping day-to-day. In response to these external changes there was a revolution of sorts internally. Management philosophy, practices, the role of employees, and organization structure changed. The most significant modification was the implementation of some form of total quality management (TQM). It was a new way to manage, radically different from management theories followed for decades.

Any long-practiced human behavior and beliefs are difficult to change, even when the benefits of the change are intellectually apparent. Change invokes insecurities—in some people, a sense of loss. People and thereby their organizations resist change, unless there is an external threat such as serious competition. This is the prime motivation for changing management style and practices.

Japan was the first nation to adopt "high quality" as a major objective for its industries. This quality objective was selected after the devastation of the country in WW II as a strategic means to get back into the world marketplace, which at the time was totally dominated by the United States. The United States had a big advantage. It had not suffered any damage to its industries and had actually increased its production capabilities to unprecedented levels. Industries could therefore convert quickly from war materials to business and consumer goods. In addition to recognizing that products with very high quality would be an entrée into world markets, Japan had to overcome its prewar reputation for producing cheap, low-quality products. To achieve that quality goal, the Japanese listened to the teachings of the Americans, Dr. Deming and later Dr. Juran, whom they had solicited for ideas to help them recover. The essence of the message from Deming and Juran was that higher-quality products and services make an organization more competitive by lowering costs, raising productivity, and satisfying the customer. Greater profits and market share are the reward. Deming also emphasized that higher quality is achieved by process control, for example, reducing process variation by using statistical quality control charts and other quality problem-solving tools, not by dependence on inspection, the U.S. practice.[1]

The Japanese openly attribute much of their subsequent success to following the Deming prescription. His work was recognized by the establishment of the annual Japanese Deming Application Prize for quality achievement, first awarded in 1956. Winning it requires a significant effort by an organization. Applicants must demonstrate, using data and statistical analysis techniques, that quality effort made a significant improvement. Highly sought after by Japanese organizations, it is an international award and has been won by an American company, Florida Power and Light.

The Deming philosophy was successful in Japan because of the lectures he gave to top industrial leaders. Once they understood the value of statistical process control (SPC), they introduced it into their companies. The Japanese concentrated on prevention; controlling the process rather than making defectives that would have to be sorted using inspection.

Since about the 1940s, quality has been a well-established activity in U.S. industrial organizations. Quality control (QC) amounted to operating an internal organization, a production police, that functioned to compare production output to standards established by product designers, and to accept or reject the output accordingly. These standards were the specified product attributes such as dimensions, tolerances, and performance limits. The American idea for controlling quality was to use inspection to prevent shipping defective material to customers. (It is still a common practice.) Process control tools such as SPC were rarely used.

Another weakness in the old QC philosophy, versus what is being done now, was the assignment of responsibility for quality to the QC organization, not to the people doing the work. Today the organization quality manager is responsible for developing and managing the quality system, a more effective and value-added activity.

The Japanese did not develop the principles of SPC. They were well documented and understood by many quality control managers in the United States, but were little understood by general managers or engineers (many still don't understand them). SPC wasn't a part of their education or experience. They didn't understand its power in managing work as a process. They didn't think in terms of process variation. Work was managed through highly autocratic, vertically organized functional organization elements—production, marketing, finance, and the like—even though the real process for doing work was across functional organization boundaries. Each function had its own special interests, and boundaries became barriers. No one was responsible for the real process; it wasn't even identified. (Process was a term used in production, but it included only the equipment and people working directly on the products.)

This boundary problem was recognized to some extent in the late 1940s, and management used organization structure to help. The added structure was (is) called program or project management. It was developed to manage large, multicompany products (not organizations) through design, development, and production. Large construction projects used a project management concept of sorts but didn't have the management planning and control tools such as those developed for building the first atomic-powered submarine. Moreover, project management isn't a panacea; it has its own organization limitations. Its main purpose is to get a product completed by the functional organizations, on time, within cost plans. In that sense, it is single-task oriented. A project pushes work across boundaries, with some resistance from the independent functional specialties, particularly when there is more than one project demanding their resources. In a sense, it recognizes that work is performed across organization boundaries. But, it did not progress to the point of managing those processes; the functional organizations remained dominant.

In a more limited scope of application, project management methodologies have been adapted to the improvement of team task management. The project is the improvement objective, and the team is working on the problem. Using project management techniques helps teams, which frequently include employee members from different functional organizations.[2] Bringing such diverse members together as a team, with an objective, also reduces organization boundary barriers. (These factors are discussed later.)

Japan was the first to move into a broader quality concept, initiating companywide quality control (CWQC), and using QC concepts in every kind of organization.[3] This changed the emphasis from maintenance and conformance (QC), to prevention and improvement. Also, customer needs and expectations—particularly quality, price, and timeliness—became a part of the improvement equation. Adjusting to CWQC also forced management to recognize that quality improvement was a top management responsibility. It was the genesis of TQM—a systems approach.

As long as U.S. business dominated the world markets from the 1940s to the 1980s, there was little incentive for management to change. However, in the late 1970s it became apparent that Japanese products such as autos and electronics were steadily increasing world market share. Investigation whereby thousands of U.S. managers visited Japanese companies disclosed that customer acceptance was due to the higher quality, higher reliability, and lower cost of their products. The Japanese companies also benefited by competing another way: Their productivity was high and product development time shorter, resulting in a shorter cycle time. This further reduced costs and added a capability to respond quickly to market changes.

There were several theories about how the Japanese did it. One early idea was that it was due to the use of quality circles. As a result, many U.S. businesses started them, looking for a quick way to catch up to the Japanese. Most didn't survive long. Inserting a "participative" tool into an autocratic organization doesn't work because management still makes all the decisions; the culture doesn't change. It was a typical American mechanistic approach. Circles were only one element in a totally different management philosophy, and the total philosophy had to be understood.

Another commonly expressed reason for the ability of Japanese companies to make employees a part of the improvement process was their culture. It was said that they were more disciplined and could work together better. American workers weren't like that, so it wouldn't work in the United States. However, Japanese companies proceeded to buy American companies and to build divisions of Japanese-based companies in the United States and produced the same or even higher-quality products, using American workers.

This different philosophy is what is most commonly called, in the United States, total quality management. Many writers and other experts have called it by different names, for example, Six Sigma, organization improvement, a search for excellence, total customer satisfaction, and so forth. Many businesses adopt it and coin their own titles, to give it a "home grown" identity, but an examination of those program elements reveals that they are variation's of TQM.

QUALITY AND THE MARKETPLACE

A driving force behind modern organizations' effort to become more competitive is the demand of the global marketplace for high quality, competitive prices, and faster delivery of products and services worldwide. The reference to a "global market" is a commonly used phrase. It is more than businesses selling their products and services—it's bigger and more fundamental.

The global markets are the most powerful force the world has ever seen, even capable of obliterating governments almost overnight. The world elimination of barriers to trade and capital, and the rise of communication technologies, have created the global financial marketplace, which informed observers hailed for bringing private capital to the developing world, encouraging economic growth and democracy. . . . They are beyond the control of any government or regulator.[4]

This "force" can quickly impact all levels of business. The Asian currency crisis in 1998 is a good example. All kinds of businesses lost markets overnight. It is one reason for organizations to become flexible, self-learning, and able to respond quickly to change.

Reduced government spending and privatization of some activities have also increased competition within government and education organizations. Here, too, using a systems approach to higher quality has lowered costs and improved productivity and effectiveness.

The common elements in all these programs are that the organization focus has to be on customer satisfaction, the effort must involve most employees, and there must be a policy of continuous development and improvement in how the organization operates and delivers its products and services.

In addition to these management philosophy and methodology changes, the modern marketplace requires a different business approach. Instead of the older first objectives of maximizing profit and price, current objectives must recognize that profits are a result of satisfying the customer. This is the policy of the world's leading companies.

Establishing prices has always been risky, and it has frequently involved an educated guess as to what the market will bear. It must be based on

$$\text{Cost} + \text{Desired Profit} = \text{Price}$$

Even when a business has a virtual monopoly, that is, a unique product or patent protection, the desired price is often not obtainable. Customers will buy a substitute or do without it. Also, to maintain profit, businesses have focused on cost-cutting methods such as staff reduction. This often has adversely affected quality and thereby customer satisfaction. The result is a constant juggling of the two factors.

With the recognition that growth and survivability require the primary focus to be satisfying customer needs and expectations, price has to be based on

$$\text{Existing Market Price} - \text{Costs} = \text{Profits}$$

Low cost is still a basic factor, but it must be attained without a reduction in quality. It has been proved that the new methodologies provide that objective.

Limitations

The process management, customer focus approach has its limitations. Successfully implementing TQM is not a panacea for satisfying all organization objectives, but it is a powerful aid to doing so. It can't change outside influences. If there is a world oil crisis for example, as in 1974, and a business using TQM makes luxury, low-gas-mileage cars, it could still develop some survival problems. Business always involves the risk that unknown or unpredictable factors can impact organization health. This risk has increased with the globalization of competition. But, a flexible, quick-reacting organization is better poised than a functionally organized traditional one.

QUALITY AND SOCIETY

Broadly speaking, the evolution of quality in industry has been from only meeting engineering or customer requirements (anything within specification limits is considered high quality) to reducing the variation in all processes—and not only those used directly in product production. The value in variation reduction can be described in monetary terms or in a representative model by Genichi Taguchi: "Quality is the degree of variation from the target (nominal) value."[5] The greater the variation from target the lower the quality. Figure 1.1 shows a product measurement, its upper and lower specification limits, and the output distribution of two processes making the same product. Taguchi selected a parabola to describe the loss function that exists as a dimension/characteristic deviates from the target value. Performance, customer acceptance, or both decrease as an increasing continuous function. This usually doesn't occur suddenly as a dimension passes through a tolerance limit. Taguchi's concept represents the customer's interest rather than that of the production line. But there can be an impact on production costs if there isn't customer acceptance. Narrowing the tolerance limit to get more parts closer to the target value may seem to be one alternative, but it will raise costs even higher. Tighter requirements produce even more out-of-tolerance products if the process isn't improved, if process variation isn't reduced.

An example of quality as a continuous function is the experience of Ford Motor Company with a transmission in the 1980s. The transmission was being manufactured to the same drawings and specifications in the United States and also in Japan by Mazda Motors. Evaluating customer complaints (as any good customer-focused organization must do), Ford found that there were fewer for the Mazda-produced units. The complaints about the Ford units related to the speed at which they shifted; the variation was greater in the Ford units, and some customers didn't like the shift point in their cars. Analyses showed that Mazda's processes produced their parts closer to the nominal, so there was less variation from nominal in the operation of the final assembled transmissions. Ford manufactured to stay anywhere within tolerance limits; they met requirements. With this approach,

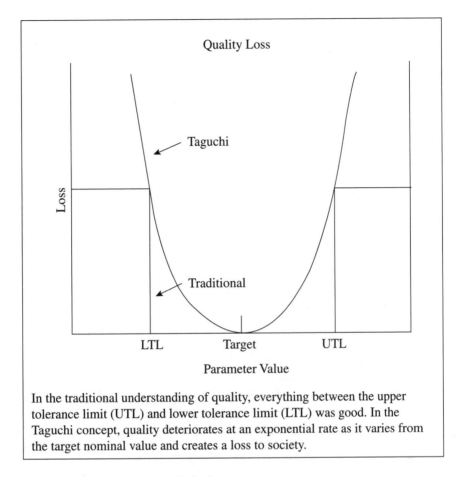

In the traditional understanding of quality, everything between the upper tolerance limit (UTL) and lower tolerance limit (LTL) was good. In the Taguchi concept, quality deteriorates at an exponential rate as it varies from the target nominal value and creates a loss to society.

Figure 1.1 *Quality, variation, and the loss concept.*

parts at opposite extremes of their tolerance range would go together but result in a greater variation in the final assembly, and thereby shift speed. This example also illustrates another of Taguchi's definitions of quality: "Quality is the loss imparted to society." At first sight this is a rather confounding definition. Taguchi is stating that *any* variation from nominal creates a loss, and that the loss increases with the degree of deviation. The loss can be expressed in monetary value. It can be composed of the loss of business as a result of customer dissatisfaction, the loss to the producer for warranty costs, or the loss to the customer from repair costs. Reducing variation reduces these costs: Products work better and longer. The same concept can be applied to service quality. A wide variation in service quality reduces customer satisfaction.

QUALITY AND PRODUCTIVITY

It has been a frequently accepted axiom in industrial management that there is a fixed relationship between cost, schedule, and quality. It can be represented by an equilateral triangle.

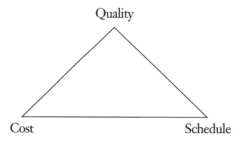

The belief is that the three factors have to be kept in balance, that if one changed they all would change. This idea has contributed to the lack of improvement in quality as an organization-wide effort. Moreover, there has been some hypocrisy in the actual practice of this "axiom" in that management frequently cut cost and shortened schedule regardless of the effect on quality. For industry, the axiom is misleading. It was based on the notion that higher quality costs more. This wasn't challenged because quality had a narrow definition. In industry, higher quality was equated with tighter tolerances. Workers would have to take more time, and more costly inspection (QC) would be needed. What neither manufacturing nor quality management considered was the concept of controlling products by controlling process variation, a means to prevent poor quality, to lower costs, and to improve schedule.

The standards of the marketplace now demand high quality and lower costs to compete. Also, the true relationship between quality, cost, and schedule has been more usefully defined. Higher quality raises productivity.

For any activity the following relationships exist

$$\text{Productivity(P)} = \frac{\text{Output}}{\text{Input}} \frac{\text{(cost of goods or service)}}{\text{(cost of input)}}$$

Productivity is the efficiency measure of an effort. It can be measured at any level, macro or micro—at the total organization level or for one task (if the proper costs are available).

A model that could apply to manufacturing activities, issuing purchase orders or selling hamburgers, is

$$P = \frac{\text{Number of items}}{\text{Cost to produce}} \frac{\text{(finished, sold)}}{\text{(labor + material + capital + expenses)}}$$

Quality is a factor in productivity since errors and defects anywhere in an organization require extra labor and frequently material—and often capital—to correct. These costs would not be required if defects were minimized. Therefore poor quality adds extra operating costs to the input and lowers productivity.

In symbolic terms:

$$\text{Total output}(O) = \text{Output with}(Qo) + \text{Output nonquality}(qo)$$
$$O = Qo + qo$$

$$\text{Input} = (RO) + (ro)$$
$$\text{Where: } Ro = \text{resources to produce } Qo$$
$$ro = \text{additional resoures required to produce } qo$$

So that:

$$P = \frac{Qo}{(Ro + ro)}$$

and $Pmax = \dfrac{Qo}{Ro}$

Also, with no (qo), schedule capability is increased since the resources that were used are available to make conforming output (Qo).

Total productivity can also be significantly improved by technological innovation and mechanization. In the United States, about 15 percent of the labor is direct factory work. It is projected to decline to about 10 percent by the year 2000. Similar reductions have happened in agriculture, where less than 5 percent of the labor force produces more food than the 40 percent it took many years ago. (Nonindustrial societies still employ most of their workers in agriculture.) About 25 percent of the total industrial labor force is professional, technical, clerical, and managerial; the rest comprises other support jobs. The service sector of the U.S. economy employs more people than industry or agriculture. These are fertile areas for productivity improvement through process quality improvement.

Productivity in the service sector is frequently more difficult to measure, and therefore to systematically improve. There are many unpredictable variables in service operations and in the demands of the customer, which make these processes more difficult to control and modify. Many elements of the service sector involve paper transactions. Productivity gains have been made mainly by process simplification and using the latest technology, for example, more electronic data transfer (less mail), bank automatic teller machines. The quality impact of those techniques has not been systematically studied, but past experience suggests that removing human participation from an ongoing, repetitive process leads to fewer errors.

A study by Huff, Fornell, and Anderson,[6] indicates that a number of characteristics of service firms contribute to a negative productivity and quality relationship.

- It is more difficult for customers to evaluate relative quality for services.

- Services are largely intangible. Strict quality specifications are difficult to set.

- Production and consumption of many services are inseparable. The quality of the production cannot be measured.

- In many services, quality is believed to be inescapably correlated with the amount of labor expended. When customers expect a certain amount of personal attention and interaction, labor cannot readily be replaced without disturbing customer quality perceptions.

Organizations in the service sector vary so much in their methods of organizing and operating that generalizations are not very useful. The relationship between quality and productivity can best be evaluated by limiting the comparison to companies that are alike and in the same market.

DEFINITIONS OF QUALITY

What is quality? A clear definition escapes most people. It is important in the task of improving performance, products, and services that there be a clear and consistent organization understanding of what quality means. Typically, quality is confused with luxury, but they are fundamentally different. Quality relates to perfection and excellence. To customers it is a value used to select products and services. In organizations of all kinds it refers to error-free and defect-free work, products, and services. Other important quality components are dependability, consistency, safety, and meeting the needs of the customer. In Dr. Juran's words, quality is "fitness for use."[7] For example, some low-priced autos are very high quality. They satisfy the criteria above.

Luxury relates more to appearance, status, extra comfort, scarcity, high cost, and sometimes extra performance—attributes that are wanted but not needed.

Table 1.1 lists some of the definitions given by quality experts. There are some significant differences among them. One widely accepted definition of quality has been "conformance to requirements." This means to produce exactly what is specified or ordered, and anywhere within a tolerance is good. The other definition, "fitness for use," brings in the customer. "Conformance" reflects the old QC philosophy of maintenance to standards. "Fitness" says do what has to be done to satisfy the customer. CWQC and TQM grew out of this approach. "Conformance to Requirements" is the minimum necessary in day-to-day operations, but it doesn't provide an organization the objective of achieving continuous improvement in order to become more competitive. It also puts the designer of a product or operator of a service in the position of "telling" the customers, not satisfying what they really want, because the provider sets the requirements. Microsoft Corporation is an example of this, with their computer operating system. They reached such a dominant position that they have a near monopoly. However, rapid technological advances may challenge their position.

There are other simple definitions, such as "delighting the customer," or, "exceeding customer expectations." They capture in a few words what the objectives of a modern organization should be.

TOTAL QUALITY MANAGEMENT

The acronym represents three facets of organization-wide quality management. *Total* represents a management method that involves everyone in the organization—every function and activity and, frequently, suppliers and customers. It is a systematic approach to achieving excellence. Total involvement is a recognition that every activity contributes or detracts from quality and productivity and that the people in those activities (processes) are in the best position to know what needs to be improved. After proper training, they are in the best position to introduce and manage improvements. The common methodology for doing this is by using multifunction teams.

Table 1.1   Common definitions of quality.

Definitions	Source
"Totality of characteristics of an entity that bear on its ability to satisfy stated and implied needs"	1
"Fitness for use"	2
"Conformance to requirements"	3

1. ANSI/ISO/ASQC, A8402-1994, "Quality Management and Quality Assurance Vocabulary."
2. J. M. Juran, *Juran's Quality Control Handbook*, 4th ed. (New York: McGraw-Hill, 1988).
3. P. B. Crosby, *Quality Is Free*, (New York: McGraw-Hill, 1979).

Quality is the characteristic used to measure this management method. It reflects the focus on improvement in the operation of all activities. It requires continuously improved process output so as to be close to the ideal. This results in less variation in products and services, a more satisfied customer, lower costs, and a better competitive position.

Management is the actions involved in applying improvement principles and techniques. It includes both old and relatively new techniques, assembled and applied in a combination more effective than either alone. It is a scientific management method in that it relies on proved, repeatable principles and methodologies. The old management principles were to provide employees with all the instruction and training needed to do a specific job, nothing more. The principles for the 1990s and beyond are to evolve the organization to train employees in process problem solving and improvement techniques, organize them into coherent work teams, provide them with the resources and overall organization objectives, and let them manage their work and processes to meet those objectives.

COMMON TERMS

The following are some terms frequently encountered in quality management language that warrant defining at the outset. More are included in the glossary at the end of the book.

System—A group or work pattern of interacting human and/or machine activities, directed by information, which operate on and/or direct material, information, energy, and/or humans to achieve a common specific purpose or objective.[8]

Process—Any series of connected work tasks or activities. Each has an input and an output. Each has a customer and a supplier. Processes can be internal, or have an external connection to an outside customer or supplier.

Variables—The factors in the operation of a process that affect the output and can be measured to determine performance. A more explicit definition is used in the discussion of some quality control charts.

Variation—The changes in process variables over a period of time. Reducing variation is synonymous with improving a process.

Process Capability—In general, the capability of a process to continuously meet requirements. In relation to variables control charting, it is a statistical measure of how well a process stays within specification requirements to indicate whether or not the process operation is acceptable.

Big Q and Little Q—A terminology resulting from the change in the quality function from a manufacturing orientation (little Q) to the inclusion of all organization activities, products, and services (big Q). Little Q is quality control (QC). Big Q is companywide quality control (CWQC), or TQM.

Multifunction Teams—Improvement teams composed of those representatives of the functional organizations whose work directly impacts the operation of a process.

Cycle Time—A cycle is the time to complete a task or series of tasks, measured from the time of input to the task, or process, to the time of its successful completion. It can be measured at the macro level—from order entry to customer delivery—or it can be a micromeasurement of the time of one process activity.

VARIATION AND STATISTICAL CONTROL

Process and Quality Improvement

What is a process and what is its quality? A process is a task or sequence of tasks, with an input and an output. What does process quality improvement mean? Most simply described, it means the measured reduction in process variation and process task completion time. The most common measurements of these factors are how well production produces close to target, error quantity, and cycle time. For example, in an office activity a defect chart might be used to track a process performance over time (Figure 1.2). The quality objective is zero errors, zero defects. This objective can be approached using the quality improvement tools explained in Part II.

Frequently zero defects is only one of the improvement objectives. Cycle-time improvement is also of great value. It can lower costs and improve competitive position. The improvements shown in Figure 1.3 are obtained by using process mapping, analysis, and other quality improvement techniques.

Process Variation and Statistical Control

It is common in an organization activity or process to make performance decisions based on some kind of data. It may be qualitative (such as on time, late, or too many errors), or it may be quantitative (such as 15 percent over budget, 75 percent yield, or 10 percent improved). Additionally, decisions are made on such things as whether commitments are met, people are performing, or costs are acceptable. Typically, all those conclusions are reached using one-dimensional data. The data may be very accurate, but they are evaluated in relation to standards or objectives based mostly on experience, practices, and what managers have learned to do. The critical missing information for intelligent decision making is, in quantitative terms, how well activities and processes are performing and how actually capable they are of performing as they operate day-by-day. One of Deming's key tenets is to manage using statistical thinking. Without the introduction and understanding of the *statistical* concept of variation

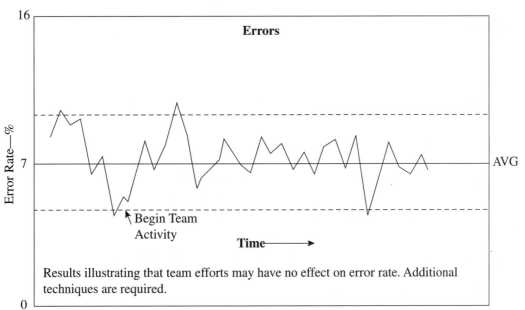

Figure 1.2   *Defect chart used for tracking performance.*

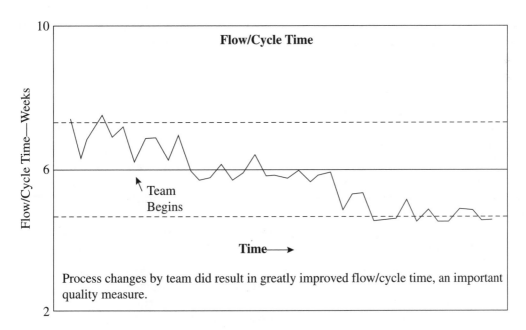

Figure 1.3   *Chart used for tracking improvement.*

applied to operating business processes, the wrong—even counterproductive—decisions may be made. This means recognizing that everything varies, including natural, industrial, office, and service processes as well as individual and combined human actions.

Failure to understand the concept of variation leads to blaming people for failure to perform as a result of their inability to control a process they don't comprehend. Some wrong decisions that result are

- Organization demotivation by looking for scapegoats when the process may be inadequate and causing the problems.
- Making changes assuming that something has gone wrong when it hasn't. The process may be doing it's best, or something unrecognized may have happened to cause unacceptable process variation.
- Purchasing new equipment when it isn't needed, or not purchasing it when needed, because the true cause of a problem is in the process but is not recognized as such.
- Tampering with a process that is working to its capability when the correct action would be to leave it alone. If a process is understood, its behavior can be improved and made predictable.
- Establishing improperly based reward programs. Performance rewards based on improving organization performance are more valuable than those arbitrarily set by management.

In industry, design engineers have recognized that variation exists in product size and performance parameters. They allow for acceptable design variation by putting tolerances on dimensions, for example, cut this piece to a diameter of 1.00+/− .01". In the past, manufacturing did their best with what they had. When a specified tolerance couldn't be held, those parts out of tolerance would end up scrapped, reworked, or in the nonconforming product review cycle. Engineering would then try to change the drawing tolerance to what the shop could actually manufacture—not a very scientific approach, and an expensive way to operate. Quality was often compromised.

What was missing was the knowledge of the measured variation—the capability—of the production process. Few managers were aware either that production variation could be measured or the value of fairly simple statistical methods to measure and aid in its control.

The same lack of understanding about variation and process control has existed in so-called "soft" processes, such as the service industry Here, variation has been even more difficult to analyze because the work systems were not defined as a process. But in fact they are processes and can be measured and improved. Many of the improvement tools discussed in these chapters, including team management, are also applicable to nonmanufacturing processes.

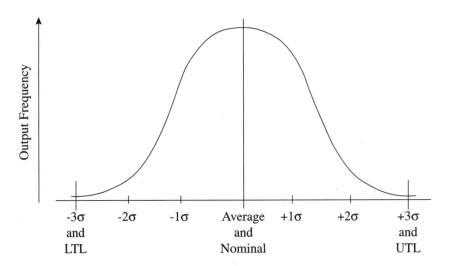

Figure 1.4 *The normal distribution. The output of a controlled process is represented by the normal distribution. Most of the output is near the average of the process output. The output spread is measured in sigma.*

Variation Measures

Sigma (σ) is a statistical measure of variation in a normal distribution.[9] It indicates the amount that a controlled process can be expected to vary from its average performance. Figure 1.4 shows this measurement. The curve, the normal distribution, represents the output variation of a process in control. The horizontal scale is sigma. The characteristics of a process with a normal distribution are such that 99.73 percent of output is contained within the range from –3σ to +3σ. The normal distribution and its characteristics are the foundation of statistical thinking in managing variation. If a process operation displays the distribution as shown in Figure 1.5 (shaded), and the product design specification tolerance limits coincide with the process ±3σ limits, the process is said to have a +/–3σ capability. If, in such a process, the specification limits were ±6σ away from the specification nominal, it would have a 6σ capability (Figure 1.5). Initially, establishing a +/–3σ capability goal is a valuable step. It makes a process minimally capable, and it leads the organization to understand process control variation and the value in managing it.

Process Dynamics

The previous discussion represents the ideal. For operating processes, the 3σ limits rarely correspond to the specification tolerance range. The factors at work in a process are dynamic and, even while remaining in statistical control, cause some shift in the average with respect to the product tolerance nominal. In that case, the ±3σ limits would sometimes fall outside the tolerance limits and the number of nonconformances would increase.

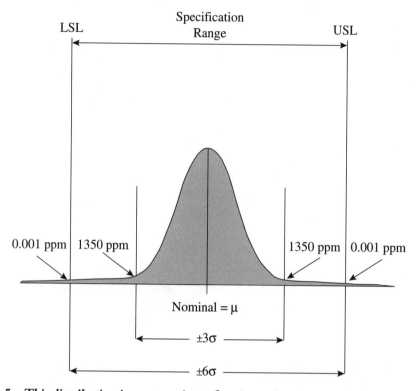

Figure 1.5   *This distribution is a comparison of a ±3σ and ±6σ process capability compared to specification tolerance limits. Also shown are the probable error rates (parts per million) in a 3σ and 6σ process.*

To allow for this shift, the ±3σ operation of the process must be smaller than the tolerance allowance. The capability of the process must provide a safety margin with respect to requirements. Another reason to have a margin is that the sigma calculations are estimates. They are based on samples and the assumption is that their distribution is normal. A common goal is to establish ±4σ as a minimum process capability initially and ±6σ as a long-term objective. If the tolerance limits remain fixed, the only way to improve the capability from ±3σ, ±4σ, or ±6σ is to make improvements that reduce sigma—by reducing process variation.

Variation and Statistical Thinking

The fundamental concept is understanding that variation in every process is a normal condition and that the state of a normal pattern should be the basis for making improvement or problem-solving decisions. If the pattern isn't known, the output can't be managed. Problems of all nature will just pop up.

It is also critical to understand that every process has an inherent capability. A process operating within this capability is doing the best it will ever do unless something in the process (such as the methods or equipment used) is changed. Countless resources are wasted trying to fix a problem in a process output, without the realization that the process is doing its best. It isn't realized that the process doesn't have the capability to meet requirements consistently.

Variation Basics

As Shewhart proved, in the 1930s, a brand new high-precision machine, perfectly set up, repetitively cutting the same diameter on similar pieces of metal, will not produce pieces with exactly the same set diameter. The diameter of every piece will vary, if ever so minutely, around some average dimension. This is the inherent capability of that machine. Shewhart identified these as common causes of variation that define the inherent capability of the machine Such common causes could be temperature variations both within and around the machine or movement of parts within. It would be impossible for every finished diameter to be within a tolerance tighter than the machine's inherent capability.

A nonindustrial example is the time-based variation of product sales in one territory. Another would be the monthly variation in the accounts payable activity. If plotted over time, they would display a pattern of variation around some average value that would represent the normal process behavior.

There are two basic principles of variation for industrial or service processes:

1. All variation is caused.
2. There are four main types of causes:
   a. Common Causes—*Random* shifts in performance due to the nature of the process. They are always present.
   b. Special Causes—Factors that sporadically cause variation, over and above the common causes. They can be identified.
   c. Structural Variation—Systematic changes in output caused by such things as seasonal factors or long-term trends (slow equipment wear).
   d. Tampering—Unnecessary adjustments made to a process in an attempt to compensate for common causes. They drive a process out of control, out of random variation.

It is critical to correctly identify causes present in a process because the appropriate action response is different for each. The wrong action may increase variation.

The alternative to identifying and correcting variation usually results in corrective actions that have no relationship to the actual cause. They are the traditional reaction of management to "do something" when there is a problem. Root cause can be difficult to identify without data or an in-depth understanding and consideration of the process and its natural (random) variation. When only the symptoms are treated, the true cause of variation surfaces elsewhere as another symptom in an endless roller coaster of hide and seek.

Before anyone can understand what variation means and how to control it, one must understand some basic statistical concepts involved in how things vary. It isn't very complicated and can provide a major increase in the power to manage for higher productivity and improved competitive position. Deming stressed that management must address the problems in process performance. The people in problem processes are victims of management ignorance—not the cause of the poor output.

Control

Another way to describe processes varying within their inherent capability (only common causes present) is to refer to them as operating in statistical control, that is, variation around the average is random and within calculated limits. Unless something new affects the process (some factor changes in an unexpected manner), the cost and quality output of a process in statistical control is predictable and constantly within limits. The range of its variation, its limits, can be calculated using simple mathematics. If it goes outside this range, some special cause is at work and can be removed. It's the sample average outside a limit that indicates the special cause presence.

A dramatic example of special causes occurred in the testing of the Salk polio vaccine in 1955 on two million children. The Salk vaccine was a killed polio virus that worked to build immunity to the live virus. One small amount of inadequately inactivated vaccine was distributed. It led to 204 cases of polio and 11 deaths among vaccinated children. Some special cause affected the production process and was not detected.

The value and power of process control knowledge is clear. When in control, you know the process will operate within the limits you establish and continue to do so. If you don't know if a process is in statistical control, it probably isn't, and its output therefore is unpredictable. Taking corrective action to "improve" its output probably won't work.

Statistical Control

When the process is not varying in a random manner, the inherent capability is being affected by something causing the nonrandomness, something not present all the time. If, in the previous example of the cutting machine, a bearing lubricant leaked out and began slowly to fail, the machine variation would likely change. A special, assignable cause would have occurred.

The tool for measuring process variation to gain statistical control (hereafter called "control") is the control chart. This is a chart that displays the process performance, using process output measurement (usually samples) at fixed time periods. The first thing it indicates is whether there are special causes of variation present. The expected statistical range of variation can be calculated once special causes are removed. Maintaining control charts signals when to take action and when to leave the process alone.

Figure 1.6 b shows control charts for sales figures for three regions. It also shows the upper and lower calculated control limits for the process (the different variables at work) in each region. There are three sets of limits, although management set goals as if there was only one. Management sets them each year, not considering what the capability of each region's process actually is. This is a common situation when statistical thinking is missing.

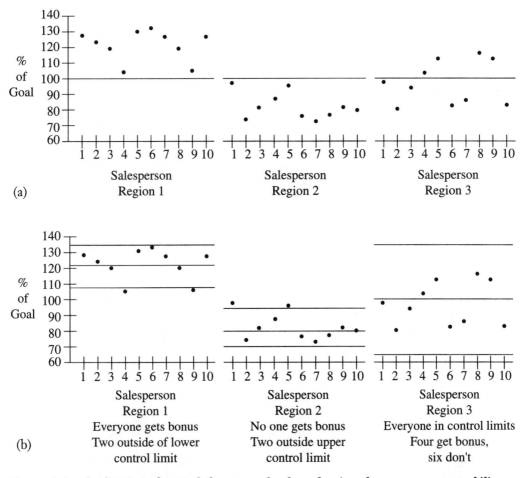

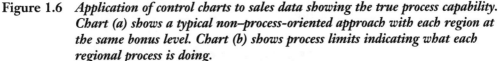

Figure 1.6 *Application of control charts to sales data showing the true process capability. Chart (a) shows a typical non–process-oriented approach with each region at the same bonus level. Chart (b) shows process limits indicating what each regional process is doing.*

Reprinted with permission of Thomas W. Nolan, from his article entitled, "Understanding Variation" (From ASQ *Quality Progress*, May 1990).

In Figure 1.6 a, the upper charts reflect a single bonus level for what is actually three independent processes. Lower charts show the performance in each. If this more rational approach had been used, the bonus awards would pay for above-average performance in the real process participated in by the sales people.

TRENDS IN QUALITY MANAGEMENT

Managing organizations as a system composed of work processes involves people, and evolving economic, political, and socially changing environments. Important trends are:

- The definition of quality will continue to evolve beyond defect-free and customer satisfaction to include corporate citizenship, environmental importance of products and their manufacture, and social responsibility–an increasing demand for excellence.

- The rapid growth and use of information technology and the internet will provide individuals and organizations with a greater quantity of information on product and service quality. This will provide more options for selection and more pressure on suppliers to provide high quality.

- Continued organization development, with reduced hierarchy, managed by self-managed employee teams.

- The continued development and adoption of international standards of quality practices and methodologies.

- Recognition of the need for a systems management approach to quality improvement.

- The growth in the need for knowledge workers will require an increase in quality training for all managers and employees and the inclusion of such education in school ciricular.

- The inclusion of quality factors by most organizations, in strategic planning.

- Further development of techniques for customer satisfaction management.

- The continued growth of quality an productivity improvement applications in a greater diversity of organizations.

- Increased success rate in improvement applications as implementation techniques are improved and managers become more proficient in their use.

- Continued market leadership positions for organizations that successfully implement a policy of continuous quality and productivity improvement, focused on customer satisfaction.

REFERENCES

1. P. J. Kolesar. *What Deming Told the Japanese in 1950* (Milwaukee: ASQ *Quality Management Journal*, 1994).
2. H. Kerzner. *Program Management: A Systems Approach to Planning, Scheduling, and Controlling* (New York: Van Nostrand Reinhold, 1995).
3. S. Siochi. "The Recent Trends in Quality Management in Japan." *The Quality Anniversary Magazine*. International Academy for Quality. (Frankfurt, Germany: 1997).
4. R. C. Altman. "The Nuke of the 90s." *New York Times Magazine*. March 1, 1988.
5. P. J. Ross. *Taguchi Techniques for Quality Engineering* (New York: McGraw-Hill, 1988).
6. L. Huff, C. Fornell, and E. Anderson. *Quality and Productivity. Contradictory and Complementary* (Milwaukee: ASQ *Quality Management Journal*, Vol. 4, October 1996).

7. A. V. Feigenbaum. *Total Quality Control* (New York: McGraw-Hill, 1991).
8. Feigenbaum. *Total Quality Control.*
9. J. M. Juran. and F. M. Gryna. *Juran's Quality Control Handbook*, 4th ed. (New York: McGraw-Hill, 1988).

ADDITIONAL READINGS

Deming, W. E. *The New Economics for Industry, Government, Education*, 2nd ed. Milwaukee: ASQC Quality Press, 1994.

Deter, H. W. *Goldratt's Theory of Constraints: A Systems Approach to Continuous Improvement.* Milwaukee: ASQ Quality Press, 1997.

Dighe, A. and C. Bezold. *Trends and Key Forces Shaping the Future of Quality.* ASQ *Quality Progress*, July 1996.

Harrington, H. J. *Business Process Improvement.* San Francisco: Earnest & Young, L. L. P., 1991.

Joiner, B. L. *Fourth Generation Management.* Madison, WI: Joiner Associates, 1994.

Juran, J. M. *A History of Managing for Quality.* Milwaukee: ASQC Quality Press, 1995.

Micklethwait, J., and A. Wording. *The Witch Doctors: Making Sense of the Management Gurus.* New York: Time Books/Random House, 1996.

STUDY QUESTIONS

1. What is the essential difference between the traditional industrial quality control (QC) and total quality management (TQM)?
2. What changes in emphasis must be made in changing from QC to TQM (or another equivalent improvement program)?
3. Why has higher quality become a major objective in organizations?
4. What is the relationship between quality and productivity?
5. What is total quality management?
6. What did Deming mean by statistical thinking?
7. What is the meaning of statistical control?
8. Discuss the trends in quality management.

Chapter 2

Management and Organization Change

- **The Need for Change**
- **A Different Operating Policy**
- **Management, Organization, and System Improvement**
- **The Role of Management**
- **Managing Change and Innovation**
- **Strategies for Managing Change**
  Leadership
  The Context of Leadership and the Management System
- **Organizations and Change**
- **Change Agents**
- **Conditions for Successful Managerial Innovation**

THE NEED FOR CHANGE

Management and quality experts Deming and Juran, Peter Drucker,[1] Alvin Toffler, and Tom Peters have all said that continued change in organization and management is needed in order to survive. But the degree, nature, and difficulty of the needed changes are frequently not fully understood. As a result, introducing change is very difficult. What is needed is a way to manage that meets modern market needs, which has driven organizations to adopt systems management and improvement. A common perception is that this form of improvement is a formula that people can learn to use without having to change the organization or the way it is managed. They think that it can be layered onto a traditional functional organization. The two are incompatible. It would be the equivalent of trying to manage a college faculty like a business.

Implementing this approach isn't that easy. There have been articles and books written about failures. Deevy, states that 75 percent of TQM and business process reengineering (a TQM-based methodology) efforts fail to deliver on their promises. It is then rejected as just another fad, another buzzword.[2]

Tompkins uses the term *Genesis Enterprise* to describe what an organization has to become in order to be successful, to survive and prosper.[3] The organization continually reaches for higher performance levels by creating a culture that continuously improves relationships with its employees and outside partners (suppliers and customers). Reaching this position requires several basic changes in how organizations operate (further discussed in following chapters)

- Changing from managing to leading
- Shifting organization relationships from individuals to a team process
- Changing the relationships between customers and suppliers, from "outsiders" to partnerships
- Changing the framework of recognition and rewards so they become effective motivators

Deevy's model for the new enterprise constitutes a new social contract between the people who run the business and the people who work for them. He refers to it as "The Resilient Organization." It emphasizes "Rapid Response." Its achievement is based on

1. Shifting from control, to commitment and removing bureaucratic constraints.
2. Developing the ability to cope with the unexpected. This is valued over order and predictability. A mechanistic approach to induce change won't produce these abilities. Also, the organization should respond to the environment and operate accordingly, rather than depend on a bureaucracy to guide it.

Organizations have to be living, adapting, resilient organisms—not mere organization charts.

Senge summarized what is needed:

Historically, upper management in large U.S. companies has avoided direct involvement in managing for quality. Instead, it delegates it, often vaguely, to some subordinate manager. It has now become evident that attaining quality leadership requires that upper management personally take charge of the quality initiative. Such has been the conclusion from a study of what happened in those companies that did attain leadership. In every case, the upper managers took charge. They did not just make speeches and then delegate all else to subordinates. Instead they carried out active roles to

- Serve on the quality council
- Establish the quality goals
- Provide the resources

- Provide the quality-oriented training
- Stimulate quality improvement
- Review progress
- Give recognition
- Revise the award system

Such a forward-looking organization could also be described by the following

- Everyone in the organization working toward the same overall objectives; the same strategic plans; a quality focus deployed.
- The creation of an environment of trust, particularly in the areas of uncertainty, where the future outcomes are not clear.
- The use of participative mechanisms, like teams, to support an attitude of respect for the individual. Teams can provide the stimulus for individual contributions. They can give people a broader outlook and more knowledge and skills to contribute new ideas.[4]

Senge also believes that the organizations that will truly excel will be those that discover how to tap people's commitment and capacity to learn, at all organization levels, faster than their competitors. This kind of learning demands that organizations, and their members, both expect and adapt to change. They are continually enhancing their capability to create the future. One basis for such goals is to reach a shared vision, which is achieved when members see the connection between their task and the overall organization vision. They do this as a community, not as competing individuals.

The ideas of these thinkers describe the initial understanding that must be reached by management of how radical the changes must be to successfully adopt TQM.

A DIFFERENT OPERATING POLICY

Another fundamental difference between traditional management and managing for the future is the adoption of a philosophy and policy of continuous improvement (CI). CI applies to every aspect of organization activity. CI means, literally, that improvement can never stop. Every objective met becomes the starting place for the next improvement objective. Status quo means atrophy. There is no status quo: Markets and competition change too rapidly.

Some managers first encountering the TQM approach, say, "I thought the main business objective was profit and to satisfy the stockholders." That is still the objective, but instead of trying to *manage/push* the enterprise to success, the nature of markets and competition today also requires leadership, with management and employees acting as a knowledgeable, flexible team, dedicated to higher performance and focused on the customer. Profits and return on investment are the result of successfully maximizing those factors.

MANAGEMENT, ORGANIZATION AND SYSTEM IMPROVEMENT

Traditional organizations still have their special responsibilities. Marketing must identify the market changes and customer satisfaction. In an industrial or software enterprise engineering has product design responsibility. Production has to produce what is ordered and usually, a quality assurance organization assesses conformance to requirements and manages the quality system. However, new management methods require all functions to operate quite differently than in the past.

The new methods represent a change from functional-procedures based, to process based management. This statement refers to the traditional management method of establishing systems and procedures that facilitate functional organizations doing the work. That seems very orderly, but work actually gets done by flowing from department to department, across the vertically structured functions. Process management recognizes, and is applied to managing, those processes—a different, more effective way to manage. But it isn't easy. It requires an understanding of the principles and application techniques of the behavioral sciences, quantitative and nonquantitative analysis, economics, and system analysis in order to continuously improve the quality of all activities and relationships.

One way to look at the relationship between the important activities in the new organization is shown in Figure 2.1. Organization activities are integrated differently than in a functional structured organization, and with different objectives. In comparison, Figure 2.2 is a generalized depiction of the typical industrial organization functions used as a basis for managing. Businesses vary widely on how they combine these functional elements to make up their structure.

In the improvement approach, organization work processes are managed to satisfy the customer. In a highly structured functional organization, the specialties operate to satisfy objectives given them by upper management, even though upper management cannot know or specify to each function objectives that will provide the best results for the overall organization. Also what happens is that specialties develop their own objectives (particularly growth and survival). The overall organization really consists of poorly communicating fiefdoms, not always pulling together. Since every organization has limited resources, this practice is wasteful. The overall organization loses sight of its purpose—satisfying the customer.

The ideal organization for the global marketplace is a loosely structured group of self-directed teams, managing their work, improving the work processes, and with a common broad objective of satisfying the customer. Xerox Corp. is an example of what happens when management changes from managing functions to managing the business processes. Several years ago, upper management identified the actual processes that got the work done. Figure 2.3 is a picture of how an organization looks when described by its processes. Also, accountability for performance and improvement was established by assigning a vice president to manage each process.

Another comparison can be made between traditional management and the participative style needed by examining the basic responsibilities of management (which stay the same) of planning, organizing, operating/directing, and controlling, described in any management textbook. This comparison is shown in Table 2.1.

Objective	Philosophy	System Elements	Key Activities
Customer satisfaction	Continuous quality improvements. Reduce variation	Management Commitment Leadership	• Operational or business quality plan • Quality deployment throughout the organization • Management audits to get feedback
		Total participation	• Company-wide involvement • Multi-function improvement teams • Supplier participation
		Internal/external customer	• Every task is a process • Next process is our customer • Customer feedback • Measure customer satisfaction
		Internal/external suppliers	• Align objectives and policies with suppliers • Select Suppliers Using Process Management • Systematic exchange between customers and suppliers
		Systematic analysis	• Common methods by all organization elements • Analyze bad, good, and best • Resources on prevention • Minimize variation • Statistical tools and techniques • Decisions based on facts • External benchmarks

Figure 2.1 *Systems improvement model. The relationship between organization activities and the system.*

General Industrial Functional Organization Top Management	
Staff	**Line**
Management Sales—Marketing Finance Procurement Maintenance Design personnel Project manager	Production line workers Computer operators Customer service Engineers

Figure 2.2 *Functional organization factors are identified by their specialties and are the focus of change. They are sometimes separated into line and staff where line people work in or on the product or service. Staff functions support the lines and report vertically to upper management. Identifying which specialties are line/staff varies with the type of organization, its products and services, and frequently by how costs are collected.*

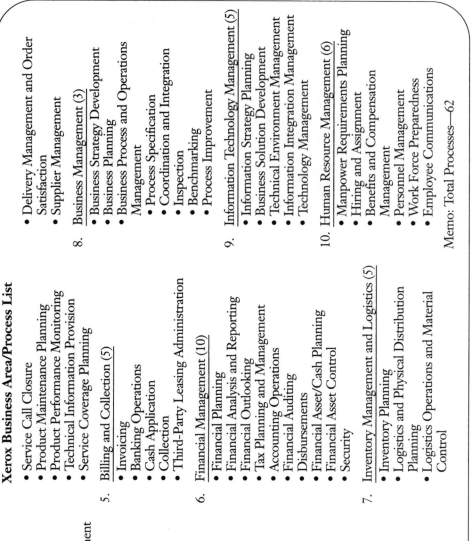

Xerox Business Area/Process List

1. Market Management (7)
   - Market Selection and Analysis
   - Segments and Customer Requirements Understanding
   - Customer Requirements Management
   - Market Planning
   - Marketing Support
   - Marketing Communications
   - Market Tracking

2. Customer Engagement (6)
   - Sales Territory Planning
   - Prospecting Management
   - Enterprise Management
   - Agreement Development
   - Agreement Management
   - Customer Support

3. Order Fulfillment (7)
   - Order Processing
   - Scheduling
   - Customer Preparation
   - Staging and Pre-installation
   - Delivery/Removal
   - Installation/Deinstallation
   - Product Production

4. Product Maintenance (8)
   - Service Call Management
   - Service Dispatching
   - Product Servicing
   - Service Call Closure
   - Product Maintenance Planning
   - Product Performance Monitoring
   - Technical Information Provision
   - Service Coverage Planning

5. Billing and Collection (5)
   - Invoicing
   - Banking Operations
   - Cash Application
   - Collection
   - Third-Party Leasing Administration

6. Financial Management (10)
   - Financial Planning
   - Financial Analysis and Reporting
   - Financial Outlooking
   - Tax Planning and Management
   - Accounting Operations
   - Financial Auditing
   - Disbursements
   - Financial Asset/Cash Planning
   - Financial Asset Control
   - Security

7. Inventory Management and Logistics (5)
   - Inventory Planning
   - Logistics and Physical Distribution Planning
   - Logistics Operations and Material Control
   - Delivery Management and Order Satisfaction
   - Supplier Management

8. Business Management (3)
   - Business Strategy Development
   - Business Planning
   - Business Process and Operations Management
     - Process Specification
     - Coordination and Integration
     - Inspection
     - Benchmarking
     - Process Improvement

9. Information Technology Management (5)
   - Information Strategy Planning
   - Business Solution Development
   - Technical Environment Management
   - Information Integration Management
   - Technology Management

10. Human Resource Management (6)
    - Manpower Requirements Planning
    - Hiring and Assignment
    - Benefits and Compensation Management
    - Personnel Management
    - Work Force Preparedness
    - Employee Communications

Memo: Total Processes—62

Information furnished by Xerox Corp.

Figure 2.3 *Xerox business area/process management list.*

Table 2.1   TQM and the classical factors in management.

Common Factors	Related TQM Factors	New Improvement Tools
Planning	Strategic quality planning • Customer focus • Quality objectives • Quality policy deployment Operational • Employee empowerment • Error/waste prevention • Process variation reduction • Supplier quality improvement	Customer surveys Quality function deployment 7 Management tools 7 QC tools Benchmarking Baldrige award criteria
Organizing	Process definition and ownership Multifunctional teams Mangement quality council Simpler management structure	7 QC tools Process mapping Team development
Operating/ Directing	Continuous process improvement Supplier quality management Concurrent engineering Team management	7 QC tools Benchmarking Design of experiments Just-in-time
Controlling	Data-based decisions Continuous process improvement	Statistical process control Quality costs

The traditional approach to fulfilling these responsibilities has been by using top-down management direction (command and control). The skills and methods to complete work were those of the special functional organizations; they decided the how and what. The process management methodologies are quite different. The emphasis is on people (as a community), customers, and continuous improvement in getting the normal work of the organization completed. Also, for the first time there is a common tool kit, most of which is useable by all organization elements, particularly in team efforts, in meeting quality improvement objectives. This commonality is also a valuable aid in communications.

THE ROLE OF MANAGEMENT

It is the prime responsibility of top management to ensure the health and survival of an organization. In organizations that are not functioning effectively—that is, not competing—management must identify what has to be done and then adopt the leadership role to induce the necessary changes. This has proved to be a difficult task—mainly the result of human behavior. Industrial management in particular has been autocratic since the industrial revolution a hundred years ago. It even adopted the military organization structure as its model. Throughout this period, new managers were selected for their authoritarian capabilities, among other things, and then further trained to be like those in charge. With lack of success, managers were blamed and they were replaced. Past methods were replicated.

In the 1950s, studies of management and employee behavior began in order to understand its psychological components. Maslow,[5] Herzberg,[6] and McGregor[7] were pioneers in this work. Using McGregor's work, Blake[8] identified a spectrum of management types from the autocratic to the participative, what characteristics they have, and their effectiveness. These studies are the genesis of modern management, whose training includes learning the role of human behavior factors in motivation—learning to lead rather than just manage and direct. Even though studied by many managers, this work had little impact; it was all too academic. The autocratic model was too entrenched. The world marketplace had begun to change, requiring a different approach to managing, but management wasn't ready to change.

More traditional organizations do not cope well in rapidly changing markets. The larger ones, in particular, find themselves noncompetitive and less profitable. Such organizations are bureaucratic and slow to make decisions; decisions are made at the upper levels of such organizations, which are highly proceduralized and characterized by slow internal communications. Not used to thinking for themselves, employees wait for direction. Typically there is little trust between management and nonmanagement. Shifting from this mode to what is required is analogous to changing religious beliefs. It will happen only when there is a greater confidence in the new way. The differences are compared in Table 2.2 by examining the changes in the role of traditional QC functions.

Table 2.2 Quality organization functions—before and after TQM.

Old Testament	New Testament
Organization management	Process not function
Definition—conformance to requirements	Customer satisfaction
Quality plans for inspection or testing	Strategic quality planning and objectives
Design to requirements	Design for robustness and customer satisfaction
Acceptable quality levels (percent defects allowed)	Continuous process and capability improvement
Manufacturing emphasis	Total organization and employee involvement
Statistical process control in manufacturing	Statistical thinking and tools used everywhere
Measure quality costs—prevention, appraisal, failure	Reduce process variation and cycle time
Quality organization controls quality	Quality organization manages quality system; process members control quality
Quality training workmanship	Quality training: everyone in problem solving and process improvement
Supplier quality—receiving and source inspection	Supplier adopts new testament supplier partnerships

MANAGING CHANGE AND INNOVATION

Establishing a climate that encourages innovation results in a growth of new ideas, with innovation piggybacking on innovation. Problems are solved in new and unique ways.

Innovation, if it is to occur, requires an openness to new ideas and a willingness to try them. True innovation is always testing the limits. The past cannot be allowed to control the future. Successful innovation requires a forward look. Organizations or functions cannot dominate actions. Innovation requires the integration of knowledge and ideas. Traditional organizations typically limit integration and control actions and events. In industry, for example, the design engineering function has been dominant. Innovation was focused on product development, not on organization development. The other organization elements—manufacturing, purchasing, and finance—focused on cost control and cost reduction. Management's task and problem is how to create conditions that stimulate innovation/creativity, how to achieve a problem-solving culture that helps to generate novel solutions.

One barrier to innovation can be organization structure. Compartmentalizing activities limits interchange and results in solutions to selected parts of a problem because there is no mechanism to integrate the parts and achieve a new and superior solution for the whole. In many traditional organizations, the members may see local manifestations of a problem and therefore seek only local solutions. There is little incentive to try to solve system or other functional group problems because this only means more work and little reward. These organizations limit member thinking to each individual's realm of assigned responsibility. A compartmentalized view affects the accuracy in assessing problems as well as the speed and effectiveness of the solution.

All these factors in traditional organizations limit their ability to cope with major external changes that occur in the global economy. The traditional organization becomes a victim of its past.

STRATEGIES FOR MANAGING CHANGE

Managing change cannot be described using a simple recipe. However, there are several principles to follow, as shown in Figure 2.4.

Leadership

Leaders are those whom people want to follow. The essence of leadership is connecting people with the purpose of the organization. Leaders create an environment that brings out the best in organization members.

It has taken the Japanese, Deming, Juran, and others many years to demonstrate the value in changing from managing and directing to leading; listening to organization members and the customers, then setting goals and objectives that will improve competitive position and to which the membership will commit themselves. These world leaders also introduced the idea that employees, empowered to work together in logical (process) groups, could continuously make and manage valuable improvements in the work they do. Leaders who accept this have gained the trust of their employees, providing a more cohesive and motivated workforce.

1. Convince people that the present state is unacceptable and that a change is necessary. Clearly describe why—on both an intellectual level and on an emotional level.
2. Describe a clear picture of what the desired state looks like. As possible, let people know what will be different for them and how they can benefit. Build excitement for the new state.
3. Allow time for people to adjust to the change.
4. Have a clear plan for getting from the present state to the desired state. Share information on the plan. Avoid surprises.
5. Get people involved in planning the change. Leave room for choices.
6. Implement the plan, and then monitor progress against the plan.
7. Be clear about the expectations and requirements in the new state.
8. Communicate updates about progress. Allow time for individuals to have discussions with supervisors and others.
9. Keep all communication channels open, and address any problems and concerns.
10. Lead by example; management needs to model the desired state.
11. Enable people to perform well in the desired state; provide training, coaching, etc.
12. Look for opportunities to positively reinforce behaviors and results that support success in the changed state. Reward and recognize early role models who have made the change.
13. Try to make it a win-win situation; avoid creating losers.

Figure 2.4   *Hints for managing organizational change.*

Adapted with the permission of The Free Press, a division of Simon & Schuster, Inc. From JURAN ON QUALITY BY DESIGN: The New Steps for Planning Quality into Goods and Services by J. M. Juran. Copyright © 1992 by Juran Institute Inc.

The Context of Leadership and the Management System

In the Malcolm Baldridge National Quality Award (MBNQA) criteria, a leadership system is "how leadership is exercised throughout the company—the basis for the way key decisions are made, communicated, and carried out at all levels." According to the Baldrige leadership criteria, an effective leadership system

- Creates clear values respecting the requirements of all stakeholders of the company.
- Sets clear expectations for performance and performance improvement.
- Builds loyalties and teamwork based on shared values and the pursuit of shared purposes.
- Encourages and supports initiative and risk taking.
- Subordinates organization to purpose and function.
- Minimizes reliance on chains of command that require long decision paths.
- Includes mechanisms for the leader's self-examination and improvement.

ORGANIZATIONS AND CHANGE

Organizations that are change oriented have a more open and integrated approach to problem solving, with several mechanisms to do so. People are empowered to act on information, which is freely exchanged. New problems are considered opportunities for improvement. People feel that they work in a community, not a function. The result is a freedom of expression and cooperative team work *across* the organization chart. The organizations also invest in new solutions in a timely manner, not after long justification procedures. Opportunities to take on larger projects represent incentives for innovation.

Executives often talk about wanting change and innovation, but the message the lower-level members get is that they are not really supposed to do anything beyond their assigned job responsibilities. It's as if there was a set of rules operating to stifle innovation. They might read like

1. Regard any new idea from below with suspicion—because it's new, and because it's from below.
2. Insist that people who need your approval to act first go through several other levels of management to get their signatures.
3. Ask departments or individuals to challenge and criticize each other's proposals. (That saves you the job of deciding; you just pick the survivor.)
4. Express your criticisms freely, and withhold your praise. (That keeps people on their toes.) Let them know they can be fired at any time.
5. Treat identification of problems as signs of failure, to discourage people from letting you know when something in their area isn't working.
6. Control everything carefully. Make sure people count anything that can be counted, frequently.
7. Make decisions to reorganize or change policies in secret, and spring them on people unexpectedly. (That also keeps people on their toes.)
8. Make sure that requests for information are fully justified, and make sure that it is not given out to managers freely. (You don't want data to fall into the wrong hands.)
9. Assign to lower-level managers, in the name of delegation and participation, responsibility for figuring out how to cut back, lay off, move people around, or otherwise implement threatening decisions you have made. And get them to do it quickly.
10. And above all, never forget that you, the higher-ups, already know everything important about this business.[9]

These conditions reflect some traditional organizations in action. If this is the environment perceived, there will be little significant improvement and no innovation. All the declarations by management about wanting to be a modern organization, implementing SPC, or benchmarking won't change anything.

CHANGE AGENTS

Organizations that need to change or are in the process of changing must have a change agent leader at the top, or the top executive must be able to use change agents skillfully within the organization. For example, Jack Welsh, CEO of General Electric, is himself such an agent. He is given much of the credit for GE's change in the way it operates and for its success in becoming a world-class company. He is leading GE to adopt the principles of measurable continuous improvement (using a Six Sigma process capability objective).

Within organizations, change agents are chartered to assist senior management in planning and executing a breakthrough or purposeful transformation. The change agent takes the lead, but others have to take part and support the process in a proactive manner.[10] Agents must have the skills to

- Educate and work with senior management to initiate and sustain the transformation.
- Support and advise other colleagues.
- Manage specific projects.
- Develop and manage a support network.
- Diagnose potential problems.
- Develop a plan to deal with issues.
- Execute the changes.

When such a leader agent exists, similar change agents in the rest of the organization frequently make themselves evident. That is their true nature, and once they recognize that upper management wants to change the culture and direction, they will surface. The author, reviewing past work experiences, can remember the occasional bright, free thinking individuals who actively proposed ideas for improvement but were considered agitators, or not team players, because they wanted to do things differently—and, they thought, better. They weren't given the chance. These people usually moved on, fruitlessly searching for an organization that wanted to change. In the past era of copycat management they were rarely successful. Enlightened management today finds ways to try innovative ideas, and consider's such ideas as possible opportunities. Management, as agent, has to look for change agents and give them open support. That is how the change message is effectively transported down through the organization.

Following this course doesn't mean that everyone is allowed to do what he or she thinks is a new and better way to work. The proper conditions must exist and organization with an operating framework established.

CONDITIONS FOR SUCCESSFUL MANAGERIAL INNOVATION

There isn't a simple prescription for organizations to follow in order to become innovative, but such organizations share the integrative form of operating just described, with somewhat common characteristics that foster improvement:

1. A culture of pride and climate of success as demonstrated by
   - Freedom and responsibility for managers to act, to do the right thing.

- Extensive dialogue and interpersonal relationships.
- Emphasis on teamwork and teams.
- Innovation as mainstream, not counterculture.
- An integrative, participative management approach.
- Managers who can handle uncertainty.
- Job charters are broad, assignments are ambiguous, nonroutine, and change oriented, areas of responsibility are intersecting.
- Local autonomy is strong, but there is mutual dependence between groups.
- There is complexity in middle-management operations: more relationships, more information, a variety of inputs on problems, more ways to get human resources involved, more freedom to investigate.

2. Entrepreneurial, innovative managers have the power they need to negotiate for necessary resources and support for an innovative action:
   - Information; open communication systems across the organization
   - Support from other organizations through networking devices:
     ~ Mobility—circulation of people through other jobs
     ~ Employment security—through long-term relationships
     ~ Use of teams at middle and upper levels, with horizontal and multifunctional representation
     ~ Complex ties both horizontal and across; access anywhere.
   - Decentralization of resources; local access to loosely committed funds

REFERENCES

1. P. R. Drucker. *Managing for the Future* (New York: McGraw-Hill, Truman Talley Books/Dutton, 1992).
2. E. Deevy. *Creating the Resilient Organization: A Rapid Response Management Program* (Upper Saddle River, NJ: Prentice Hall, 1995).
3. J. Tompkins. *The Genesis Enterprise: Creating Peak-To-Peak Performance* (New York: McGraw-Hill, 1995).
4. P. Senge. *The Fifth Discipline: The Art and Practice of the Learning Organization* (New York: Doubleday, 1990).
5. A. H. Maslow. *Motivation and Personality* (New York: McGraw-Hill, 1960).
6. F. Herzberg, B. Mausman, and B. Snuderman. *The Motivation to Work*, 2nd ed. (New York: John Wiley & Sons, 1959).
7. D. McGregor. *The Human Side of Enterprise* (New York: McGraw-Hill, 1960).
8. R. R. Blake, and J. S. Mouton. *The Managerial Grid* (Houston, TX: Gulf Publishing, 1964).
9. R. M. Kanter. *The Change Masters* (New York: Simon & Shuster, 1983).
10. D. W. Hutton. *The Change Agents Handbook: A Survival Guide for Quality Improvement Champions* (Milwaukee: ASQC Quality Press, 1994).

ADDITIONAL READINGS

Hesselbein, F. M., Goldsmith, and R. Beckhard, eds. *The Leaders of the Future.* The Drucker Foundation, 1966.

Kotter, J. P., *Leading Change.* Boston: Harvard Business School Press, 1966.

Peters, T., *The Persuit of WOW!: Every Person's Guide to Topsy Turvy Times.* Milwaukee: ASQC Quality Press, 1994.

Plsek, P. E., *Creativity, Innovation, and Quality.* Milwaukee: ASQ Quality Press, 1997.

STUDY QUESTIONS

1. What are some of the key reasons that change is difficult to implement in an organization?
2. Why is change necessary in today's organization environments?
3. What is meant by a learning organization?
4. What are the basic differences between managing an organization that is functionally organized and one using process management?
5. What are some key characteristics of a successful organization leader in today's business environment?
6. What are some of the factors that stifle organization innovation?

Chapter 3

Employee Empowerment

EMPOWERMENT AND WORK GROUPS

At the beginning of the industrial revolution, in the last half of the nineteenth century, organizations were formed around machine processes. Work decisions were all made by management. There was very little teamwork among employees.

The first effective teamwork structure in the United States started in the 1930s, was called the Scanlon Plan, in which groups of employees met regularly to devise ways to reduce production costs and share the savings. Management gave them complete access to production costs. The plan is still used in some Midwestern companies.

Quality circles (quality improvement teams) began in Japan in the 1950s as a development of the top-down process of statistical and quality management education. The quality circle is a problem-solving, morale building method that uses group participation to prepare improvement recommendations for management acceptance. The quality circle process in problem solving involves group use of brainstorming, data gathering, cause-and-effect analysis, problem identification, and recommended solutions. If accepted by management, results are measured and circle members receive feedback, recognition, and sometimes rewards.

From quality circles, a team-based approach to managing has evolved. These teams are usually empowered with authority far beyond what circles experienced. They can more freely act on ideas that lead to process improvement, often interacting with other teams when solutions affect other processes. Companies more advanced in their use of team management even allow teams to schedule work and manage the process. Teams are a part of a systems approach to managing since they work to improve system elements.

Empowerment is a major factor in process improvement in customer-oriented organizations. It is giving employees the authority to decide and act on their own initiatives. Tompkin's definition is, "the leadership process of building, developing and increasing the power of an organization to perform through the synergistic evolution of teams."[1]

Empowerment implies a significant degree of discretion and independence for those empowered—with some limitations, such as that changes apply only to work or process improvements and do not require capital expenditures or committing the company to any outside agents. Managers have always been empowered in their job scope and authority. Much of that now has to be shared with their subordinates.

Employee/team empowerment is also a way to manage change. But it is very difficult to implement. In general, the larger the organization the more difficult to implement change.[2] To provide for an empowerment culture, the management style must be open and participative with a team structure. This requires managers with the skills to support, coach, and develop people doing the work in teams. Managers need to encourage employees to become more responsible for their own decisions and their own work-based learning. In-depth management development is required before employees can be empowered effectively because it requires a supportive, open style not commonly found in traditional organizations.

Empowerment differs from delegating. In delegation of work, an employee still has to consult with a supervisor before taking any significant action. Empowerment means giving employees more authority. It does not mean autonomy, whereby employees can act without limits. Since there is confusion about what empowerment does mean, organizations contemplating its use should establish and promulgate a clear definition of authority and limits.

Empowerment is of value because successful organizations have found that it results in more effective and productive employees and significant innovative process improvements. It permits decisions—more likely based on an understanding of the process and customer needs—to be made more quickly.

Applying the empowerment concept successfully requires the appropriate organization structure and management style. It is not effective in a hierarchical structure or under autocratic management because it requires management to surrender some of its power.

Some degree of empowerment, the transfer of authority and responsibility, is necessary for effective management when delayering and downsizing an organization.

However, the appropriate management training and development must precede those kinds of changes. Success in changing to a team-based empowered organization requires attaining employee trust and a feeling of security. Suddenly announced reductions have the opposite effect, creating turmoil, mistrust, and anxiety, as well as attitudes that will resist constructive improvements.

The need for management preimplementation study can be critical. It is not uncommon for traditionally trained managers to underestimate the power shift that occurs when evolving to team empowerment. Later, when they recognize it and are not prepared to accept it, they may react autocratically and thereby sabotage the improvement effort. Teams falter, if not dissolve, and the team empowerment concept gets a bad reputation.

EMPOWERED ORGANIZATIONS

Some features that highlight the differences between the traditional and empowered organizations are

- There are changes in decision making rules. In a traditional organization, decisions are passed down through management. In an empowered organization, issues are handled by process employees. Teams solve operations problems and make decisions.

- Organization structures in traditional organizations are managed by functions with specialized members. Responsibilities are defined by organization chart. In empowered organizations the structures are broad and more integrated, with teams knowing the overall objectives, managing at least the main work processes.

- Traditional, more vertical organizations have a narrow span of control. Decisions are management controlled. Using empowerment, authority is shared, and organizations need fewer layers.

- Communication differences are significant. Traditionally, management controls information. Communication is mostly vertical. When empowered, organizations (teams) share information widely and in all directions, to the points where needed. There is open communication of all types.

TEAMS

Some of the leaders in the quality movement have formulated their own description of teams.

Juran—A group of individuals, each with specific skills, knowledge, and interests, that enable members to contribute to the accomplishment of a common purpose.

Deming—A group formed with an aim, a job, and a goal, to improve the output of any stage.

Scholtes—A group of people pooling their skills, talents, and knowledge to improve quality and productivity.

Cartin—Two or more people working together toward a common goal for which they hold themselves mutually accountable.[3]

A more fundamental look reveals that teams are the expression of employee empowerment and involvement. They become essential as an organization makes serious progress in becoming more customer driven and process focused. Teams represent a basic and characteristic methodology for managing. Their formation and development are vital if they are to be effective. The guidelines and objectives in forming teams are

- Use teams to manage the important processes.

- Train teams to solve process problems and reduce variation. Introductory training would begin as teams are formed and continue as new problem-solving skills are needed, that is, as problems get more complex.

- Provide continuous, visible management support and effective facilitation, until teams mature.

- Allow different teams to evolve at their own rate. Replace team leaders or members to maintain effectiveness.

Managing through the use of teams is a complex process. Mismanagement can easily occur, with serious consequences to ongoing operations. The tendency of those who don't perform well is to plan poorly and rush the team training and development process, trying to get quick improvement results. Both management and employees need time to adjust to what is a different way to manage. Moreover, during the transition period, the two different structures and cultures don't mix well, resulting in conflict that must be managed.

Implementation

Conversion of a traditional organization to empowered employees takes time, careful planning, and continuous follow-up by top management through visible support and adjustments as needed. It is an evolutionary process. The first step is to examine and understand all facets and ramifications of the concept, its organization implications and management resources required to succeed. The basic long-term objective would be to develop an organization that is trained and motivated to make customer-focused work management decisions, with little supervisory direction.

Upper management must develop communication paths and methods that will constantly reinforce its new objectives. It must earn employee trust. For example, mistakes/deficiencies must be treated as opportunities for improvement, not for blame and scapegoating. This is very difficult as it goes against many years of conditioning that to be the boss one gives directions and places blame.

Successes and Failures

As would be expected, there is a large variation in the success rate in implementing of the modern approach. In a survey by Lackritz, Fortune 500 companies were asked about their experience with TQM and SPC. The results indicate that even the economically successful 500 companies still have a way to go on their quality journey.

1. A formal quality management program and philosophy that had been shared with employees were indicated by 91.5 percent.

2. Teachings were observed as follows
   - 68.8 percent Deming
   - 47.5 percent Juran
   - 35 percent Crosby
3. Figure 3.1 summarizes the success rates of companies using a 0–100 rating scale.
   100—complete success
     50—an effectiveness of about 50 percent
       0—quality management never incorporated or a total failure
4. Figure 3.2 compares the rating of different groups of employees in using QM and SPC.
   100 = SPC and other quality tools successfully implemented throughout the organization[4]

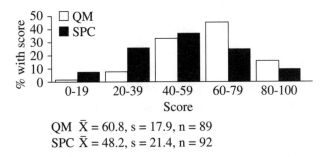

QM $\bar{X}$ = 60.8, s = 17.9, n = 89
SPC $\bar{X}$ = 48.2, s = 21.4, n = 92

Figure 3.1 *The surveyed companies success rates with their quality management and SPC programs. The average X, sigma s, and sample size n are for the complete histogram.*

Reprinted with permission from ASQ *Quality Progress*, February 1997.

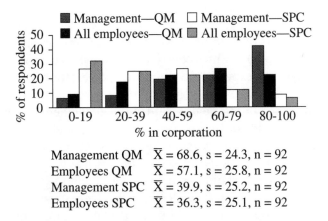

Management QM $\bar{X}$ = 68.6, s = 24.3, n = 92
Employees QM $\bar{X}$ = 57.1, s = 25.8, n = 92
Management SPC $\bar{X}$ = 39.9, s = 25.2, n = 92
Employees SPC $\bar{X}$ = 36.3, s = 25.1, n = 92

Figure 3.2 *The level of quality management and SPC knowledge of different groups of employees, as perceived by managers of their organizations.*

Reprinted with permission from ASQ *Quality Progress*, February 1997.

Most respondents thought their quality management program was only moderately successful. However, far fewer thought they were successful in the use of SPC tools. Deming didn't separate them. Success in quality management requires success in understanding SPC because it goes to the heart of the management of variation and improvement.

These companies also reported that less than 80 percent of the management teams were sufficiently knowledgeable of TQM, but that about half were knowledgeable of SPC tools. All the companies reported that they used quality teams. (There was no information as to how long companies had been working on implementation or how aggressively they had pursued it.

Several current authors such as Senge,[5] Tompkins,[6] and Deevy suggest why TQM "fails." They say it differently, but a common thread is that management typically has a mechanistic approach to TQM implementation. Management delegates a task that cannot be delegated. It

1. Hires a consultant to train upper management.
2. Organizes and trains teams, but leaves it to lower management to use them.
3. Supports team efforts financially.

A mechanistic approach—a "force fit" on the organization—will not work, or work effectively, and is the cause of many failures. A TQM effort is not a "one size fits all" method. It has to be tailored to the organization, and success requires leadership at the top.

QUALITY EDUCATION AND TRAINING

Even a cursory review of all the factors involved in managing quality in the modern organization makes it obvious that it is a complex and dynamic arena. This also means that it requires new knowledge and skills for everyone, which implies the need for new and continuing education and training. Quality management in the past meant the management of a functional organization responsible for the quality activities. It now includes the quality aspects of everyone's work in the overall organization, plus those of the customers and suppliers. This requires new knowledge and skills, reeducation and training. With change expected to continue, reeducation and training should never end.

The reeducation and training begins with the management group, shifting their emphasis away from individual competition to becoming skillful in collaboration, teamwork, and long-term customer–supplier alliances. These techniques require high-level interpersonal interactions. Also, the shift is not just a matter of changing style; it requires a basic understanding of behavior (including management's own), motivation, team management, and leadership. As a demonstration of leadership, managers from the very top down should make a visible commitment to increasing their own learning. Much of the downsizing and restructuring that have taken place is the result of the awakening of some management to the reality that the old ways of managing, utilizing old knowledge and skills, won't keep an organization competitive.

Juran believes that training must be customized to fit an organization needs and subsequently planned.[7] Major issues to be considered are

1. Quality problems and challenges that face the organization.
2. Knowledge and skill level needed to solve the identified problems and meet the challenges.
3. Assessing the knowledge and skills actually possessed by the people within the organization, and determining those needed.
4. Availability and appropriateness of training facilities.
5. The current climate toward training within the organization.
6. The determination of what is to be different from present practice, at every level. (Repeat after every organization change.)

Education and Training Defined

Education is the process of acquiring knowledge and information, usually in a formal manner. Some examples are the study and understanding of science, technology, human behavior, team dynamics, and the principles of statistics.

Training is the process of acquiring proficiency in specific skills. Some examples are team leadership and facilitation, and the application of the seven quality control tools for problem solving (discussed in Part II).

Management Support and Strategic Planning for Quality Training

Change is a major theme in the business marketplace, as well as in government agencies. Creating rational change is the responsibility of management. There are two approaches being followed. One is the result of chasing short-term financial gains. The other is based mainly on strategic planning. The press has reported both but provided little information on their differences.

Short-term change is simple cost cutting to show improvements to investors, or to improve top management bonuses based on profit targets. Sometimes it is the only option because management has allowed an enterprise to drift into a serious noncompetitive position and survival actions are required. Other actions such as a 10 percent cut in personnel merely to improve the financial picture, are a different matter. These leave organizations in turmoil, and the actions are frequently short-sighted. They limit an organization's ability to change into what the future marketplace will require, because there is no trust between management and employees (or among management itself).

In utilizing the strategic planning process, a company might identify an approaching decline in the demand for its product or service. Perhaps it would take the form of a growing technological obsolescence in the company's product based on a competitor's product announcement (such announcements are frequently made long before the product becomes available). Management can then plan its reduction, explain the situation to employees, and follow the plan. It wouldn't make the employees happy, but having been informed, they would be less likely to lose trust in their management.

A good example of this approach was the announcement, in early 1998, by the CEO of AT&T of a planned two-year elimination of 2000 management positions. The announcement was accompanied by new, generous changes in the early retirement benefits for the positions affected. AT&T is an "old line" company that was viewed as overstaffed and poorly structured to compete in the very competitive world communications market. The new CEO analyzed company needs and began the reengineering of the corporation. The company common stock reacted positively, even though some financial analysts were critical about the projected two-year timetable for the reduction.

This reflects two schools of thought—both approaches to change. One says make a company more competitive by quick, radical cuts in costs (cut staff, sell some product lines). This view is that "the bottom line is all that matters." The other approach is to look long-range, identify changes, plan for them, and operate to the plan in an orderly manner, taking the impact on employees into account. In the second category are companies that base their changes, that is, downsizing, privatizing, restructuring, reengineering, spin-offs, and the like, on the results of planning.

A critical element in organizational success, then, is good planning, particularly strategic planning. Policies, projected structure, and identification of needed knowledge and skills evolve directly from this activity. (Planning is discussed more fully in Chapter 5.) Strategic plans are a look into the future, and, based on where the organization is, involve deciding what the organization should be, where it has to go, and how it will get there. They provide a picture of what goods or services customers will expect and what competitors might do about it. This has traditionally been the limits of business planning, but the next critical step is to define what new knowledge and skills the organization will need, which they no longer need, and then make plans on how and when new expertise will be attained and the resources required.

For example, if the strategic plan sets a goal of a 15 percent improvement in product quality, this must be followed by the identification of how that goal will be met, that is, how it will be measured, and what facilities, equipment, financing, skills, and other resources will have to be on-line by the plan time. Those who are well into becoming a new organization recognize the nature of the changes and reeducation and training that are, and will continue to be, required. Just consider the potential effect on education and training needs of entering the global market, that is, new languages, new cultures, new business practices.

A newer element in long-range planning is, rather than identifying how much bigger the organization will have to be, addressing the question of how best to meet revised needs and to stay flexible, ready to meet the unexpected. Many organizations are deciding that isn't wise to accumulate more debt, facilities, or people, particularly for special skills. They have decided that they can be stronger by keeping and developing a core organization specifically related to their market, and using some form of outsourcing for other needs. New skills may be located in subcontractors, and this is becoming a common approach for filling a need for expertise that is different from what currently exists within the organization.

Up until about the 1980s, organizations mostly depended on the employment marketplace to find the skills they needed, and the approach generally worked. Skill needs changed slowly, and the fluctuations in various business sectors provided a reasonable supply. But now, as reported in the business news, employment markets are in turmoil. As a result of considerable downsizing, people have become available. Simultaneously, management is complaining about limited availability of new employees with the skills needed for the modern workplace, particularly in reading and math. As a result, more businesses are doing their own training and education. One example is the Motorola Corporation, which developed its own "university" and spends more than $150 million a year on a broad spectrum of training and education topics. The curriculum is relevant to the company, the individual, and the job. This is a clear demonstration of both the need and support for learning.

Upper management support for quality training is based on how thoroughly it does strategic planning and in what depth it evaluates and understands the full implications of any newly identified needs.

Training Topics

Effective training will focus on the following

- Base examples and case studies on the business.
- Base the assessment of specific training needs on job categories and existing skill levels.
- Design training to fit existing tools, techniques, and methods (if effective).
- Design training to fit the existing learning culture.
- Design the material to fit management's vision of improvement.
- Customize the material to fit the company.
- Include implementation, the tracking system, and course evaluation in the design of the course schedule.
- Design course prerequisites and specific skills needed to make each module effective.
- Design exercises that contribute to a work situation.[8]

The criteria of the Baldridge National Quality Award (discussed in Part II), have become the basic reference for describing a comprehensive competitive organization. The award reflects the need for employee education, training, and development in what could be called the management quality principles. It asks award applicants to describe how the company's education and training address company plans, including building company capabilities, contributing to employee motivation, progression, and development, and the knowledge and skills that employees need to meet their work objectives. The Baldridge Award reviews

- Leadership skills
- Communications
- Teamwork
- Process analysis and problem solving
- Interpreting and using data
- Meeting customer requirements
- Process improvement
- Cycle time reduction
- Error proofing
- Priority setting based on cost and benefit data
- Training that effects employee effectiveness, efficiency, and safety

Considering our diverse society, it might also include basic skills such as reading, writing, language, and arithmetic.

The subject list is comprehensive and far different from only a few years ago, when quality training was mostly in measurement, blueprint reading, work tools and procedures, and safety—in other words, only the minimum for employees to do their jobs, as management described them. The Baldrige criteria go further. They describe how education and training could be evaluated to address

- Impact on work unit performance
- Cost effectiveness of education and training alternatives

A continuous training process is required by the international standard, ANSI/ASQC Q 9004-1. It requires that training needs for all personnel be identified and documented. Particular attention should be given to the qualifications, selection, and training of new employees in their new assignments. It further describes the requirements for training quality executives, technical personnel, process supervisors, and operating personnel. It is a good training structure for any organization, except that it omits TQ training for upper management, as well as the point that training needs evolve from strategic quality planning.

Training is also required to meet other international standards. The training requirement to comply with ISO 9001 and 9002 states

> The supplier shall establish and maintain documented procedures for identifying training needs and provide for the training of all personnel performing activities affecting quality. Personnel performing specific assigned tasks shall be qualified on the basis of appropriate education, training, and/or experience, as required. Appropriate records of training shall be maintained.

Summarizing, the Baldrige and ISO training requirements reflect the extent of the increasing scope of training and education needs in modern organizations—to increase quality and remain competitive.

Training Needs Analysis

Training is expensive and important to the success of the organization. Modern organization education and training needs are greater and more comprehensive than were those of pre-TQ management. More significantly, trained personnel are needed to support change and improvements that the organization must make to succeed or survive.

Small businesses have other problems with training and education. They typically operate in a small market area. Their main interest is satisfying the immediate needs of their customers, most of whom are larger business. They may not be aware of the magnitude of the changes occurring in their customer's markets that will affect them.

In most cases, small businesses cannot afford significant training. Most of them rely on their customers to tell them what is needed; however, the relationship has traditionally been almost adversarial, and there is little likelihood of forward-looking information exchanges. In any case, the supplier/customer partnership concept (described later) can offer small companies the opportunity to find out what new skills are needed and even obtain customer assistance in providing training.

Training and education should be managed, like any other important investment, beginning with planning. Training needs should be derived from the overall and functional strategic and tactical quality plans. The following steps provide a measure of the gap between what exists and what the plans identify as future needs.

1. Prepare an inventory of the present organization skills and who has them. Managers and employees should also identify what they think they need.
2. Analyze the strategic and tactical plans and objectives for quality improvement.
3. Identify the skills required to meet those objectives.
4. Compare projected skills requirements with the present inventory to identify new needs, or an increase in the quantity of present skills.
5. Prepare a plan for when the skills are needed, when and how the training will be provided, who will receive it, and what resources will be required. This plan should also be the basis for deciding if and when recruitment will be necessary and a schedule for any new job/position descriptions. This plan may highlight the magnitude of the training problem so that management can decide whether future outsourcing or an acquisition is a better alternative.
6. These plans should be coordinated with the overall organization to prepare a master plan for training.

Figure 3.3 is one possible outcome of the training needs planning activity. It provides a basis for scheduling and planning specific training to fill different employee needs.

Students	Consultant	Total quality seminar	Team leader training	Facili-tator	Leadership/ people skills	Advanced problem solving	Process control methods	Introduction to design of experiments	Design of experiments	Data gathering	Implementation
Team leader	●	●	●	▲	▲	■	▲	■	■	■	●
Team member	■	■	■	■	♦	■	■	■	■	■	▲
Facilitator	●	●	●	●	▲	■	▲	▲	■	▲	▲
Statistician	●	●	●	●	▲	■	●	●	●	■	●
Improvement manager	●	●	●	●	●	●	●	●	■	■	●
Nonmanagement	■	■	■	■	♦	■	■	■	■	■	■
Other key members	■	■	■	▲	▲	▲	▲	▲	▲	▲	■
Manufacturing	■	■	■	■	▲	■	■	■	■	■	■
Engineering	■	■	■	■	▲	▲	▲	▲	▲	■	▲
Office/ administrative	■	■	■	■	▲	■	■	■	■	■	▲
Management	●	●	●	▲	●	▲	▲	▲	■	■	●

● Required ▲ Recommended ■ Optional ♦ Not required

Figure 3.3 *Quality improvement education and training plan.*

REFERENCES

1. J. Tompkins. *The Genesis Enterprise: Creating Peak-to-Peak Performance* (New York: McGraw-Hill, 1995).
2. P. Hersey, and K. Blanchard. *Management of Organizational Behavior: Utilizing Human Resources* (Englewood Cliffs, NJ: Prentice Hall, 1988).
3. T. J. Cartin, and D. Jacoby. *A Review of Quality Management and a Primer for the Quality Management Certification Exam* (Milwaukee: ASQ Quality Press, 1997).
4. J. R. Lackritz. "TQM With Fortune 500 Corporations." ASQ *Quality Progress*, (February, 1997).
5. P. Senge. *The Fifth Discipline: The Art and Practice of the Learning Organization* (New York: Doubleday, 1990).
6. Tompkins. "The Genesis Enterprise."
7. J. M. Juran, and F. M. Gryna. *Juran's Quality Control Handbook* (New York: McGraw-Hill, 1988).
8. J. A. Miller. "Training Requirements to Support Total Quality Management." *CMA Magazine* (November, 1992).

ADDITIONAL READINGS

Hutton, D. W. *The Change Agents Handbook: A Survival Guide for Quality Improvement Champions*. Milwaukee: ASQC Quality Press, 1994.

Katzenback, J. *Teams at the Top: Unleashing the Potential of Both Teams and Individual Leaders*. Boston: Harvard Business School Press, 1997.

Kotter, J.P. *Leading Change*. Boston: Harvard Business School Press, 1996.

STUDY QUESTIONS

1. What is employee empowerment? How does it differ from management delegation?
2. What are some of the practices and policies in operating an empowered organization versus a traditional one?
3. Formulate your definition/description of a quality improvement team and compare it to the descriptions used by quality experts.
4. What are the key roles and responsibilities of improvement teams?
5. What are some of the reasons improvement teams fail?
6. Why should training requirements be tied to strategic planning?
7. What are the knowledge and skills that employees need to contribute to continuous improvement?

Chapter 4

Customer Satisfaction and Focus

CUSTOMER FOCUS

The most significant change in managing for quality in recent years is the focus on customer satisfaction as the prime organization objective. Satisfying customer needs and expectations has become the driving force for quality improvement. It is the highest priority of management. It requires a systematic approach. Research has shown that superior quality increases market share.

Changing the focus of the typical organization, away from satisfying self-interests, to a dedication to the needs and expectations of the customer (internal and external), requires an understanding of what is involved.

Customer focus is important for several reasons. It determines

- How the organization communicates on a daily basis with its customers to better understand their needs and wants
- The degree of commitment to customer–supplier relationships and how they will be managed
- Employee roles and responsibilities and the culture of the organization
- How problems are handled and the speed with which they are resolved
- What feedback is important and how data are collected and used
- The foundation for a companywide strategy permanently focused on the customer
- Whether companies retain customers

TYPES OF CUSTOMERS

In its most general usage, the term *customer* is viewed as anyone who buys a product or service. It is a reference used mostly in business. Professional service sellers commonly use *client* or *subscriber.* These customers are all external. The new approach adds the concept of internal customers. And, in relation to actual business market structure, it is useful to add another category, intermediate customer.

- *Internal* customers are the people, or process, in an organization who receive work from another person or process, work on it, and deliver it to the next step, to either another internal or an external customer. For example, an internal customer could be manufacturing, which receives the output of the engineering process, the product design package; or a patient care process that receives the output of a blood test evaluation.
- Businesses often have a customer between them and the ultimate end user— their *intermediate customer,* such as a distributor. The intermediate customer is actually a forward extension of the producer's processes, a stop on the way to the end user. The intermediate customer, too, being an important part of the total process, is an important focus for customer satisfaction.
- The third type of customer is, then, the final, *end user*—the one who receives and uses the final product or service.

Adopting the concept of internal and external customers creates a more holistic view of the process in a traditional or functional organization. It changes the view of organization members to see beyond divisive territorial attitudes.

The dedication to satisfying the external customer is enhanced by maintaining a similar internal focus, that is, by using the internal supplier–customer relationship. If external customer needs/requirements are reflected in strategic and tactical quality planning, and planning objectives are deployed down throughout the organization and translated into related process improvement objectives, they will become the needs of the internal process customers. Internal improvements will then be connected to the external customer, and the entire organization will be customer driven.

ELEMENTS OF A CUSTOMER-DRIVEN ORGANIZATION

Whitely identifies several fundamental imperatives that produce a well-integrated organization that can deliver high quality in products and services. A totally focused organization must meet these imperatives.

1. Create a customer-keeping vision in everyone in the organization.
2. Establish the voice of the customer in every organization decision. Become close and communicative with the customers.
3. Study, adopt, or adapt methods of the leaders from every kind of organization in products or services.
4. Employees must believe that the customer is their number-one job. Managers must demonstrate this in all their activities and lead by example.
5. Break down barriers between and within organizations that inhibit serving the customer. This should happen through the adoption of the policies and proper application of the continuous process improvement methodologies.
6. Develop and use performance and effectiveness measures. They must be tied to customer satisfaction measurements. Other organizations can be benchmarked to identify useful measures.[1]

Whitely also recognizes customer-driven organizations by

Reliability—the ability to provide what was promised, dependably and accurately

Assurance—the knowledge and courtesy of employees, and their ability to convey trust and confidence

Tangibles—facilities and equipment, and the appearance of personnel

Empathy—the degree of caring and individual attention provided to customers

Responsiveness—the willingness to help customers and provide prompt service

THE ROLE OF MANAGEMENT

Organizations with a strong commitment and dedication to customer satisfaction exhibit some distinctive characteristics in the way they are managed and operate, that don't exist to the same degree in non customer driven organizations. The key elements usually present are

1. Total customer satisfaction is an all-consuming objective of all members.
2. The relationship between customers and suppliers is based on practices reflecting a partnership. Improvement decisions are made with supplier–customer input.
3. Operating policy and practice are structured for continuous improvement in process, product, and service quality.
4. Comprehensive strategic and tactical planning, containing quality objectives for processes and products, are given equal weight with schedule and profit.
5. Human resource development is ongoing to meet quality objectives.
6. Products and services are competitive.[2]

Management has to play the key role. The continuous activities in managing a customer, market driven organization are

1. Internal support—organization development, to develop the right structure, management, and employee skills for growth and marketplace changes
2. Use of knowledge—application of market research and analysis tools; getting customer feedback, assessing changing customer expectations and needs
3. Use of metrics—establishment of market-based process performance measures that result in improvements tied to the customer rather than to the interests of an internal function
4. Communications—publication and reporting within the organization of progress toward meeting customer needs

CUSTOMER NEEDS, EXPECTATIONS, AND "VOICE"

Determining customer expectations, needs, and priorities is a demanding and never-ending task. It is not a single objective but a moving target. Expectations and needs are never fully satisfied. Expectations measured at one point in time, when satisfied, become the new standard taken for granted. The customer then develops new expectations. It's a never-ending cycle. Anticipating, and satisfying customer expectations is critical to remaining competitive.

Expectations, needs, and priorities are also interrelated. This complicates the job. For example, people buying a car now expect, need, and give a high priority to reliability and style, within various price ranges. An expectation met creates a new norm and further demand, and the benchmark continues to rise. As a further example, automobile reliability has improved dramatically in recent years. According to the J. D. Powers quality survey of new car owners, there is still a gap between Japanese and American cars. The Japanese have steadily improved; the United States has not caught up, but is progressing.

A manufacturer, before committing any model to production, must decide (years ahead) what combination of attributes the buyers of the future will prefer—a very difficult and risky task. There are many variables to satisfy, not the least of which is assessing future competition and trends. A few years ago, Chrysler started a new trend when it marketed the minivan. Other manufacturers scrambled to enter that market. Because Chrysler had anticipated and defined a need and market, it held a competitive advantage for several years As markets become more global, customer needs, expectations, and priorities become even more complex to identify and satisfy. The Ford Taurus was not well accepted in Europe, but it subsequently became a big success in the United States. To complicate matters further, buyers often don't have a clear idea of what their expectations are; they tend to confuse needs and expectations in their thinking. A business must continually search for customer information that will provide a basis for making decisions, which is the function of market research.

Needs of business customers are usually more definitive than those of the consumer, but it is still important to communicate with them regularly. Their needs and expectations can change or be changed by a competitor. Suppliers using continuous process improvement, and all that it entails, should be able to keep customers satisfied by raising quality and lowering cycle time.

Organization elements driven to satisfy internal customers, knowing their expectations, needs, and priorities, are key to satisfying the external customer. It hasn't been common practice, individually or as an organization, to sit down with internal customers, the receivers of work or process output, and determine exactly what they expect, need, and in what form and in what order. When satisfying the internal customer becomes an organization practice, there is a chain reaction in overall organization effectiveness, that extends to the external customer. It becomes a way of thinking and acting.

CHANGING TO CUSTOMER FOCUS

A growth company needs an organized way to challenge its thinking. It can begin by answering these five questions:

1. What are the customer needs and expectations, and which matter most to them?
2. How well are we meeting those needs and expectations?
3. For external customers, how well are our competitors meeting them? What are they doing?
4. How can we go beyond the minimum and truly delight them?
5. For internal customers, do we routinely determine and satisfy their needs and expectations?

Methodologies
An approach to defining customer needs and expectations is to focus on answering these questions:

1. Do we have a practice of doing effective market analysis, that is, what's new, who is buying what, where, at what price?
2. Do we get data from customers and others, analyze it, and act on results?
3. Do we do an analysis of competitors' products, services, and practices?
4. Do we use benchmarking of our processes to find the best?

The voice of the customer is a term used to identify the existence of customer requirements as the main objective of all processes. If this voice is lost (if requirements are changed or diluted), customer and market needs will less likely be met. A powerful tool used to keep the voice of the customer in the process, from the initial to final organization activity (delivery), is quality function deployment (QFD). It is a planning tool that begins with a complete identification of customer requirements and translates those requirements, throughout the work processes, as the basis for each process design, assuring that the true customer requirements end up in the final product. QFD is finding applications in all kinds of organizations and activities. It is described in Part II.

QUALITY IN INDUSTRY AND SERVICES

Industry

Historically, any reference to quality activities referred to industry activity, quality control. It was pretty well confined to the production process, which is where the basic process quality control techniques were developed. Statistical techniques such as inspection sampling and SPC, based on probability mathematics, were developed in the 1930s.[3] Both were used in the high-volume and expanded production processes in WWII. After the war, SPC use declined to a minor role in industry. It didn't become well known and was not taught in management or common college programs.

Quality in industry is used in reference to the attributes of a product and its parts during production and to some degree in customer use. It is in this context that the "conformance to requirements" quality definition developed. Adopting this definition, although it is not "wrong," has had several ramifications that limited Western industry's ability to meet new market quality standards. Figures 4.1 and 4.2 illustrate this point. Engineering specifications identify the dimensions of a product using a center value, or nominal, with upper and lower limits that define the acceptable range. It is a tolerance range based on the ideal. Providing tolerances is a recognition that no process can produce everything at the nominal value. *All* process outputs vary.

In Figure 4.1, following the "meets requirements" doctrine, a product measuring at point B would be accepted, although it is almost outside the tolerance. The same product measuring at point A would be unacceptable. If the two points represented something like the speed at which an automatic transmission shifted, a customer would probably not recognize the difference between A and B, but would between A and B and C. In other words, if everything measures close to nominal, less variation has occurred in the process of making the parts. Products work better longer. Customer satisfaction would be greater, and that is the important measure of acceptance, not just specification tolerances.

It is the recognition of this concept that supports the principle of continuous improvement, illustrated in Figure 4.2. The three curves represent the distributions (output range), of three similar processes making the same part. The output under A is producing mostly within tolerance limits but with a little waste outside the limits. Curve B is a process producing widely but within tolerance limits. C is a process with

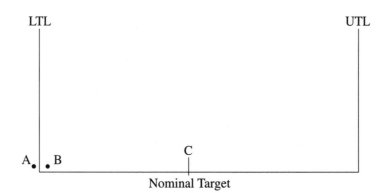

Customer would not likely consider operation at point A much different than B, but would notice the difference between A and B compared to C.

Figure 4.1   *Following the "meets requirements" definition results in accepting a part anywhere within upper tolerance limits (UTL) and lower tolerance limits (LTL) and rejecting anything outside a limit (measurement A).*

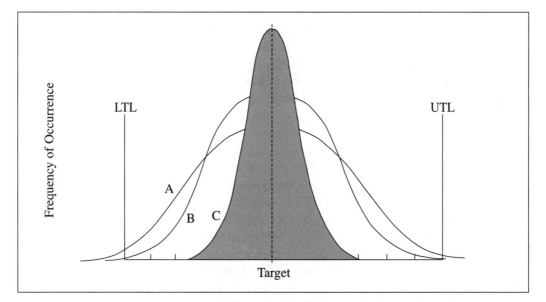

Products A or B could be the outputs of processes anywhere in their distributions as shown. Better product performance and customer satisfaction would be achieved if all process variation was as close to the target as C.

Figure 4.2   *These curves represent the idea of comparing the variation in the outputs of the same product form three different processes. The width of each curve repesents the total variation of each process.*

much less variation, producing higher quality than A or B, more frequently. Most of the output is near nominal. The waste in process A requires extra labor and material to replace it, as well as more production equipment, thereby reducing productivity. Process B is better, but those parts near the tolerance limits, when matched to their mating part, may not look like or function as well as those in C.

Quality in Nonproduction Activities

From the time of the development of CWQC and TQM, attention in industry has been given to improving organization activities that do not work directly on the product, such as

- Quality planning
- Product conception and formulation
- Design—engineering
- Purchasing
- Finance
- Human resources
- Management systems
- Quality assurance
- Customer service

Their actions/outputs of these activities directly affect product quality, productivity, cost and customer satisfaction. The processes they use are identified, measured, and improved in conjunction with the production processes. (One of the tools used early in a product-planning and development stage to effectively combine the skills and knowledge of various staff organizations is concurrent engineering, discussed later.)

Quality in Services

The service sector in the U.S. economy is the largest in both sales and employment. It includes everything not industry or agriculture (although there are many service activities within industrial organizations). Some large components of the service sector are communications, transportation, medical care, finance, government, and sales. They are highly competitive within their own spheres.

Until the introduction of TQM, there was little systematic activity to improve service quality. The energies of the organization were not focused on satisfying the customer. The worldwide application of TQM methodologies has resulted in business and quality management literature replete with descriptions of methodologies and examples of success, in all kinds of service organizations. Most of the team tools and techniques to be discussed, properly modified for the application, are useful in any kind of process improvement effort.

One of the conditions that limited the use of "production" quality improvement techniques is the functional isolation that has existed between the different economic sectors, and even within sectors. Managers in one kind of business don't believe that managers in another kind of business can teach them anything. They didn't consider their similarities such as purchasing function, human resources, and finance. Many in all sectors have transportation systems, warehousing, production, communication systems, computer systems, and the like. Also, managers haven't thought in terms of systems, and there is a human tendency to think that they and their organizations are different, rather than to recognize their similarities. Systems/process thinking and managing have changed much of that limited viewpoint. Benchmarking, a powerful improvement tool discussed later, is used to overcome this "tunnel" vision. Moreover, organizations compare and evaluate similar activities and systems in different, outside organizations, in order to find a better way. For example, Xerox Corporation, in looking for ways to improve its replacement parts customer response time, benchmarked the L. L. Bean catalog clothing company, who are well known for a short order-to-delivery cycle time.

HARDWARE AND SOFTWARE QUALITY

The quality objectives of meeting requirements and fitness for use apply to hardware and software. But the methods for achieving those objectives in software, or for knowing how well they have been achieved, are radically different. The tools and techniques for attaining high quality in products are included in this book. However, the fundamental difference between hardware and software development and production makes the common QC tools unusable. In fact, there is no agreed way to even measure software quality or reliability—just as there is no good way to measure the quality of product designs.

Software is ubiquitous in our lives, but it's a different animal than a physical product. Software has no physical presence. It can't be measured or counted, and that is the root of the difficulty. It is a generally accepted fact that all software programs, when used, will contain bugs. They are the result of software encountering new environments, applications, and interactions that cannot feasibly be anticipated during its development. In the physical world, the consequences of an action or a bug are closely related in time, space, and severity to the cause. "I call this the Principle of Locality. In the software world the consequences of a bug are *arbitrarily* related in time, space and severity to the cause. Simple bugs in simple software often have a localized impact; but as the size and complexity increases, the locality principle is increasingly violated."[4] The symptoms of a bug can be manifested arbitrarily far away from the cause and arbitrarily long after the execution of the faulty code. The symptoms of a bug are arbitrarily related to the cause.

One well-known example of a bug that has been in software for 50 years and only recognized in the late 1990s is the so-called "millennium bug." In the first computers, punched cards provided program memory as well as the source and method of input data. To conserve space, only the last two digits were used for the year dating. This two-digit date became imbedded in old and new programs (and using old computer languages that few people know). Recently, it was recognized that when the year 2000 arrives, computers will read this as 1900 and do things such as closing files as though they were finished. This could, for example, stop payments or stop orders for material that is still needed. Costs to fix the software have been estimated to reach a billion dollars, and no one really knows.

However, there are procedures for minimizing software errors. The first step in software development is the most critical in producing a high-quality product. It is in the preparation of the program requirements specification. The subsequent development outcome depends on how accurately and completely the application/user requirements were captured. But even the best requirements specification will not eliminate all bugs.

Quality is also dependent on following a disciplined development procedure. Module testing is a development tool that can disclose the simpler problems, but it can't test quality into the program, it can't test all possible applications or combinations when many are unknown and unknowable. There isn't a known way to confirm that all requirements have been met. QC methods such as charting defects found in testing are locally useful but of limited value.

There are some quality improvement tools that have application in software development. Quality function deployment (QFD) is a good requirements planning tool. There has been some value in using it as a methodology to aid in identifying all the requirements and in describing the final structure.[5] Benchmarking, another technique, can be used to find ways to improve a development process. Both tools are discussed in Part II.

IMPORTANT FACTORS IN PRODUCT QUALITY

Managing an industrial enterprise to achieve customer satisfaction requires an understanding of not only business and improvement principles but also of the basic factors that affect product quality in the design–production cycle. These factors determine quality and, to a large degree, product cost. They are successful product operation, design margin, reliability, complexity, producibility, and the manufacturing capability. They are all interrelated and interdependent, making management complex and difficult.

Customer satisfaction with a product is directly related to its quality and reliability. These are determined primarily by the design margin. The greater the design margin (that is, a product's capacity to withstand all the stresses of the manufacturing cycle and customer use), the lower the failure rate in use. An effort to increase a design margin can then result in greater satisfaction and lower production costs (less rework). This indicates the need for more integration in the design and development cycle with the production process. The production process role in this equation is to provide capable processes (little variation) to produce products closer to the design nominal. Conversely, the design has to match process capabilities. This allows products to approach their design reliability. Without high process capability, simply producing product parts anywhere within the tolerance limits increases the in-process failure rate and lowers the product reliability.

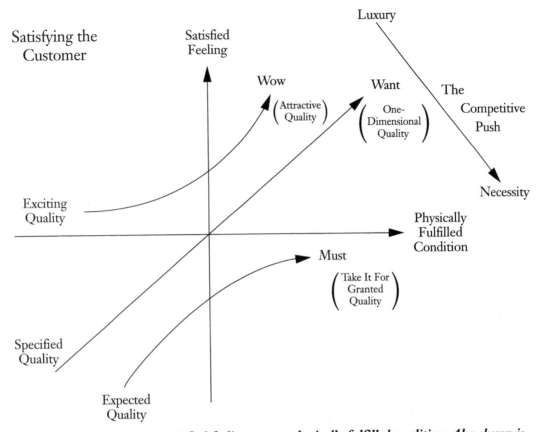

Figure 4.3 *A customer's satisfied feeling versus physically fulfilled condition. Also shown is the reality that luxury factors become expectations as all competitors add them.*

Customer Requirements

The first and most critical step is to identify customer wants, needs, and expectations. Extensive research is required to develop accurate descriptions. Thoroughness is important because these factors determine the product cost, quality, and reliability. Figure 4.3 shows the relationship between various customer requirements. Customer satisfaction, measured vertically, is achieved by going beyond one-dimensional quality and discovering unexpressed customer expectations. It is also necessary to identify what would be new, exciting, and attractive to customers. The sloping line on the upper right shows that the relationship between factors is dynamic. Products and features once considered a luxury become necessities when they are widely available. This trend has to be considered when identifying features to be offered.

Following the customer research, the requirements must be translated into product characteristics. For example, a kitchen product must be dishwasher safe, which controls the materials that can be used. The translation is commonly done between marketing and engineering. One knows customer requirements, whereas the other has the technical knowledge to describe a design to fit the need.

Frequently used tools for this translation process are the seven management tools:

- Affinity diagram—to identify and organize ideas and information
- Interrelationship chart—to identify relationships (dependence and influence) between ideas
- Tree diagram—to illustrate the form of influences, from the purpose through its roots
- Matrix chart—a summary diagram/chart of the strength of each idea
- Matrix data analysis—a chart providing values/rankings between problem causes
- Process decision program chart—to show possible sequences leading to a desirable result
- Arrow diagram—to show estimated or planned time values for key problem elements, to reach a solution

These tools are particularly appropriate for this activity, which is often complex and conceptual in nature. They are described further in Part II.

Product Planning

The purpose of a product is to satisfy customers' needs or desires. This satisfaction has several components—some obvious, some that must be discovered. The latter might be in the nature of unexpressed customer expectations. For example, for many years U.S. consumers wanted more reliable and economical cars. If these factors, rather than style and higher profits, had been more important to U.S. auto designers, the requirements would not have existed for the Japanese to fill (and consequently put themselves so heavily into the U.S. market). Not listening to the customer led to a major mistake in business strategy.

Product planning should thoroughly identify customer needs and expectations and ensure that all engineering and manufacturing decisions are based on filling those needs. It must be a thorough, disciplined, documented process that identifies customer needs, wants, and expectations and deploys them throughout the design and production cycles. To ensure this, the Japanese developed QFD methodology. This technique, similar to task analysis, was first used in the 1960s and is now used widely in Japan. Its use is growing in the West. It requires a significant effort before the design is started or released to manufacturing. It results in a shorter design cycle and more reliable, producible designs with very few changes required after production begins—which is very expensive. It also results in higher-quality products and greater customer satisfaction. The products satisfy every definition of quality to a degree never before achieved on a large scale. QFD is primarily comprehensive planning. It results in a series of interlinked, interdependent, detailed descriptions of design decisions, process identifications, and procedures, as well as process controls. The entire design production process is described, through to customer delivery. The quality to satisfy the customer is fully deployed through every activity and task. Figure 4.4 shows an overview of the QFD technique. It is more fully explained in Part II.

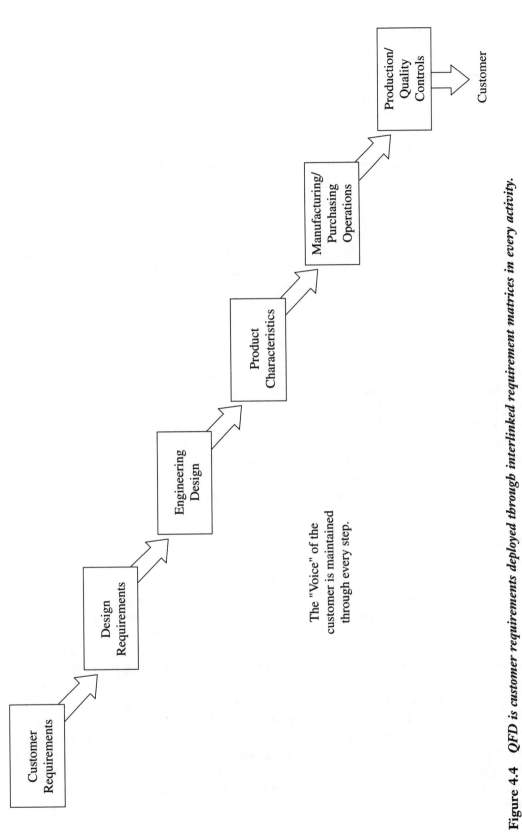

Figure 4.4 QFD is customer requirements deployed through interlinked requirement matrices in every activity.

The Design Process

Product development is a sociotechnical activity. People in organized groups use various technologies to produce a detailed product description (a specification). Managing to achieve this is complex. All factors involved must be effectively integrated to succeed. One impediment in the design process can be organizational structure. Traditional organizations are structured vertically according to function: marketing, engineering, production, personnel, and so on. Most work and responsibility flows vertically; however, important information and communication flow horizontally through the boundaries between organizational functions. Communications and data bridging this barrier are often distorted, and employees don't always communicate well with organizations outside their own. Organizations tend to develop their own cultures and goals. The organizational boundaries are also perceived as the limits of responsibility. When engineering releases a product to manufacturing, there is then less interest in the product because the engineers' work is done. Often the original designers are assigned to another project. After receiving the design package, manufacturing then begins the production process design activity. Sometimes there is some early interaction between engineering and manufacturing, however, it is of limited value as practiced. Designs keep changing up to and after the turnover time, which frequently requires production process design change.

One effective response to this has been to change organizational structure from the common vertical, military pyramid to a flatter organization with fewer layers. Combined with the multifunctional team concept for process management, this has simplified communications and has forced interorganizational cooperation because the teams have an interest in improving the quality of the design to production processes. The result is a product development/production process that contains all the work elements that affect the product, with the members working to produce what the customer and company want.

Quality of Design

Product design determines cost, quality, reliability, and, ultimately, customer satisfaction. Manufacturing can affect these factors. It does not control them, however, and it cannot enhance what the design has established. In fact, it takes careful planning and execution for manufacturing to approach its achievement. Therefore, the design–manufacturing sequence is critical to success in industry.

Product development is essentially a one-time event (and therefore impractical to measure.) If it is not done correctly and effectively (if it fails to meet the proper design goals), it results in less than the best. At the same time, to remain competitive, it is of strategic importance to reduce the development time for marketing a product. The result is a conflict between thoroughly designing and evaluating a product, and shortening the time to market. Too often this conflict is resolved in the direction of starting production too soon. The Japanese developed techniques such as quality function deployment (QFD) and applied older ones such as design of experiments (DOE) in concurrent engineering, to resolve this conflict. Development time and costs were reduced, and higher quality resulted.

Before companies began using these techniques, products typically entered production while still immature and not evaluated for producibility. The result was production delays and higher costs due to design changes to eliminate shortcomings. Such changes also frequently compromised the design in order to maintain production. In addition, the changes often caused secondary problems that were thought to be resolved but had bred further problems, resulting in a continuous fire-fighting cycle. Much of this was caused by product designs in which requirements were poorly defined, characteristics and tolerances were not scientifically established, and design requirements were not compatible with the manufacturing process capabilities.

Tolerances were the best estimate of the designer. It was normal and expected that changes would be required in production. In many industries, it was common to include the cost of the number of expected changes (based on past experience with a similar product) in the product development cost estimate. Little improvement was expected. Also, manufacturing processes were frequently not designed for a specific product; they were generic. It was expected that they could be adjusted to make the products being designed. The processes and the product would be debugged as production progressed. Inspection would sort good from bad, and the bad would be scrapped or reworked.

This approach was the norm. Figure 4.5 schematically depicts the way the typical design production process has worked. It is a sequential process with functional independence. Problems are fixed when they are found. Few integrated prevention activities take place.

Quality Design Reviews

Design reviews by specialists are intended to improve the design production process, but they haven't been effective. They fail because the review is done after design decisions are made; the scheduled time has been used, and manufacturing is impatient to start production and meet the schedule. Too much has been expended to change anything by then, other than to correct blatant errors. Culture and ego factors also limit the effectiveness of design reviews in the United States. Many designers resent being second-guessed by personnel from other organizations who were not involved in their design decisions. This was a common problem, initially, with U.S. engineers who worked for Japanese companies or U.S. companies taken over by the Japanese. The Japanese practice is to finalize designs through consensus. It is expected that designs will be reviewed and questions asked. Every engineer is not expected to know everything. Some studies have shown that American engineers in these companies first resented this peer review but came to understand its value and intent: to take advantage of the collective knowledge of the group objectively.

Fortunately, there are several interlinked and powerful tools that provide a better system for optimizing the design manufacturing process. They can produce high quality, shorter development cycles, and lower cost of products in Japanese-owned companies. They are all a part of the design development process commonly called concurrent engineering or team engineering, which will be discussed later.

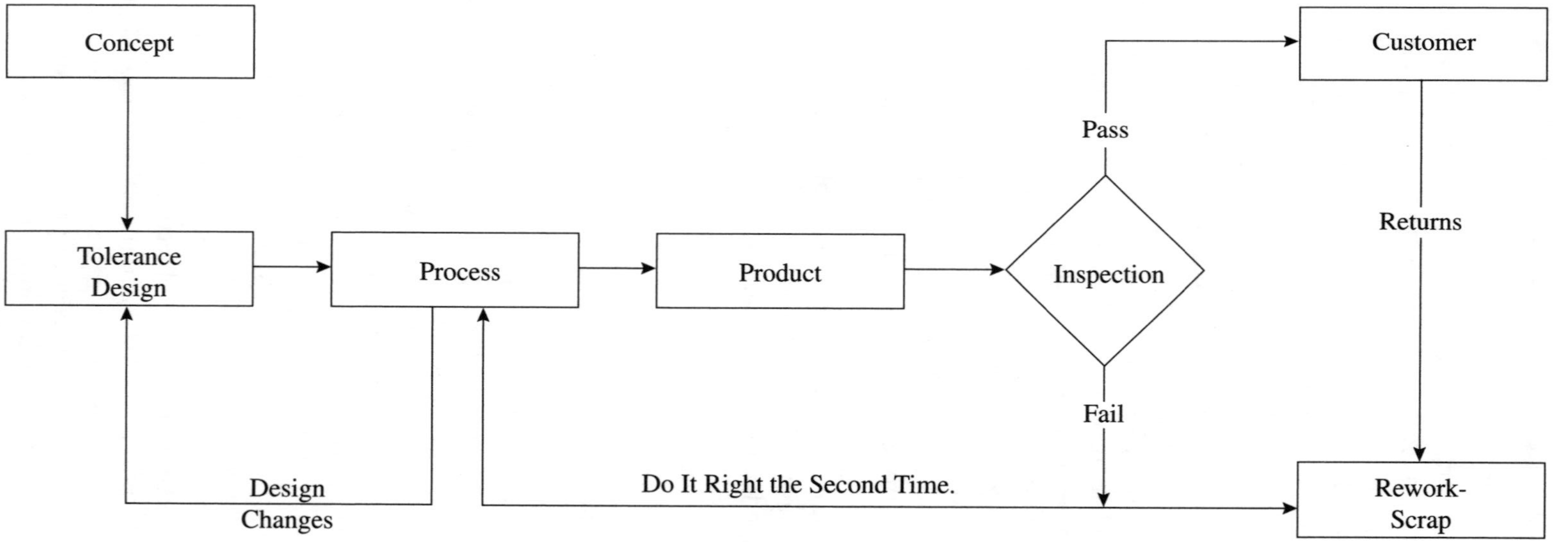

Figure 4.5 ***The predominant design–production–delivery process before TQM offered a better way.***

Design Control

The function of engineering is to interpret customer requirements and provide the detailed description of a product to manufacturing in a form—usually drawings and specifications (on paper or through the use of software)—sufficiently detailed so that the product can be produced at a competitive cost. Typically, for products of some complexity, the design steps are an evolution from concept through development, preliminary design, pilot production, and then release for manufacture. There are many terms used to describe this process, with variations in different industries. The complexity can vary tremendously depending on the technological advances required and the nature of the product. There would obviously be a difference between developing an electric toothbrush with relatively few parts for a benign environment, and a communications satellite with around a half million parts for a hostile space environment.

Design and Manufacturing

Following the definition of the engineering approach to be followed, the detailed design decisions are made, followed by the manufacturing process descriptions. Also at this time, the critical control points are selected for process control. It is during these decision steps that the DOE techniques should be used to select the critical design and process parameters. Forcing this process to a conclusion discloses many design and manufacturing problems to be resolved early rather than when a product is in production or use. Correction at these later stages is more costly and even damaging to a company's reputation. In addition, late fixes often force a compromise in the product design integrity.

The documents resulting from this effort represent an outstanding product history and are a communication tool for everyone in the organization because they describe not just the product but the basis for all decisions Employees can also identify where their jobs fit into the process of satisfying the customer.

The Modern Approach in Design

The modern approach (much simplified) to designing and producing a product is to use the appropriate tools. For example

1. Modern marketing research tools are used to define what customers need, want and expect.
2. A multifunction team, including marketing, engineering, and production specialists, employing the seven quality management tools and a QFD methodology, translates customer responses into product characteristics.
3. The engineering-led team would produce a design that meets those product characteristics and one compatible with production capabilities. (It is assumed that process capabilities have been quantified.) Final design tolerances would be established using DOE.
4. Established process improvement teams would continue to improve process capabilities.

This approach would result in a product that satisfied customer wants, needs, and expectations.

REFERENCES

1. R. C. Whitely. *The Customer Driven Company: Moving from Talk to Action* (New York: Addison-Wesley, 1991).
2. Whitely. *The Customer Driven Company.*
3. W. A. Shewhart. *Statistical Method from the Viewpoint of Quality Control* (Milwaukee: ASQC Quality Press, 1993).
4. B. Beizer. "Software Is Different." *Software Quality Professional* (August, 1997).
5. R. E. Zultner. "Software Quality Function Deployment: Applying QFD to Software." Denver, CO: ASQC Rocky Mountain Quality Conference, 1989.

ADDITIONAL READINGS

Hayes, B. E. *Measuring Customer Satisfaction: Survey Design, Use, and Statistical Analysis methods*, 2nd ed. Milwaukee: ASQ Quality Press, 1997.

Kessler, S. *Total Quality Service: A Simplified Approach to Using the Baldrige Award Criteria.* Milwaukee: ASQC Quality Press, 1995.

Lawton, R. L. *Creating a Customer Centered Culture: Leadership in Quality, Innovation and Speed.* Milwaukee: ASQC Quality Press, 1993.

STUDY QUESTIONS

1. What is the basis and value of the modern organization focus on customer satisfaction?
2. Identify the factors that create conflict between quality and productivity.
3. What is meant by internal and external customers?
4. What are the key elements/activities present in a customer-driven organization?
5. What are some differences in quality factors between industrial and service organizations?
6. What technique is used to maintain the requirements of the customer in the final product?
7. Discuss how the basic QFD matrices are connected.
8. Discuss how the techniques QFD, DOE, and concurrent engineering are used.

Chapter 5

Quality Planning and Deployment

- **The Role of Planning**
- **Strategic Planning**
- **Strategic and Quality Planning**
- **Goals and Metrics That Drive Organization Performance**
  - **Quality Goal Deployment-Management by Planning**
  - **Goal Basis**
  - **Goal Types**
  - **Goal Criteria**
- **Metrics-Measurement**
  - **Process Capability**
  - **Quality in Terms of Failure Rate**
  - **Common Metrics**
    - **The Six Sigma (6s) Quality Goal**
    - **Parts Per million (ppm)**
    - **Cycle Time**
    - **Cycle Time Reduction Methods**
- **TQM Versus Management by Objectives and Management by Exception**

THE ROLE OF PLANNING

The goal of planning is to make an organization better than its competitors, now and in the future. This could be market competitors, or in the case of a nonprofit, competitions for a budget. Planning is also a continuous process since the competitive environment is dynamic. Competitors often copy each other's successes, so new and innovative competitive strategies are needed to achieve or maintain a leading position.

Planning is based on strategy, mission, vision, and objectives. They are interrelated, but their development is not a three-step sequence. All must be reflected in a strategic plan. Planning is a difficult and complex task, an iterative process, not something only done on a fixed schedule. Also, competitors are strategizing, which may very well result in everyone's having to change. Strategic planning, therefore, is describing the organization future, destination, difficulties, and paths to success.

The information input into the strategic planning process is largely the result of the insights into the external competitive world, as well as the nature and capability of the organization (particularly its creative capability). The variables involved can change rapidly and in a way that challenges previous decisions.

Without effective, continuous planning an organization has no guide to achieving goals and is unprepared for changes in outside factors that can threaten its future. This is particularly true of the present, when operating environments are changing rapidly and unpredictably.

Planning is identified by type and time scale. Planning is *Strategic* for the future and is usually based on a 3 to 5 year projection. Each organization should determine its own strategic time frame. *Tactical* planning is short term, usually a year. It commonly coincides with the financial or budget year, but it should be flexible. Rapid changes in tactics may become necessary to meet a new challenge.

The two types of planning are used by the overall organization as well as the internal functional units, that is, marketing, quality, facilities, and so forth. Planning is the road map and actions identified to describe how an organization is going to continue to operate and grow. Some general reasons why it is required are

- The change in the scope and type of competition
- The increase in deregulation, privatization and changing markets
- Changing customer expectations toward higher quality
- The globalization of economic and financial factors
- Changes in world government policies, cultural issues, and trade agreements
- The rapid change in technology and information systems
- The change in workplace skills
- Widespread downsizing in all types of organizations
- The mobility of work/jobs

In light of the dynamic nature of all these factors, upper management has to frequently ask

- What business are we in or do we want to be in, in the next 5 to 10 years? What plans do we need?
- What do we do in response to the answers to those questions?

- How is the market changing? How will that affect us? How do we prepare for it? How do we organize for it? How do we lead the organization toward the new objectives?
- What are the organization strengths and weaknesses?
- What will the opportunities be as well as what will the threats be?
- Who and what will the competition be?
- What are the probable timing factors?
- What will the customer want?

STRATEGIC PLANNING

According to Mintzberg, a strategy is the embodiment of an organization's vision[1]. For example, a vision statement could be, "to become a leader in the field of health care delivery" (the external strategy). This reflects the strategy of the organization management, from which they will devise the actions to achieve it (the internal strategy). Some of the elements of these strategic actions may include: (1) become a systems-thinking organization, (2) become a learning organization, or (3) develop a management methodology using self-directed process improvement teams.

Strategic planning is the process by which organizations formulate strategies. It is not the strategy itself. The planning should be integrated with internal goal setting (including quality goals). In autocratic organizations, planning is done by upper management and dictated to the lower levels. Team-based organizations solicit and include individual and team ideas. Planning activities involve the solicitation and discussion of the strategic and other quality objectives submitted from every level. Each level of the organization is expected to meet its goals. An open management style will allow members to contribute. This kind of activity is rare in autocratic organizations because upper management thinks not in terms of employee participation but rather that planning and goal setting are management's job and the organization should accept the results. The basic elements of strategic planning are listed in Table 5.1.

A part of the ongoing strategic planning process is to fully define whether previous plans were met and if not, why not. The objective is not to assess blame but to learn whether the planning process is flawed and needs improvement, whether objectives were unrealistic, or if any organization weaknesses were a factor. (One way to evaluate the planning process itself is to benchmark the processes of other similar and successful organizations.) The strategic and other internal quality planning processes are the foundation of successful organizations and critical to the development of an organization collectively working to excel.

One of the critical questions in strategic planning is the subject of quality. What will its role be in being competitive and satisfying future customers? What has to be done internally to assure that quality goals are met? What are the key quality goals? (Nonquality strategic factors might be to increase market share, expand to other countries, introduce a new product, make an acquisition, or sell off some product line.)

Table 5.1   Basic elements of strategic planning.

1. Vision and Mission
Vision statements describe what the organization wants to be—what it hopes to achieve in measurable terms. Mission statements describe why an enterprise exists. They define an organization's scope of business. Some organizations develop separate vision and mission statements. Other organizations incorporate the vision into the mission statement. Vision and mission statements are often included in the annual reports of publicly held companies.
2. Core Beliefs and Value Statements
Such statements describe items such as an organization's beliefs, values, assumptions, credos, philosophies, principles, and priorities. These statements are the basic beliefs that drive organizational behavior. Core beliefs and value statements are representative of the organization's personality and culture—or "the way we do things around here." Similar to vision and mission, core belief and value statements often appear in an organization's annual report.
3. Strengths, Weaknesses, Opportunities, and Threats (SWOT) Analysis
A SWOT analysis evaluates key internal strengths (e.g., financially strong market, employees) and weaknesses (e.g., young company with a high debt load) and external opportunities and threats. The analysis considers factors such as the industry and the organization's competitive position, as well as functional areas and management. Opportunities are identified and limitations acknowledged to provide information for reasonable goals (e.g., competition, internal capabilities).
4. Goals and Objectives
An organization sets specific goals and objectives to help fulfill its mission and give it direction and purpose over a long period of time.
5. Tactics
Once goals and objectives are defined, the organization creates tactics—strategies and processes that will help them arrive at their objectives. Organizational and divisional business plans develop goals within their appropriate budgets to support the tactics.

STRATEGIC AND QUALITY PLANNING

Business managers commonly make strategic plans for new product or service development and introduction, as well as penetration into new markets, but only in recent years have they included quality improvement because it is now a market requirement. Quality planning is an integral part of the strategic planning process. The objective in linking quality planning with the total strategic plan is to fully integrate quality and operational planning with the business plan (the business plan is how to meet all objectives). The primary objective of the quality plan is to meet the strategic quality objectives. The overall organization quality plan is usually prepared annually, after the strategic plan. It may contain one-, three- or five-year steps, reflecting the overall strategic plan structure. This quality plan includes what each organization element does to meet the immediate and long-term quality objectives.

Some quality objectives in the quality plan could be

- Reduce process variation by 5 percent; cycle time by 20 percent. (Key processes would be identified, as well as the metric.)
- Benchmark three (named) processes for breakthrough improvement.
- Improve cycle time: Reduce new product development-to-market time by 10 percent per year. This could also be a strategic plan item.
- Introduce quality function deployment planning on one new product/service this year

Satisfying quality objectives of this nature will reduce variation, cycle time, and cost; increased productivity will provide better products and services to customers, putting the organization in a better competitive position.

GOALS AND METRICS THAT DRIVE ORGANIZATION PERFORMANCE

A goal, or objective, is the target to reach by a specified time. Targets are usually identified by the metrics (measurement) selected to indicate achievement. Managers are frequently not comfortable with using resources unless they can see numbers that show a benefit. But initially, quantitative goals—although desirable—are not always necessary or wise. An argument supporing this is that setting quantitative goals is frequently arbitrary, selected when it isn't known how they can be achieved. On the positive side, though, there can be a sense of progress, of achievement, and of winning if the goals are met. Whatever goals are set, they must be meaningful to top management to gain its total support.

The other aspect is that not meeting goals is often considered failure. However, is coming to within 90 percent a failure? There is also the potential problem in setting quantitative goals mentioned in the discussion on management by ovjectives, later in this chapter, that long-term benefits can be sacrificed for short-term gains. In comparison, just using continuous improvement as a goal and measuring the trend is a simple concept that can be a motivation to continued improvement. This approach is particularly useful in the early stages when people are learning the philosophy, understanding the process and methodology. The complexity of measurement can be added after the data are collected and understood.

Benchmarking (Part II) is an excellent goal-setting technique that is being used more frequently. If an organization discovers that another company can operate a similar process at a lower cost and higher quality output, this establishes an improvement goal. It is frequently found that benchmark goals are more difficult than an organization would normally set, but since they have been proved achievable they are accepted.

A different idea has been initiated by the Motorola Corporation and adopted by others, such as General Electric. It sets quantitative quality goals for all organizations and processes. A goal to achieve Six Sigma capability in all its processes (discussed later) sets a quantitative goal for the entire company. It is difficult but achievable for the company, its elements, and its suppliers. It is also a rather sophisticated statement. It requires an understanding of basic statistics and statistical thinking about process management.

Quality Goal Deployment—Management by Planning

The Japanese have for many years used a unique form of planning to deploy quality throughout a company. It is commonly called hoshin kanri. Hoshin kanri is different because, although there is organizational goal setting involved, the focus is on the planning process itself. The objective is to improve the planning process continuously and thereby become better at setting goals. The emphasis is not only on meeting goals but on learning how to set them better. The result is that targets normally are exceeded.

The process begins with the setting of a few key goals for the company by top management. Then down through the organization, managers and employees establish goals that correlate with those of the company. Peers then meet to make sure that their plans are complementary. They are then reviewed by management. The final plans/goals are posted in the work area.

After developing their targets, individuals document a monthly self-assessment that is given to their supervisors, who combine it with their own and send it to their supervisors and so on up to the top. Everyone in the chain knows what is going on. Flexibility and continuous improvement are reflected in the procedure, whereby measured gains become the new standard and from which further progress is planned. The new standard becomes the level for daily control. There are then two activities involved: meeting standards and making improvements. Other unique features include the monthly audit to analyze what was learned. Also important is an annual presidential audit to assess progress in order to determine how the planning process is improving and how the president can assist. Every level of management stays involved.

Goal Basis

Goals have often been based on historical performance. Marketing made the sales forecast, engineering and manufacturing equated them into effort, and budgets were set. Any improvement objective was supplementary. A number was selected based on what organization managers thought could be done. Very often the number was "negotiated" with higher management. There wasn't a clear picture of how it would be accomplished. The concept of work processes or the tools for improving variation were unknown or only vaguely recognized. The term *process* was pretty much assigned to what manufacturing used to make things. Modern improvement goals are based on what is required to satisfy the customer and become more productive and competitive. In process managed organization, where process status and capabilities are known realistically, goals can be set more rationally and accurately.

Goal Types

The two general types of goals are incremental and breakthrough. Both are necessary to maximize improvement. Incremental refers to the small continuous process improvements contributed mostly by team actions. Breakthrough goals are set to provide a significant process improvement, beyond what the incremental trend would indicate. They can be achieved by methodology or equipment changes and the reduction of common

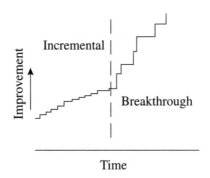

Figure 5.1 *Relationship between incremental and breakthrough goals.*

causes of variation. As shown in Figure 5.1, breakthrough goals are dramatic increases in performance in a short period of time. Goals resulting from Benchmarking can be among the most significant and challenging, as well as a breakthrough.

As an example of a goal for the overall organization, the Institute of Electrical and Electronic Engineers *Spectrum Magazine*, October 1995, reported a landmark type of agreement between Boeing and a major customer, United Airlines, for the purchase of the Boeing 777 airplane, prior to its design. At the time it was projected to be the largest and most advanced and complex commercial two-engine jet ever produced. The agreement was not a stack of specifications but a note that simply stated

From day one, the plane would

- Have the best dispatch reliability in the industry.
- Have the greatest customer appeal in the industry.
- Be user friendly, with everything working.

The Boeing approach was to launch an airplane, on time, that would exceed the expectations of flight crews, cabin crews, maintenance and support teams, and ultimately the passengers and shippers. Boeing met those objectives. The biggest breakthrough aspect was the application of concurrent engineering and advanced computer-aided design techniques on such a large and complex product. Design time was significantly shortened, costs were reduced, and a design was formulated requiring few production changes. Of course, Boeing did a great deal of detailed planning and goal setting to be successful.

Goal Criteria

Goal-setting criteria should be

Measurable—Objectives that can be stated in numbers can be communicated with precision.

Optimal as to overall results—Objectives which "suboptimize" performance of various activities can damage overall performance.

All-inclusive—Activities for which objectives have been set tend to have high priority but at the expense of the remaining activities.

Maintainable—Objectives should be designed in modular fashion so that elements can be revised without extensive teardown.

Economic—The value of meeting the objectives should be clearly greater than the cost of setting and administering them.[2]

No less important is the list of criteria as perceived by those who are faced with meeting the objectives. To these people objectives should be:

Legitimate—Objectives should have official status.

Understandable—They should be stated in clear, simple language, ideally the language of those faced with meeting objectives.

Applicable—The objectives should fit the conditions of use or should include the flexibility to be made adaptable.

Worthwhile—Meeting the objectives should be regarded as benefiting those who do the added work, as well as the organization that established them.

Attainable—It should be possible for the typical organization member to meet the objectives by applying reasonable effort. However, it is very valuable to set stretch-goals for improvements vitally needed.

Equitable—When using goal attainment in merit reviews, it is important to be fair and to consider the relative difficulty between objectives.

Goals related to customer satisfaction should be stated in terms of exceeding those of the competition in such factors as

Reliability—Having a product work for as long a time as economically attainable.

Service—A no questions asked replacement policy; Convenient, rapid service available.

Safety—Products must be safe, not only to satisfy the customer but because of the high cost of liability lawsuits.

Style—The style of the design is a critical factor in many products. It is the emotional quality factor that can be the reason for a customer selection.

METRICS—MEASUREMENT

Process measurement is necessary in order to know where a process is performing, that is, how far it is from the improvement goal, and to indicate status as improvements are made. The primary purpose of measurement is to support continuous process improvement.

As a metric fundamental, the system or process to be measured must be completely defined. The boundaries of the measurement must be established. Selected measures should only be those vital factors related to performance. Vital factors are those which effect the goal of satisfying the customers and providing comparison to competitors. Both internal and external goals should include customer input. Some vital measures and metrics examples are

Cycle time

Process variation—Errors per unit, process, or supplier

Value added— (nonvalue-added reduction)

Cost—per task, unit, hour, or rework

On time—tasks or items

It is also important to select the best measurement point in a process. The idea of critical or vital measurement points is illustrated in Figure 5.2.

Other temporary measurements can be devised and tracked by the process improvement teams to evaluate the effect of their incremental changes. Frequently, measurements characterized by great accuracy are difficult and expensive to obtain. In such cases, good estimates, established by consensus, may be all that is necessary since the most common application of process measurement is for comparison from first measurement to when improvements are made.

Organizations/teams involved in measuring need to be alert and avoid getting overly involved in making measurements, thereby forgetting improvement as the real objective.

Process Capability

Process capability is a statistical measurement comparing the range through which a process functions (varies) to the tolerance limits of a part being produced in an industrial process.

If the manufacturing processes varies outside what the tolerance allows, defective products are produced. A major factor in producing high-quality products (very few defects) is to maintain processes with a high capability. Process capability is described more thoroughly in Part II.

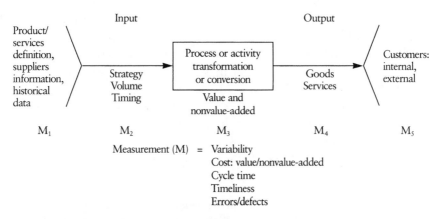

Figure 5.2   Process-quality measurement points.

Quality in Terms of Failure Rate

A low product failure rate is an important objective for customer satisfaction and low warranty costs. Product complexity affects failure rate (reliability). In fact, failure rate is inversely related to design complexity. Complexity creates more opportunities for failures and defects. It results in a higher failure rate during manufacture and in use. Complexity also adds to product cost in labor and materials. Latent defects, those occurring during customer ownership, are largely a result of inadequate design margin, complexity, and low process capability. They must be minimized during design and production. The effort to increase the ratio of design margin to process capability is therefore critical to achieving customer satisfaction and reducing costs.

Common Metrics

Organizations need goals to focus their energies and resources on common values; goals are important for unifying efforts and measuring achievement. At the same time, it is also difficult to set single meaningful goals for the entire organization. They tend to become so broad that organizational elements and individuals fail to see the connection between their efforts and some generalized goal. A goal, "to be number one in five years", is meaningless unless it is supported by strategic and tactical plans describing how it will be reached. The following discussion identifies some successful approaches that make goal setting more meaningful.

The Six Sigma (6s) Quality Goal

Some leading companies such as General Electric, Motorola, Allied-Signal, IBM, and others have set a goal to achieve a Six Sigma capability in their organization processes.* This would translate into a process that would produce only two defects per million tasks/operations— a very ambitious goal by any standard. It has been proved to provide good motivation and to engage all organization members in working to improve the quality of their work and work processes. To be effective, it requires management leadership and a systems approach to organization development and process improvement. It also requires the tools and techniques used in TQM, with the added emphasis on financial measurements. Implementing improvement programs requires an investment. Because management is responsible for assuring a fair return on an investment, many top managers have adopted programs like Six Sigma that include financial improvement measures as well as quality measures.

Management adoption of a Six Sigma quality objective is intended to convey continuous process improvement and the achievement of very high quality in internal processes as well as in their products and services. The overall objective is often quantified in terms such as, "We want to improve from where we estimate we are, at 20,000

---

*Note: Some literature uses 3.4 errors per million in relation to Six Sigma. This goal is set by assuming that any process in average operation will itself vary at least +/- 1.5 sigma. This could produce, on average, 3.4 errors per million.

errors per million operations, to five errors per million operations, in five years and two errors in 10 years."

Statistical rigor is not intended in this kind goal setting. A "sigma" capability does not have meaning in many internal processes. A "sigma" goal can be applied to specific processes. There are relatively simple statistical process measurement tools that measure process variation in terms of sigma and can be used to measure a process operating condition. (This methodology will be discussed in the next chapter.) Suffice it to say at this point that one should determine whether 6s is being used as an "objective slogan" or as a true process measure.

Parts Per Million (ppm)

Parts per million (ppm) is another way to express a goal equivalent to a sigma capability. It means defects or errors per million process operations, or in products produced. As an illustration of this concept, Figure 5.3 relates number of defects per million typically produced in some common activities (processes), and the equivalent sigma. It shows the high process capability, the sigma measure, required to approach zero defects. For example, errors in doctors' prescriptions are about 10,000 per million written. That process demonstrates a capability of about 3.9 sigma. If an objective were set to reach a 6s capability, defects would have to be reduced to two per million prescriptions. A great deal of organized effort by many different doctors would be required to reach it. The best-in-class notation is made in comparison to the average company performance. The best-in-class notation is the benchmark process to equal or exceed.

Cycle Time

Another important goal is cycle time reduction.[4] From a macro viewpoint, cycle time is the time between the receipt of an order to the delivery of a product or service. This is an important measure of company performance and productivity in satisfying the customer. This macro measure is, of course, made up of and determined by the many internal (micro) cycles, and it is these that are the targets for improvement. Cycle times for new product development to market time are of growing importance and can provide a major strategic advantage. The company first to market with a high-quality product or service will reap the highest profit before competition drives prices down. Cycle time can also be a factor in retaining market share. Intel Corporation has retained the world market share lead by supplying ever-improving products that have kept the customers satisfied.

Cycle Time Reduction Methods

Cycle time reduction involves looking at the process from the point of view of the task within the process. The task in this context could be to make something or to complete paper work. Cycle time reduction then evaluates all the activities in the process to determine whether each is necessary, can be done more simply, and adds value.

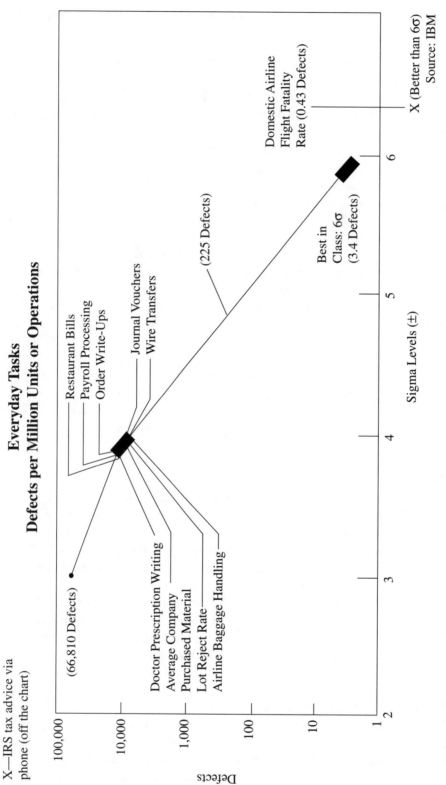

Everyday Tasks
Defects per Million Units or Operations

X—IRS tax advice via
phone (off the chart)

(66,810 Defects)

Restaurant Bills
Payroll Processing
Order Write-Ups

Journal Vouchers
Wire Transfers

Doctor Prescription Writing
Average Company
Purchased Material
Lot Reject Rate
Airline Baggage Handling

(225 Defects)

Best in
Class: 6σ
(3.4 Defects)

Domestic Airline
Flight Fatality
Rate (0.43 Defects)

X (Better than 6σ)
Source: IBM

Defects

100,000
10,000
1,000
100
10
1

Sigma Levels (±)

2   3   4   5   6

Figure 5.3 *Some common performance capabilities.*
Copyright of Motorola, Inc. Used with permission.

82

Juran, in his *Juran on Quality Design*, outlines a series of actions to reduce cycle time:

- *Diagnosis of cycle time:* Analysis of total cycle time and the time consumed by the vital few steps.
- *Diagnosis of the process:* Analysis of how the process has been designed and operated.
- *Diagnosis of major influences:* Analysis of those major forces that are all-pervasive and must not be ignored.
- *Identification and implementation of remedies to reduce time:* Identification of those improvement methods and technologies that will generate the time reductions.

Basic steps in cycle time improvement in simple processes are

1. Define the process and its specific objectives.
2. Identify all activites.
3. Flowchart/map the process.
4. List the elapsed time for each activity.
5. Identify nonvalue-added tasks.
6. Simplify and eliminate the nonvalue-added.*

TQM VERSUS MANAGEMENT BY OBJECTIVES AND MANAGEMENT BY EXCEPTION

In addition to teaching the world how to raise quality and improve competitive position, Deming was a constant critic of American management practices. His ideas, proved to be effective when understood and properly implemented, conflict directly with the old American model, represented by the command and control management style and such fads as management by objectives (MBO) and management by exception (MBE).

Peter Drucker is credited with coining the term *management by objectives.* It is defined as "a process whereby the superior and subordinate managers of an organization jointly identify its common goals. They then define each individual's major area of responsibility in terms of the results expected of him/her, and use these measures as guides for operating the manager's unit and assessing the contribution of each of its members."[5] The key factor is that the individual should play the primary role in setting his or her own objectives and not merely accept those dictated from above, which has been the most prevalent practice. Typically the objectives were "negotiated" between manager and subordinate, but the manager was always in the position of control. MBO was practiced more successfully in the upper levels because the lower level conditions were more dynamic. Objectives agreed to one month became inappropriate a month later because some unforeseen event changed operating conditions—a contract cancellation, landing a new contract, the appearance of new competition, or new product manufacturing problems.

---

* Cycle time can also be reduced in more complex processes by using the appropriate process improvement tools.

MBO emphasizes functional performance measurements supposedly under the control of individual managers. However, when an organization doesn't understand and use process management, individual managers, and their objectives, can become victims of events outside their control. Yet by MBO policy, they are held accountable. Even if upper management accepts the fact that uncontrollable events have prevented the achievement of objectives, the whole process was of little value.

As so frequently happened in the typical MBO methodology, a manager and subordinate would agree to an objective when neither really knew how it could be done. Managers who were resourceful and lucky enough to succeed were rewarded. If they failed, they lost some stature with the boss. In either case, success or failure, no one was sure how the objectives were met or missed, or what negative effect success may have had on some other organization element or the overall organization. It was something of a lottery. It should also be obvious that giving managers individual objectives in a team-managed organization would at a minimum be counterproductive, if not destructive to team objectives.

This not to say that some form of MBO tool cannot be used in team-managed organizations. If objectives are set in coordination with organization and team objectives, the best results for the organization can be achieved. For example, in an organization with operating teams, a team leader manager could reasonably agree to reduce process variation by say 20 percent in a year, if the team was functioning and understood how and what approaches were required to make the improvement. If, in an organization oriented quality improvement, MBO is used to incentivize process improvement management, it approaches what the Japanese call quality deployment or Hoshin planning.

Management by exception (MBE) is also another common management technique. It is an old method for identifying targets for management attention and action. For MBE, reporting systems are established to identify variables (cost, quality, volume, or schedule) that are performing outside established forecasts, targets, or budgets. By definition, such items are problem indicators and need correction. It is a simple concept, but it doesn't produce long-term results required for survival because

1. Performance outside arbitrarily set limits is usually a symptom rather than the problem.
2. Performance (action) limits are not set based on the capability of the process (they are often set in relation to MBO). Without the knowledge of the capability of the process, performance limits can easily be set that the process will never meet. Managers under pressure to "do something" will force some temporary change, which will be short lived or cause some other problem, with the connection never realized.
3. No action will be taken when a favorable variance occurs, yet this may indicate the existence of a special cause of variation that needs to be identified. It may be a clue to achieve permanent performance improvement.

MBE, like MBO, can be a useful management action indicator if the "exception" levels are tied to variation outside the measured process capability, or if in the case of exceeding error levels, cost limits, or missed schedules, the process was examined for the cause.

REFERENCES

1. H. Mintzberg. *The Rise and Fall of Strategic Planning* (Upper Saddle River, NJ: Prentice Hall, 1994).
2. T.J. Cartin, and D. Jacoby. *A Review of Quality Management and a Primer for the Quality Managers Certification Exam* (Milwaukee: ASQ Quality Press, 1997).
3. J. M. Juran, and F. M. Gryna. *Juran's Quality Control Handbook* (New York: McGraw-Hill, 1988).
4. P.R. Thomas. *Competitiveness Through Cycle Time* (New York: McGraw-Hill, 1990).
5. R.G. Greenwood. "Management by Objectives," as developed by Peter Drucker, assisted by Howard Smitty. *Academy of Management Review* 6, No. 2 (1981).

ADDITIONAL READINGS

Hayes, B.E. *Measuring Customer Satisfaction*. Milwaukee: ASQ Quality Press, 1997.
Morgan, M.W. *Measuring Performance with Customer-Defined Metrics*. ASQ *Quality Progress*, December 1996.

STUDY QUESTIONS

1. What is meant by organization planning? What is it based on?
2. Why is strategic and tactile organization planning needed?
3. Why should quality planning be part of overall stategic planning?
4. What is the value in devising management quality goals and measures?
5. What are the criteria for setting goals, objectives?
6. What are some common basic process measurements?
7. What is the meaning of a Six Sigma quality goal? How does it differ from other improvement programs such as TQM?
8. Why is cycle time an important quality and productivity measure?

Chapter 6

Quality Systems and Improvement

- **Systems Thinking**
- **A Systems Approach**
- **The Quality System**
- **Continuous Process Improvement (CPI)**
- **The Improvement Concept**
  - Kinds of improvement
  - The Quality Trilogy
  - Breakthrough Quality Improvements
  - Process Characteristics
  - Process Description
  - The Context of Improvement
  - An Approach to Process Management
- **Quality Improvement Techniques**
  - For Variables
  - For Attributes
  - Design of Experiments (DOE)
  - Concurrent Engineering
  - Quality Function Deployment
  - Reengineering
  - Reengineering and TQM

- **Organization/System, Assessment, Audits, and Surveys**
    The Assessment Process
    Assessment Structure
    Assessment Criteria
    Terminology
    Process and Personnel

SYSTEMS THINKING

Systems thinking is the belief that an organization is more than the sum of its parts, that it is an integrated system that cannot be divided into independent parts. Moreover, organizations cannot function effectively if viewed as functioning parts of a large machine. They must be viewed, organized and managed as social systems (a community) if they are to survive, let alone prosper.[1]

Systems thinking is important to effective management because it indicates that a piecemeal, problem-patching approach won't fix the system or make it work better. When one element is changed, the effect on all elements must be evaluated. For example, implementing improvement teams in only one organization element can have a negative effect on attitudes and behavior in other elements unless they fully understand management's intent and rationale. Another example would be to allow one organization element to set quality goals that were not in alignment with overall quality objectives.

A SYSTEMS APPROACH

In complex product development, engineers use a systems engineering methodology to assure that all subassemblies and parts work efficiently, and reliably, and will consistently perform to requirements. Software program developers use a systems framework that recognizes the interdependency of a program's elements. Therefore, a system is the product of the interaction of its parts.

In contrast, the most common approach to organization problem solving and making improvement has been to use a piecemeal rather than a systematic approach. Most problems are approached and resolved by an organization function, even though most are interfunctional systems problems. One reason for this is the practice of managing using organizational structure and specialization that evolved in American business.

Historically, as the economy and population grew, the size and complexity of organizations also increased. For example, up until about the late 1930s, foreman in industry hired their own workers as they needed them. Hiring then devolved to the responsibility of a personnel function, then to an industrial relations function, and commonly now, a human resource function. (Drivers behind this growth were the increase in technical skills required and the increase in federal government employment regulations, the introduction of extensive employee benefits, and greater training needs—all requiring special knowledge in hiring and managing the workforce.)

Also during this period, quality requirements became more complex; by inspection, quality control was performed, then by quality assurance, and sometimes by product assurance. (Again this expansion was driven by government requirements imposed during WWII and the increased complexity of products and production processes.)

The practice of using organization specialists continued. Unfortunately, operational barriers grow as more ornaments are added to the organization tree. This led to each functional organization's solving problems, or the part of the problem they determined were within their responsibility, even though many problems were interfunctional, system problems. Usually there was no mechanism to resolve system problems because no system/process had been identified, so no one was responsible. The functional organizations were expected to "work it out." Constantly working out individual problems also had the weakness of not providing the means or serious interest in making system improvements.

Until the 1970s, while the United States used the pyramid, functional structure, the Japanese went in another direction. They simplified and flattened their structures. This brought upper management into better contact with the lower echelons, improved communications, and reduced cost. Also, with the development of the quality function deployment technique, the Japanese introduced a systems planning and improvement management practice. Organization barriers were reduced, and overall efficiency and effectiveness was improved.

THE QUALITY SYSTEM

Organizations using TQM, Six Sigma, or any quality management improvement program must develop , manage, and improve the quality system. The International Standard, ANSI/ISO/ASQ A8402 (1994), defines the quality system as the "organizational structures, procedures, processes, and resources needed to implement quality management."

A quality system should satisfy the managerial needs of the entire organization and not only customer-defined requirements. The system elements are those needed to focus the organization on satisfying the customer and competitive markets. The system should be designed to facilitate meeting strategic quality objectives. The quality system should also facilitate the production of facts and data needed to improve performance and competitive position.

Quality management manages the system. Other organization members work in the system. The system should be documented and understood by all organization members. It is not only for management-designated quality specialists. One example of a good quality system would be the policies, procedures, practices, and measurements needed to satisfy the criteria of the Malcolm Baldrige National Quality Award (chapter 12).

CONTINUOUS PROCESS IMPROVEMENT (CPI)

Most managers, if asked, could identify and describe improvements they have initiated or in which they participated. Change would probably be things like methods improvement, procedure clarification, suggestion writing, or assigning special training. Most efforts probably had some positive effect. They saved time, for a while at least. But the dynamic events of the workplace kept these managers busy reacting to problems—fighting fires. The different functional organizations continued to do their own thing. Functions such as manufacturing operations satisfied their own needs; quality engineering documented the inspection procedures, records, and reports; finance decided what cost data it would collect and report; and so on.

The common element in these activities is that each functional organization operated for its own interests. The boundaries of their interests were pretty much the boundaries of their organization structure. There wasn't an overall organization, systematic approach.

Work gets done through a process (good or bad) crossing organization boundaries. If work is a continuous or sustained process, improvements not based on that reality wouldn't have much effect. Functional organization boundaries and self-interests would inhibit any changes.

Management has always been interested in and receptive to ideas on how to improve. But there have been some unstated and critical constraints as to what management would allow. It maintained command and control. It has tried changing some things such as various organization responsibilities, but the power base, operating methods, and policies didn't change in any significant way. This situation is one of the reasons the adoption of CPI often does not meet management's expectations. Too often management has embraced the idea of constantly improving and can see the advantages to team problem solving, but is reluctant to give up control. The thought of change can be unnerving, but like the need for major surgery, the alternative is more serious.

CPI is not just an activity, it is a management philosophy and methodology fundamentally different from the traditional practice of managing specialized functional organizations. It is the core operating principle for an improvement-oriented organization.

What has often happened is that a CPI activity has been *added* to the existing organization. This approach can provide some improvements but will not lead to the most valuable changes because it is soon limited by the old management and organization barriers. More importantly, it doesn't lead to a change in management's thinking about what kind of an organization is required for tomorrow's marketplace. CPI can't be considered just another organization activity. It should be considered a means of providing one methodology in the evolution toward becoming *the way* organizations operate.

THE IMPROVEMENT CONCEPT

CPI is a management operating philosophy as well as an objective. It says that the organization will seek never-ending improvements in the important, if not all, organization activities, with the primary focus on improving internal systems and processes, as well as those externally connected to suppliers and customers.

One way to conceptualize CPI is to analyze a picture of it from initiation to reaching tough improvement objectives. A process is a sequence of steps, tasks, or activities that converts an input into something else as an output. The sequence of steps can be the activity of one person, or the linking of tasks to define a more complex process. A valuable concept is to treat every process activity, as well as the entire process, as having a supplier and a customer. In actual operation, each "producer" has the responsibility, when possible, to add value and strive to improve its supplier–customer relationship.

The process depicted in Figure 6.1 is for a process in which *variables*, numerical characteristic measurements, can be made—meters, cycle time, cost, etc. The process represents the concept of time-based variation reduction. For other processes involving *attributes* measures—that is, good-bad, number of errors—improvements can be pictured using a trend chart that shows the process functioning over time. Improvement efforts would reduce variation, and as typically plotted, would show a downward trend.

Kinds of Improvement

Performance improvements can be incremental (steady progress, step by step, each problem solved in order) or breakthroughs (big jumps). As Juran defines them in his "Trilogy,"[2] these are quality planning, quality control, and then quality improvement where a major breakthrough advance is made. Both incremental and breakthrough approaches are needed. Also, if the improvement activities are going to become the theme of the organization on a long-term basis, they also must involve improved relationships, both between managers and employees and of the organization with its customers and suppliers.

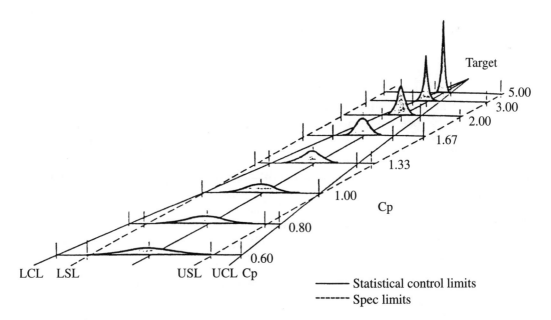

Figure 6.1 *Continuous measurable improvement.*

The Quality Trilogy

Managing for quality is done by using the common managerial processes of *planning, control,* and *improvement.*

Planning—This is the activity of developing the products and processes to meet customer needs. It includes identifying and describing the following

- The customers
- Customer needs
- Product or service features to satisfy customers
- The processes, in detail, to produce those features consistently
- The performance of the processes need for and affected by the planning
- The status of completion of the outstanding quality plans
- The demonstrated capability of the organization in the quality function
- The improvements suggested by improvement teams
- Upper management selection of the overall quality objectives
- The resources required to meet objectives
- The internal organization's plans to meet overall objectives
- The related plans to be used by the process operators

Control—This is the activity used to collect, evaluate, and report on actual performance, such as

- Evaluate ongoing, operating process performance.
- Compare actual to goals.
- Assure action to eliminate differences.

Improvement—One theme and strategy of modern management is continuous process improvement. It applies to every process that may affect the product or service received by the customer. It involves the concept of measurable objectives and the use of feedback loops. Improvements are then tracked against the objectives in the strategic quality plan.

The typical Process Improvement(PI) teams will provide a steady stream of incremental improvements. However, this will not usually provide the products and services that will result in the organization becoming a leader in its field. Imagination and innovation are required to provide breakthrough improvements—improvements in leaps, on top of the incremental. This will result in market leadership.

Breakthrough Quality Improvements

The following is the basic Juran trilogy sequence for achieving a "breakthrough" rather than incremental improvement.

- Proof of Need—Loss of market share, lower costs, shorter cycle time, competitive advantage.
- Project Identification—An important problem selected for solution. An important process needing significant improvement.

- Organization to Guide Projects—Multifunction innovative project team.
- Organization, for Diagnosis—Make project team responsible for diagnosis.
- Diagnosis—Identify and analyze symptoms and causes.
- Development of Remedies—Choose a remedy for dominant causes and recommend corrective action.
- Proof of the Remedies—Prove remedy effectiveness under operating conditions.
- Dealing with Cultural Resistance—Evaluate social impact of change. Determine how change will be introduced.
- Control at New Level—Make gains permanent, as basis for next improvement, breakthrough or incremental.
- Benchmarking—Use it to find stretch goals.

Process Characteristics

A process is a sequence of activities or tasks completed by a person, group, team, set of equipment, or their combinations. As Figure 6.2 shows, outputs are generally inputs to another process.

- No two process outputs are exactly alike, even when one is the replica of the other.
- Sources of variation vary.
- Some randomly occurring variation is normal.
- Some variation may be due to assignable, removable causes.

Reducing process variation provides higher quality at lower cost. A sequence of related processes is a system. Processes and systems have the attributes of efficiency and effectiveness in terms of their performance.

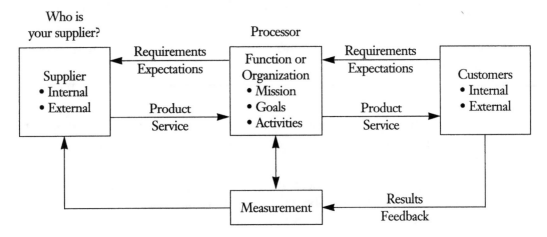

Figure 6.2   *Systems approach to improvement.*

A comparative efficiency can be determined quantitatively by comparing cycle time and costs prior to improvement with those after improvement. Effectiveness can be determined in terms of internal or external customer satisfaction.

Interrelated processes act as both a supplier and customer. In providing requirements to a supplier, a customer becomes a supplier. In receiving the output of another process, a supplier becomes a customer. This process model is universally understood and represents reality, to which various tools and techniques can be applied for improvement.

A high-quality process

- Achieves intended results and satisfies the customer.
- Uses resources efficiently.
- Displays variability at the lowest economically achievable level.
- Uses key quality measures to assess performance.
- Adds value to the organization objectives.

Process Description

The *macro* process of the total organization is the sequence of tasks performed from order entry to delivery, or as an analogy, from when a patient is admitted to a hospital, to the satisfactory delivery of the product or service: The patient exits from the hospital after satisfactory treatment. The *micro* processes are each of the linked tasks required to complete the macro task, such as registration of the patient, forms completion, and the like.

A generic process module would look like the one in Figure 6.2. This module can represent the macro or micro level. This module idea represents a tool for a systems approach to improvement. The system is the linkage of modules. Individual tasks or an entire process can be described, and then analyzed. The central element of a process module is the processor/producer. The module illustrates the concept of every producer/processor having a supplier (input) and a customer (output), and that the role of each can vary at different times.

- The producer supplies requirements to its suppliers, and goods and services to its customers.
- Suppliers may be internal, that is, the other connected modules, or external, another organization or end user.
- Customers can act as processors (producers) in that they provide requirements to their suppliers and are receivers of a product or service from their suppliers.

The module approach can be useful in CPI because modules represent processes that improvement teams can describe, measure, and improve. It can be a useful concept tool used in conjunction with its extension, process mapping, discussed later.

This kind of modeling also supports one of the fundamental ideas in TQM—that work should be managed as it really gets done, as a process.

Process improvement results in

- Reducing/eliminating errors and defects.
- Reducing cycle time to shorten the development - to- delivery time, or in any process sequence.
- Reduction in overall resources needed for a given output.

The Context of Improvement

A process is improved by reducing three measurable values—variation, cycle time, and nonvalue added activities (simplification). The results are higher quality, lower costs, and higher productivity.

For processes providing a variables measurement, reducing variation means reducing the output dispersion around the process average and keeping the process near the tolerance center.

For attributes, reducing variation means, in practical terms, driving the trend toward zero. Improving cycle time means simplification, technological improvement, and reducing errors and other nonvalue added activities.

Attributes and cycle-time improvements are valuable in both internal and external processes. Improvements can be made using an incremental approach—small steady improvements—or, as many leading companies do, combining the small, steady changes with breakthrough improvements, which as previously described, are big and rapid.

An Approach to Process Management

Process management is not a procedure or canned approach that can be hauled to an organization. In considering its use, management must first understand its theory, practices, and implications, for management and the entire organization. It requires significant change in the way the organization is managed, at every level, and in the particular role of all employees.

- It takes years to fully implement, particularly in the transition period, because it is an activity *in addition to* building products or providing a service.
- It requires an investment of resources to implement (training, team development, and operation).
- It changes responsibilities and organization relationships.
- It permanently changes the way organizations behave—the culture.

The chart in Figure 6.3 depicts a methodology that will suggest the character and scope of the process improvement methodology. This model suggests a procedure that could be used after overall quality objectives have been set and are to flow down through the organization.

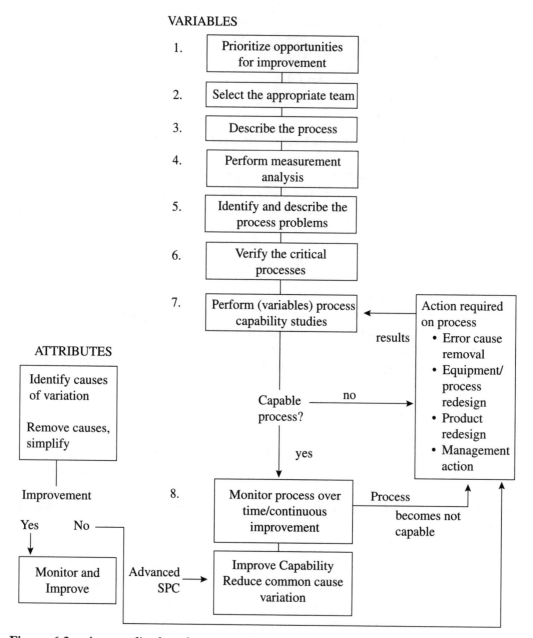

Figure 6.3   *A generalized product process improvement methodology.*

QUALITY IMPROVEMENT TECHNIQUES

There are technical techniques and organization operating methods being used in industry to reduce variation, cycle time, and cost. They are discussed further in Part II, but are introduced here to associate them with improvement methodologies.

For Variables

1. Prioritizing is done at several levels. The first priorities are the strategic quality objectives. In consonance with these, functional organization short- and long-term objectives are defined. This will provide several objectives for the multifunctional teams. The functional level managers next prioritize these objectives.

2. After key process identification, managers select and prioritize the objectives for these processes and select the improvement teams. This requires consideration of the level of knowledge and skill required. If the goal is pursuing an opportunity involving product and process design, a concurrent engineering team may be the best approach. If it is to reduce cycle time, an entirely different team may get the assignment.

3. Describe the process. The core of the team is those people knowledgeable of the process and those from important peripheral activities that have significant inputs or are customers. Peripheral activities could be an outside supplier or a quality control function that has pertinent records. The tools for adequate process description are the flow chart and its extended methodology, process mapping.

4. Perform measurement analysis. Before process analysis and improvement is pursued, some critical process performance measures should be established as well as the place in the process where they are be measured. These measures are needed to establish a baseline to which improvements will be compared.

5. An initial part of the team action, along with the process definition, is to clarify/define the process output and identify the process problems.

6. Output requirements must be verified and explicitly described. Verifying the process involves detailed descriptions and analysis to the degree necessary.

7. The team must describe where/how the process is operating with respect to requirements. When the process involves variables measurements, a definitive process capability must be established. If the process is capable, further improvements should be identified and quantified and their value and cost estimated. Their pursuit will depend on this cost as well as the priorities in the expenditure of resources. It might be more valuable to work on another process first. When a process is measured using attributes, the same capability concept is not appropriate. The measures in these processes are usually errors/defects, good/bad, cost, and cycle time. Control limits can be calculated for such a process to show what it will continue to do if improvements are not made. Many such processes can be brought into statistical control at some average defect level. This would at least indicate stability and provide a baseline to measure the effects of changes. The objective in improving these processes is to drive poor quality to the lowest level economically justifiable.

8. These steps describe the decision-making methodology based on whether a process is or is not capable. The last condition describes actions involved in continuous improvement. Processes that are capable are further improved. Those that require remedial action are identified by feedback paths. Processes that are in statistical control and capable will require the reduction of common cause variation to obtain further improvement. Technological changes or advanced statistical techniques such as DOE will be required.

For Attributes

Attributes processes require basically the same approach, except that the process capability measure does not apply. The objective is to constantly reduce variation.

DESIGN OF EXPERIMENTS (DOE)

It was not until in the late 1980s that U.S. industrial companies began to educate design and manufacturing engineers in the use of the experimental technique called DOE. One of DOE's greatest values is in determining how to reduce product variation and improve yield beyond what SPC can provide. It is a major tool in improving process capability.

The techniques were first developed by Ronald Fisher in England in the 1920s to evaluate agricultural experiments in the natural conditions while in the fields. The techniques determined which factors (sun, temperature, rainfall, soil, or fertilizer) had the most effect on growth, and determined the effect of different factor levels on results. These are analogous to questions that should be asked about a product. What effect do manufacturing process and customer use variables and stresses have on product performance and quality?

The critical difference in this method over others is that it provides quantitative answers when the variables are applied or exist together, as they are in operating the processes of manufacturing and in customer use. One of its greatest values is that it provides the results (effects) of interactions between the variables. The typical one-dimensional testing (one variable at a time in the laboratory) cannot provide this. Yet it is frequently critical to know the effect of interaction in order to optimize both the design and manufacturing process for maximum yield and lowest variability. Applications of this method, common in the chemical, textile, and pharmaceutical industries for some time, had not made the transition to other manufacturing industries to any extent. The work of Taguchi in the 1950s changed that. Adopted by the Japanese, DOE has a direct correlation with the high quality of Japanese products. Taguchi made experimentation more practicable so that engineers would use it. His "cookbook" approach, using predesigned experiment set-up matrices (arrays), increased its acceptability and economy over the classical approach. Used by engineers experienced in design and production, similar to the approach of a chef versus a cook, and as a result of tests using the experimental results to confirm their values, the benefits of the Taguchi approach far outweigh the risks of a wrong selection. (Anyone doing designed experiments should understand the principles involved and consult with a knowledgeable statistician about the design and risks.) There is some controversy over

Taguchi's simplification, particularly with more than two levels. (A level is, for example, a test temperature at which you want to examine several performance variables [factors].) Taguchi's fixed test matrices (arrays) with three or more levels can fail to indicate the interaction between variables and thereby lead to erroneous conclusion. However, there are ways to avoid this possibility and still realize the great benefits of DOE. They are beyond the purpose of this book but can be understood through the works of George E. P. Box and Dorian Shainan. See Part II for further details on DOE.

Benefits

Experimentation provides data that

1. Allow engineers to optimize the design characteristics so that performance variation can be minimized in the manufacturing and customer-use environments.
2. Make products less sensitive to variations in their internal components.
3. Identify the best material, design, or method that provides adequate performance.
4. Produce the lowest cost design (avoid overdesign).

The method is an experiment and not simply a test. The experimenter must be alert to events as the experiment progresses. Sometimes the unexpected occurs with valuable results. An unanticipated problem may be resolved.

Concurrent Engineering (CE)

Concurrent engineering (CE) involves the appropriate application of process improvement tools and techniques combined with those of modern engineering, such as computer-aided design, engineering, and manufacturing. The key ingredient in CE is teamwork in the early product design phase. Representatives from the key functional organizations—marketing, engineering, manufacturing, quality engineering, procurement, and, frequently, suppliers—collaborate over the life of a product, from concept to obsolescence, to ensure that the products fully satisfy customers' needs and expectations. It is a sustained effort to develop a functioning, reliable product that is highly correlated with a minimum variation between product samples. CE is a change from serial engineering, with organization functions contributing sequentially (Figure 6.4), to organization functions contributing as a team (Figure 6.5), with the emphasis in the product design phase. Design is not an end to itself. It must be done reflecting the other needs identified. CE is also a valuable organization development tool. The participants from the different functional organizations learn about the decisions, compromises, and limitations in the other function's activities.

The results, demonstrated by Japan and companies initiating CE in the West, are products that are more desired by the marketplace, more competitive, and with lower engineering and manufacturing costs and shorter design delivery cycle times. It should be a major element in every industrial improvement methodology. The Japanese, who pioneered industrial CE, have, for example, reduced by one-half the labor expenditure to develop and deliver a new automobile, such as the Lexus, in

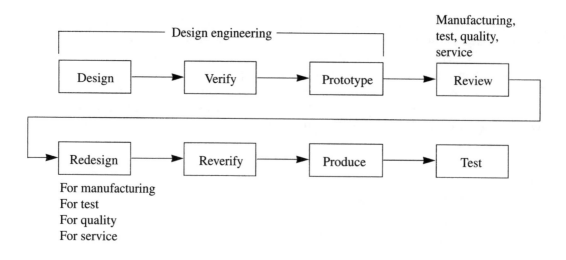

Serial engineering is characterized by departments supplying inputs to design only after a product has been designed, verified, and prototyped.

Figure 6.4 *Serial engineering.*

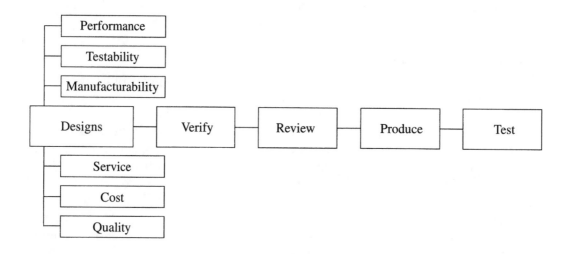

During product design, concurrent engineering draws on various disciplines to trade off parameters such as manufacturability, testability, and serviceability, along with the customary performance, size, weight, and cost.

Figure 6.5 *Concurrent engineering.*

two-thirds the normal time. These factors alone provide a significant market advantage, but, in addition, the successful practitioner doesn't have its resources tied up in correcting errors and defects (serial engineering) but can apply them to the development of new and advanced products that it can also bring to market rapidly.

Quality Function Deployment (QFD)

QFD is a technique that provides a qualitative and quantitative detailed plan to assure that customer requirements (the "voice" of the customer) are thoroughly identified and maintained in the product throughout the stages of concept, design, manufacture, and delivery. The result of this planning effort is a detailed requirements specification for all organization activities involved, completed before any work begins on the product.

Benefits

1. Customer requirements are the basis of all organization planning. They do not become subordinate to the special interests or operating methods of any organization function.
2. The interorganization required avoids costly mistakes and design changes commonly found when a new product enters production. The production process, tools, and controls have been designed along with the product.
3. QFD is a valuable organization development tool.
4. QFD can significantly reduce design lead time.

The common organization methodology used in applying QFD is the first phase of concurrent engineering.

Reengineering

The technology revolution has resulted in a rapid increase in the options on how to do work. There are many new products that can tap human potential to work more creatively and efficiently. Organizations, in all economic sectors, have been trying to exploit this phenomenon while still using traditional structures and work organization. American business has traditionally met new challenges by reorganizing, adding or removing functions and changing responsibilities, but, remaining under traditional concepts of management and structure.[3] It's an ancient activity. From the writings of Gauss Pertains about changes in the Roman Empire:

> We trained hard to meet our challenges but it seemed as if every time we were beginning to form into teams we would be reorganized. I was to learn later in life that we tend to meet any new situation by reorganizing; and a wonderful method it can be for creating the illusion of progress while producing confusion, ineffectiveness and demoralization. (Sounds like the original Dilbert scenerio.)

It is also common for management to adopt new technological solutions to improve productivity and quality, but management has found it difficult to integrate this with a coherent strategy. Also, in many cases, focusing only on the internal customer–supplier relationship process improvement has enabled the barriers created by functional hierarchies to remain intact.[4] A poor success record has led to the organization reengineering approach, starting over from scratch to find a structure that fits today's needs. The term implies a rational, information-based analysis and decision-making process to determine what the organization should be and how it should operate in the modern marketplace.

Reengineering has been a popular activity and another name for making major organization-wide improvements. It is not simple restructuring or downsizing; those are decisions by management based primarily on cost reduction. It has also become more than just business process improvement and simplification.

Within reengineering there are two expert methodologies. Hammer and Champy describe it as starting all over, from scratch.[5] The existing process configuration baseline is not used. Their approach uses only a highlevel understanding of the what and why, not the how of a process. (The how is going to change as a result of the reengineering.) Hammer and Champy define reengineering as, "The fundamental rethinking and radical redesign of business processes to achieve dramatic improvements in critical contemporary measures such as, cost, quality, service and speed."

Harrington[6] and Morris and Brandon[7] emphasize process simplification and improvement, determining where processes are and then improving them from that point. It is analogous to continuous improvement.

Reengineering and TQM

There is argument about the similarities and differences between TQM and reengineering. It is based on the differences in the accepted definitions in the two approaches. Table 6.1 illustrates key reengineering concepts.

Table 6.1   Key reengineering concepts.

Topic	Concept
Reengineering	Fundamental rethinking
	Radical redesign
	Process
	Dramatic improvement
	Measures
	Return
	Risk
Process	Activities
	Customers
	Measures
	Work ordering
	Time
	Space
	Beginning
	Ending
	Inputs
	Outputs
	Structure
	Action
	Baseline
Redesign	Process configuration
	Design flows
	Process transformation
	Redesign alternatives

TQM is frequently interpreted as emphasizing incremental improvements and reengineering to emphasize breakthrough improvements. The differences are a matter of degree. Juran has long emphasized both incremental and breakthrough improvements in his Trilogy concept. Also, benchmarking, which preceded reeengineering, frequently has yielded breakthrough improvements. On the other hand, reengineering sometimes produces only incremental change. Most experts and practitioners believe that both approaches are needed. For example, improved processes from reengineering can benefit from an incremental continuous improvement effort to refine them. Methodologies reflecting both approaches might involve the activities listed in Tables 6.2 and 6.3.

Breakthrough redesign and process improvement—not structure reorganization—is the usual objective of reengineering. It is the reorganization of the work people do in different organizational functions into new methods, processes, and structure. Nothing is sacred. Companies may change structure in reengineering but it is a *result of defining new processes and responsibilities*. It is related to what has been discussed in other chapters, clarifying the responsibility between organization functions about how

Table 6.2   Critical Redesign activities.

Understanding and improving existing processes
1. Describe the current process flow.
2. Measure the process in terms of the new process objectives.
3. Assess the process in terms of the new process attributes.
4. Identify problems with, or shortcoming of, the process.
5. Identify short-term improvements in the process.
6. Assess current information technology and organization.
Designing and prototyping a new process
1. Brainstorm design alternatives.
2. Assess feasibility, risk, and benefit of design alternatives.
3. Select the preferred process design.
4. Protype the new process design.
5. Develop a migration strategy.
6. Implement new organizational structures and systems.

Adapted from T.H. Davenport. *Process Innovation: Reengineering Work Through Information Technology* (Boston: Harvard Business School Press, 1993).

Table 6.3   High-level reengineering activities.

1. Identifying processes for innovation
2. Identifying change levers (that is, enabling or transformation technologies)
3. Developing process visions
4. Understanding and improving existing processes
5. Designing and prototyping the new process.

Adapted from T.H. Davenport. *Process Innovation: Reengineering Work Through Information Technology* (Boston: Harvard Business School Press, 1993).

work actually gets done, what processes are needed, and how they should relate. It eliminates work not contributing to goals.

A critical factor in limiting the success of many reengineering applications is the failure to understand the effects on the human resources. Reengineering often fails to change attitudes and culture.

ORGANIZATION/SYSTEM, ASSESSMENT, AUDITS, AND SURVEYS

A basic management responsibility is to evaluate and monitor organization performance and effectiveness. There are three commonly used techniques to do this—assessment, audit, and survey.

Assessment is a comprehensive evaluation to determine performance, effectiveness, and compliance. It involves quantitative and qualitative determinations to assess how well an organization is being managed, that is, whether management is doing the right things right for the future success of the organization.

Performance refers to the results/information obtained from processes, products, and services that permits evaluation and comparison relative to goals, standards, and past results as well as to competitors. Performance can be expressed in quantitative or qualitative terms.

Effectiveness is a more intangible and subjective factor. It involves describing organization attitudes: Are most people satisfied to meet minimum requirements? Do they know and work toward meeting objectives? Are the objectives in line with the desired end? Do they reflect current customer/market needs? And so forth. Management needs the insights an assessment can provide so that it can determine what the character of their organization is and whether it is on the path to what is wanted.

Compliance refers to whether established policies and procedures are being followed, including applicable government regulations, or if special customer requirements are being satisfied.

An assessment can be made by an agent external to the organization, or it can be a self-examination. A self-assessment can be conducted by the organization itself or by another internal function, such as quality auditing. Using both approaches may reveal even more useful and comprehensive information. An important factor in the selection of assessors is their independence from the assessee and its management. Another useful approach is for an organization to make a self-assessment, make whatever improvements management wants, and then have an assessment performed by an outside professional. The differences in perception can be very educational.

Application

As previously discussed, success in developing an organization requires a change in culture. In order to change something, its current status must be determined or assessed. One method of achieving culture change is to begin with a technique called culture gap analysis, which can be adapted to the development of a desired quality culture. The six steps in this method are as follows:[8]

1. Identify quality competitors and their attributes. Determine whether the organization is primarily competing on

   - Tangible product quality attributes
   - After-sales service and support
   - Customer interface
   - All of the above

2. Identify necessary organization quality values to suit the competitive environment.
3. Identify target groups that must have the desired values listed in step 2.
4. Identify the current quality values of the target groups and compare them to the desired quality values.
5. Decide formal and informal mechanisms to introduce the desired quality values in the targeted groups.
6. Review each target group's quality performance and repeat appropriate steps.

The Assessment Process

An effective organization self-assessment can be conducted only if there is a climate of trust. An accurate self-assessment is a form of self-revelation. Flaws in people and processes are revealed, as well as their strengths and weaknesses. Without a climate of trust, exposing weaknesses can create fear and cover-up.

Trust of management is developed starting at the top by assuring lower management and employees that flaws will not be punished but will be treated as opportunities for improvement. One basis for developing trust and making decisions that are effective is to make decisions based on assessment data, not opinions.

One example of a corporation that has successfully used the self-assessment process is AT&T. It used self-assessment as a way to achieve two major goals:

1. Aligning its business management systems more closely with customer needs
2. Integrating quality principles into every business practice

To achieve these goals, an assessment process was introduced. A Chairman's Quality Award was established at an early step, with a process modeled after the Baldrige Award. Business units assessed their performance against published, objective criteria and shared their successes. This assessment also identified areas for improvement. The assessment guidelines are shown in Figure 6.6.

Within three years, the eight business units involved scored improvements of 50 percent against the seven Baldrige-related criteria. Two of the units later became Baldrige Award winners.

Assessment Structure

The approach in designing an assessment procedure is to not only consider adequacy and compliance issues, but to identify the broader issues affecting organization success now and for the future, such as culture, communication, evaluation of human resources, strengths and weaknesses, and technology. The example shown in

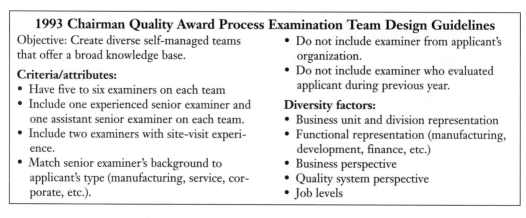

Figure 6.6 *AT&T examination guidelines.*
Reprinted with permission from ASQ *Quality Progress*, January 1995.

Figure 6.7 includes questions that would elicit the kind of information needed for management to evaluate its strategic position and to decide what improvements should be made in objectives or operating methods.

Additional issues in an assessment include

- Basic questions on quality practices and results, common to all organization elements. They should cover quality planning, adequacy of training, management perspectives at every level, and effectiveness of improvement activities in support of continuous improvement by management.

- Special questions to be asked of all functional organization members, such as their participation in the quality function, customer relations (internal and external), their awareness of competitor quality, what they perceive are the top quality problems, supplier relationships and problems, whether process yields are adequate or improving, problems with management, and whether they understand the quality responsibilities of their organization.

- Other such factors such as culture, communication, learning from mistakes, career paths, and personal growth.

Assessment Criteria

Modern organization performance assessment has evolved from the criteria used for the Malcom Baldrige National Quality Award (MBNQA). This award, discussed in Part II, requires a comprehensive assessment. It uses seven subject categories with criteria for each:

Leadership

Strategic Planning

Customer and Market Focus

Information and Analysis

Human Resource Focus

Process Management

Business Results

As an example of a broad survey, a consultant was engaged to evaluate the operations of one division of a large processing company. The objectives of the survey were stated in broad terms:

Objectives
1. To discover where the company wants to be with respect to quality
2. To discover where the company is now with respect to quality
3. To recommend plans and policies which can economically move the company closer to its objectives

Operations were studied in six different plants, various data were reviewed and discussions were conducted with plant personnel and with personnel in manufacturing and nonmanufacturing functions at the division level. The consultant reached five conclusions.

Possible Conclusions
1. The division was generally well equipped to do a good quality job in terms of adequate processes, modern technology, capable personnel, a favorable organizational climate.
2. Personnel were doing a good job on meeting the quality policies as interpreted by them.
3. Personnel interpretation of policy, however, did not match that of most division executives.
4. A considerable amount of money was being wasted as quality losses, without anyone having a clear idea how much this was or how much of it was readily avoidable.
5. There was a good chance for worthwhile cost reduction, while at the same time improving outgoing quality.

The consultant then presented 14 specific recommendations in areas such as quality policy, losses due to poor quality, machine capability studies, responsibility for deciding when the machines may run, supplier relations plans, measuring ongoing quality, evaluation of the usefulness of process control charts, and evaluation of the effectiveness of lot acceptance plans.

In a different type of survey, a consultant was asked to define specific responsibilities in the quality program for all major departments of a health care company. The consultant used five questions to interview the department managers.

Organization Questions
1. What tasks in your department affect quality?
2. Should any additional quality-related tasks be performed in your department?
3. Should any additional quality-related tasks be performed anywhere else in the company?
4. What quality-related tasks have unclear responsibility?
5. What quality-related tasks currently done in your department require more definitive written procedures?

Figure 6.7 *Creating a self-assessment survey.*
Source: J.M. Juran and Frank M. Gryna, eds., *Juran's Quality Control Handbook* (New York: McGraw-Hill, 1988). Reproduced with permission of The McGraw-Hill Companies.

The award criteria are widely used for self-assessment by all kinds of organizations, since they are designed for industry, services, and government agencies—large or small.

Audits of organization accounting systems, practices, and results have been conducted for many years, conducted by internal/external functions. Nonfinancial audits have been a common practice in business contracting with DOD when contracts require a comprehensive quality control system. They are conducted for compliance with established policies and procedures, regulations, and customer requirements.

Surveys, another common quality evaluation activity, are conducted to determine the quality capability of a potential supplier or compliance to requirement by an active supplier. The usual objective is to determine whether the supplier has the quality system elements required and is using them effectively.

As will be discussed in the next chapter, companies are combining assessments, audits, and surveys into one comprehensive practice.

Terminology

There is little consistency in the application of the three evaluation terms, so no specific content can be assumed. The assessment function has grown as a quality function primarily as a result of the Baldrige Award. The term *assessment* does not appear in Feigenbaum's *Total Quality Control*, a basic reference since the 1960s. *Juran's Quality Control Handbook* prefers the term *survey*, but his description is closer to what is now commonly meant by an assessment. The Japanese use the term *survey* for companies competing for the Deming Prize, but their process is closer to what those in the United States call assessment. Juran suggests that a comprehensive view of quality assurance should provide management with nonspecific quality factors such as those related to the marketplace, self-analysis, and customer and employee perceptions on quality. He identifies this approach as a quality assessment or comprehensive audit.

International standards (ISO) are ambiguous. Quality evaluation is sometimes called "quality assessment," "quality appraisal," or "quality survey" in specific circumstances.

Process and Personnel

An effective organization assessment, audit, or survey uses resources. These activities should be planned and carefully staffed. Assessment requires the most comprehensive planning. It frequently takes months, require some full-time staffing, and at least touches on the work of everyone. Selecting the key people to conduct the audit is very important. They must be knowledgeable of the organization policies and practices, have good interpersonal and communication skills, and be objective. People with these attributes are usually key people and difficult to free up to do the assessment. Many organizations beginning an assessment establish it as a project, establishing plans, procedures, methodologies, budgets, and schedules. A useful assessment requires a high level of management commitment.

REFERENCES

1. R.L. Ackoff. *The Democratic Corporation* (New York: Oxford Press, 1994).
2. J.M. Juran, and J.M. Gryna. *Juran's Quality Control Handbook*, 4th ed. (New York: McGraw-Hill, 1988).
3. W. Ouchi. *Theory Z* (Reading, MA: Addison-Wesley, 1981).
4. K. Gadd, and J.S. Oakland. "Chimera or Culture? Business Process Reengineering for TQM" ASQ *Quality Management Journal* Vol.3, Issue 3 (1996).

5. M. Hammer, and J. Champy. *Reengineering the Corporation: A Manifesto for Business Revaluation* (New York: Harper Business, 1992).

6. H.J., Harrington. *Business Process Improvement* (San Fransisco: Ernst and Young, LLP, 1991).

7. D. Morris, and J. Brandon. *Re-enginering Your Business* (New York: McGraw-Hill, 1993).

ADDITIONAL READINGS

Bemowski, K., and Stratton, B. *101 Good Ideas: How to Improve Just About Any Process.* Milwaukee: ASQ Quality Press, 1998.

H.J. Harrington. *Business Process Improvement: The Breakthrough Strategy for Total Quality, Productivity and Competitivness.* Milwaukee: ASQC Quality Press, 1991.

R.S. Johnson. *TQM: Management Processes for Quality Operations.* Milwaukee: ASQC Quality Press, 1993.

W.E. Trischler. *Understanding and Applying Value-Added Assessment: Eliminating Business Process Waste.* Milwaukee: ASQC Quality Press, 1996.

STUDY QUESTIONS

1. With respect to an organization, what is a system and what is system thinking?
2. What is a quality system?
3. What is the difference between traditional functional management and using continuous process improvement?
4. In simple terms, what does process improvement mean?
5. What are the characteristics of a high-quality process?
6. What are the benefits of using design of experiments in product/process development?
7. What is concurrent engineering?
8. Compare reengineering and TQM.
9. What is an organization assessment and how does it differ from an audit or survey?
10. What seven subject categories does the MBNQA use as a basis for organization assessment?

Chapter 7

The New Quality Assurance

ORGANIZATION CHANGES

Implementing the new quality management has had a significant impact on traditional quality control organizations (quality control or quality assurance). The new organization, where there still is one, differs from the old in size, scope, and responsibility.

The largest and most comprehensive quality organizations were those doing business with the Department of Defense (DOD). This was a result of the way the DOD used comprehensive military specifications for quality programs when contracting for equipment. The quality activities a contractor had to initiate were extensive and defined. The specifications described not only what had to be done but often gave strong direction on how to do it. It was also a required practice to have a quality organization. In addition, the DOD used its quality personnel to confirm that the contractors' quality personnel were effective in ensuring that all contract requirements were fulfilled. It was a redundant and expensive approach directed toward merely meeting minimum requirements, not toward improving quality. Quality organizations grew to be large and expensive adjuncts to contracting with the DOD. This had a strong influence on how quality assurance* developed throughout all industry. The model was an emphasis on inspection by a quality organization. There was some attention given to corrective action, but it was event (symptom), not system/process, oriented.

Military specifications didn't require that quality activities had to be the responsibility of a separate quality organization. It just evolved that way. However there was some justification for the customer to insist on it. Without the presence of a contractor quality police, the military received considerable defective material. With a contractor quality function, thre was much less.

In the late 1980s, the DOD and major contractors began to embrace the idea of process control—continuous improvement and less reliance on inspection. Implementation took years because both parties had to change long-held practices and beliefs. The change also required retraining of all elements of both organizations. In the early 1990s, the DOD changed from reliance on military quality specifications and accepted the international ISO 9000 series quality standards. (The genesis of the ISO standards was the DOD military specification MIL Q 9858, " The Quality Program.")

It is interesting to note that during the period from the 1950s onward, while industry was concentrating quality efforts on a "conformance to requirements" inspection approach, the Japanese were listening to W. E. Deming on how to use existing statistical techniques to improve quality through process control.

The Quality Function Within the Total Organization

As a result of the world trend in recognizing quality as a critical objective for all types of organizations, both organization structures and their quality functions have changed. The quality function that used to be viewed as the responsibility of a separate special organization, such as Quality Assurance, has evolved into an identifiable responsibility of all organization elements.

The quality functions within organizations are

- Those activities necessary to meet the overall organization quality objectives, both short term and strategic
- Those quality improvement projects and objectives selected by any organization function for self improvement

The specific kinds of quality activities vary widely based on such factors as

- Type and size of organization
- Products and services

---

*Note: There are no standard practices in naming quality organizations. In general, quality control is the inspection function, quality assurance is used when quality engineering and prevention activities are included, and product assurance is used when reliability engineering is added.

- Nature and source of regulatory or special customer requirements (ISO-9000, GMP, MIL), covered in Part II
- Management philosophy
- Degree of commitment to TQ principles
- Organization structure

Traditional Quality Organization Functions

Traditional industrial organizations, regardless of structure but dependent on size and nature of the business, have been functionally organized, for example, marketing, engineering, manufacturing. They had separate quality functions, focused on material quality, with the responsibility to manage the work elements listed in Table 7.1.

If organizations were working on defense contracts, they tended to have the most comprehensive quality activities and organizations because they were required by military specifications, particularly MIL-Q-9858. (This specification can be replaced by the ISO Standard, 9001, 9002 or 9003.) Organizations using a project or a matrix management structure usually had a quality functional organization that operated like the other functional units. The project/program office included a quality representative to assure that the project quality requirements were met, operating through the quality functional unit.

The New Quality Organization Functions

The common transition from the traditional to team-managed organizations has resulted in a significant change in the nature and accountability for quality functions. Table 7.1, just referenced, also identifies those typical quality functions, shifted to all organization units. Only a general guide can be presented, since the responsibility for quality functions and work elements varies so widely and is often in a state of transition. The important point is that responsibility for quality and improvement is shifted from quality specialists to the people doing the work.

The fundamentals in each organization are that quality work elements need to be identified, and that some person or unit is responsible and accountable for their effectiveness and improvement.

Service Organizations Quality Functions

Most organizations in the service sector do not have a tradition of managing for quality or identifying and assigning responsibility for quality activities. This situation has changed with the growth of the service industry and the recognition of changes in competition and the market. Many have adapted a version of TQM that fits their operations. As might be expected, depending on size, they may have a designated quality leader responsible for coordinating and facilitating the process improvement activities.

Table 7.1   Quality organization activities.

Reliability engineering working elements (frequently part of design engineering organization.)
 Establish reliability goals
 Reliability apportionment
 Stress analysis
 Identify critical parts
 Failure mode, effects, and critically analysis (FMECA)
 Reliability prediction
 * Design view
 * Control of reliability during manufacturing
 Reliability testing
 Failure reporting and corrective action system

QC engineering
 Process capability studies
 Quality systems and strategies planning
 * Establish quality standards
 Test equipment and gage design
 * Quality troubleshooting
 * Analyze rejected or returned material
 * Special studies (measurement error, etc.), DOE
 * Software QA
 * Product safety

Quality assurance
 * Development, maintenance, and improvement of the quality system
 * Write quality procedures
 * Maintain quality manual
 * Perform quality audits–system, products, services
 * Quality information systems–in house, supplier
 * Quality certification–in house
 * Quality training
 * Quality cost systems–management and analysis
 * Supplier selection–certification

Inspection and test
 In-process inspection and test
 * Final product audit
 * Receiving inspection
 * Maintain inspection records–documentational
 * Gage calibration
* In TQM, prime responsibility of quality organization.

Adapted from J. M. Juran and Frank M. Gryna, eds., *Juran's Quality Control Handbook* (New York: McGraw-Hill, 1988).

THE TOTAL QUALITY FUNCTION

The quality function in an organization consists of the activities of all organization elements in meeting planned quality objectives to produce products and services to satisfy customer needs and expectations. Organization elements have their assigned responsibilities for their specialized normal activities, but are also assigned their share of the quality function. This is somewhat analogous to their responsibility for meeting other organization-wide objectives in finance and human resources. Top-level leadership is necessary to develop and manage the quality organization mission. This is frequently provided by some form of management group such as a quality council.

A Quality Council

A Quality Council is usually composed of a group of key upper management. Its function is to set quality policies, objectives, give the quality program direction, and track the activities and results.

If there is an organization designated as quality control or quality assurance, it serves with upper management, in oversight and leadership functions, respectively. The functional quality organization operates to assure that the other specialized organizations fulfill their obligation to meet quality objectives, satisfy customer requirements, measure and report quality status, maintain standards, and measure customer satisfaction. The scope of quality organizations' responsibilities varies widely with different kinds of companies and markets.

The Quality Mission

For an enterprise with a specialized quality organization it is useful to have a mission statement to describe to everyone what its purpose and objectives are. Such a statement gives the quality organization a legitimacy and authority to do its job. This requires crossing all organization boundaries to gather (quality audit) and analyze data from all the important organization systems and to conduct any product or service evaluation and publish the results.

Mission statements vary widely from platitudes to specific responsibilities for the quality organization. The statement should be forward looking. It should not be mixed with specific objectives, which belong in the quality plan.

The quality organization statement is primarily for internal use, but it should be available to outside reviewing agencies. The statement should identify the role the quality organization, or leader, plays in achieving strategic goals as well as its participation in meeting the tactical quality plan. It is useful to also note the principal quality functions it performs.

The mission of all organizations to satisfy their quality improvement responsibilities is related to the fact that the collective efforts of all organization elements produce customer satisfaction.

Formulation of Quality Principles and Policies
Policies

Quality policies are the strategic direction to the organization on quality matters:

- They set the course of action for the overall organization.
- They represent a statement as to what the overall organization stands for, its principles, and what it wants to be to both insiders and outsiders.
- They are the foundation for the formulation of objectives at all levels.

- They can identify the quality leadership the organization wants to take.
- They are as important as other organization factors.
- They are the basis for all quality procedures.
- They must go beyond platitudes and generalities to the important specifics.
- They should be widely circulated internally and to customers.

Formulation

Quality policies vary with the size and nature of the organization, but there is a basic commonality. Frequently included subjects are

- The importance of quality to the organization
- Quality with respect to competition
- Customer satisfaction: internal/external
- Employee involvement/empowerment
- Continuous improvement
- Policy toward suppliers: partnerships, fairness
- Guarantees: types
- Audits: types, scope

CHARACTERISTICS OF AN EFFECTIVE QUALITY FUNCTION

In a systems view, the quality function is a means to an end, not the goal of the system. Quality, in and of itself, is the priority and the focus.

An effective quality function would have the following characteristics

- Top management commitment and leadership
- Continuous and breakthrough improvements
- Customer focus/satisfaction
- Team building, training, rewards/recognition programs
- Employee involvement and empowerment
- Fact-based management
- Prevention-based operations
- Partnership building with stakeholders
- Cycle-time reduction
- Long-range outlook

TOTAL PRODUCTIVE MAINTENANCE

As an expansion of the responsibilities of production teams, the Japanese developed the concept of total productive maintenance (TPM).[1] It involves team members taking responsibility for the condition and maintenance of their work areas and equipment, which includes lubrication, adjustment, and minor repairs. This can be considered an expansion of the concept of cell manufacturing used worldwide, whereby a production team performs many if not all of the operations on a product in it's work area. Adding TPM gives workers more control of all the factors affecting their ability to improve quality and cycle time. They have more control of the process and of some of it's variables.

Implementing TPM requires team training on equipment maintenance, particularly preventive maintenance. A separate maintenance organization may also exist to do more complex work, but it is at the call of the teams.

The benefits of TPM, in addition to keeping tools and equipment from creating defects, is motivational. Teams feel they have more control of their work and so can take owerniship of the production process. The General Electric Company uses its version of TPM in its appliance division teams.[2] TPM is a common factor in the performance of America's top plants. It provides critical support to defect-free processes when it is religiously practiced.

REFERENCES

1. D.A. Turbide. "Japan's New Advantage: Total Productive Maintenance." ASQ *Quality Progress* (March 1995).
2. T.B. Kinni. *America's Best: Industry Week's Guide to World Class Plants* (New York: John Wiley & Sons, 1996).

STUDY QUESTIONS

1. What is the quality function in an organization?
2. What are some important organization quality policies?
3. What are the characteristics of an effective quality function?

Chapter 8

Supplier Quality Management

- **Buying Policies and Quality**
- **Suppliers and Variation**
- **Supplier Quality Management Techniques**
    Certification
- **Supplier Partnerships**
    External Partnerships
    Agreements
    Benefits to a Buyer
    Benefits to a Supplier
    Strategic Alliances
- **Factors in a Quality and Productivity Improvement Approach**
- **Just in Time (JIT) and Improvement**
    JIT Themes and Concepts

BUYING POLICIES AND QUALITY

It has been the normal practice of most organizations (industry, services, and government), to seek the lowest price for what they buy. Supplier selection by the lowest price has been a firm policy in most cases and a legal requirement for most government agencies. This policy is often driven by providing purchasing management with financial incentives to reduce purchased product material costs.

In many organizations, business, and services, the quality of purchases is critical to the buyers success in achieving quality improvement objectives. What is purchased is a part of what is delivered to the buyers' customers. Purchased materials can vary from those that are consumed in the process, those that are made a part of the end product, those shipped directly from a supplier to a customer as part of the purchase, or equipment used in the process that affects process variation. Purchased services can vary from training programs or manuals, quality auditing, laboratory analysis, or customer repair service.

Organizations have often used their procurement activities to make their own prices more competitive, passing on some of the savings in the form of lower market price for their own products.

Buying at the lowest price is based on several beliefs and practices:

1. Tough competition between potential suppliers will drive the price down.
2. Suppliers are essentially interchangeable for like products or services.
3. Making suppliers compete against each other creates buying leverage.
4. One must keep a tight leash on suppliers and control all information to and from them.

Of course, low material or service process costs will help the buyer control costs. But following those four policies maintains distrust between the two parties and is a short-term view of a buyer–seller relationship.

One consequence of making the buyer's competitive advantage dependent on supplier pricing alone is that internal purchasing inefficiencies are never corrected, improvements are never made, and suppliers deliver the lowest quality they can achieve, to just meet requirements, rather than the best quality they can achieve using modern quality methods. Deming[1] considered this issue of such importance that it became one of his 14 points for management: End the practice of awarding business on the basis of price tag alone.

Deming's view was that a more important measure for supplier selection is the total cost of a purchase. Total cost includes the cost of incoming inspection, the cost of handling defective material, and the cost of material of unknown variability entering the buyer's processes and products. Cost versus price means to consider the total buyer cost that is experienced in dealing with a supplier instead of only the purchase price. The cost factors in addition to price are late deliveries and poor quality. Late deliveries can increase buyer cost when they impact production, causing stoppages, workarounds, and overtime. Poor quality raises cost as a result of extra handling, paperwork, problem analysis, inspection, and rework. It can also result in scrap, reorder, and delay. It impacts cycle time. Nonquantified supplier material quality variation can be a critical issue for a buyer who uses statistical process control and continuous process improvement methodologies. Such material can create a special cause of process variation.

SUPPLIERS AND VARIATION

It is common for more than half of products (computers, airplanes, automobiles, and the like) to be made up of purchased material. It is poor economy for a manufacturer to establish process controls in house and use purchased material from processes of uncontrolled/unknown variability. It would have an unpredictable effect on final product quality and, thereby, customer satisfaction. Suppliers have to be managed as direct extensions of in-house processes.

One way to use statistical requirements would be for a buyer to require a supplier to deliver products, from a statistically controlled process, with a capability of +/– 4 sigma. It would define the kind of supplier a buyer needs. It means that a supplier must think in terms of developing processes that deliver products that measure mostly near the nominal (without using inspection to choose the best). Products that are just within the tolerance are not good enough.

These ideas apply not only to product suppliers. It is to a buyer's advantage in contracting with deliverers of a service to select those that practice continuous process improvement. They, too, will deliver the highest quality consistently and competitively.

A product supplier who delivers parts within tolerance 95 percent of the time, or is on time in 90 percent of deliveries might be considered by many to be satisfactory. However, with the advent of customer demands for very high quality, that perspective changed; that supplier performance may or may not be adequate. The reason is that just knowing that specifications have been met is no longer sufficient. What a buyer has to know is the statistical distribution of the performance parameters for the delivered material, with respect to the requirements. Statistical thinking has to be brought into the supplier performance evaluation and selection. Another factor is also important in judging the value of doing business with a supplier: the operating philosophy of the supplier management. If it does not include a demonstrated practice of continuous process improvement, that supplier will not deliver consistent quality at a competitive price.

The statistical principles involved can be demonstrated by Figure 8.1. It shows the distribution of a critical product performance factor for an ordered part measured as it is outgoing from the supplier.

Distribution 2 is the minimum desirable. Most parts will measure around the nominal and, if the process remains stable, almost every part will be within tolerance and randomly distributed around the nominal. A process producing such output yields higher quality at a lower cost because such a process output requires little inspection.

Distribution 4 depicts what is most desirable. It would meet a +/– 4 sigma process specification. All parts would be randomly distributed around the nominal, and some process center shift (highly probable) would not result in defective parts.

Distributions 1 and 3 show that in the as-made condition the supplier would have to *select* parts that met specifications. The balance would have to be scrapped or reworked—at extra cost.

SUPPLIER QUALITY MANAGEMENT TECHNIQUES

Certification

Inspection of purchased material on receipt has been a standard industry practice for many years. Recognizing that it is an expensive nonvalue-adding activity, many manufacturers use a procedure to certify important suppliers that demonstrate a steady history of delivering material as ordered. The material of certified suppliers goes directly to the stockroom without inspection. In some cases of manufactures using a just-in-time (JIT) technique, the material goes from receiving to the point of use in production. The resulting savings are significant and hinge on the supplier quality system.

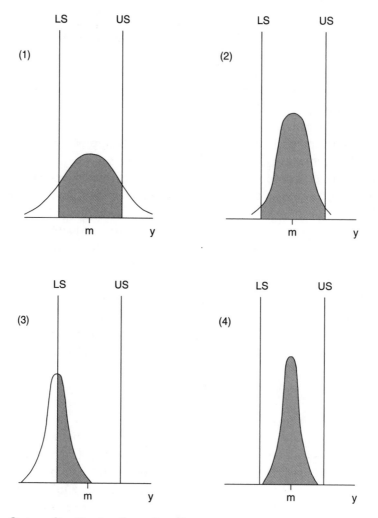

Figure 8.1 *Output distribution from four factors.*

The basic supplier certification steps are

1. Document the requirements and procedures for a certification program. Invite discussion and proposals from prospective supplier candidates.
2. Define the procedures to be applied.
3. Select a key supplier and negotiate a certification agreement. This first application is to refine the procedures.
4. Audit supplier compliance. The audit should include process control plans and implementation as well as all other requirements.
5. The first material received should be inspected, using tight sampling or screening as needed.
6. Certify suppliers when requirements have been satisfied.
7. Conduct periodic supplier audits and random inspection of received material.
8. Take corrective action according to contract agreements.

Certification mutually benefits buyer and supplier. The supplier can depend on continued business because the buyer would incur an additional certification expense if a new supplier is chosen. The buyer benefits through the reduction in inspection costs and by having a dependable source of supply. However, the conventional certification process is less effective and more costly than one invoking a continuous process requirement that would result in the supplier adopting process control. This approach would lead to both parties being in a more competitive position.

One method being used to overcome the disadvantages mentioned is to require a supplier to implement statistical process control (SPC) and a continuous process improvement policy. When such a supplier achieves process control and a capability to consistently stay within tolerance, there is a very low probability of producing outside the tolerance. Evidence of this achievement would be the delivery of a copy of the process control chart. There is then a low risk in eliminating buyer inspection, and shipping to stock. Periodic audits by the buyer would assure that control was maintained.

SUPPLIER PARTNERSHIPS

External Partnerships

The traditional relationship between corporate customers and suppliers has been for the customer to dominate the relationship. Buyer criteria were used to select a supplier. The supplier who wanted the order accepted the buyer's requirements and then tried to meet them. Suppliers were rarely asked for ideas, or how the item might be changed to improve quality or lower price. There was little loyalty by the customer to any one supplier, and the buyer usually didn't care if an order was profitable to the supplier. Contracts were based on the understanding that either party had recourse to the law if terms weren't met. This approach is to some degree adversarial, with disadvantages to both parties. The relationship is much more positive when they become partners, with the same objectives.

Partnership Agreements

In the partnership agreement, the supplier agrees to process quality control and continuous improvement. Sometimes the supplier dedicates production capacity to the one customer. The customer, with a multifunctional buying team, works with the supplier to establish both design and customer quality criteria compatible with the supplier capability, and will often help the supplier establish process controls to improve process capability (in both the technical and general sense). Price is negotiated based on maintaining an economically stable source of supply, recognizing the savings from costs expended establishing new sources. The supplier is treated as an extension of the customer's process. The supplier usually will become quality certified by the customer and ship directly to customer stock, without inspection. Note: This kind of partnership arrangement is usually not practicable for purchases of short-run or infrequently purchased material.

Benefits to a Buyer

The buyer gets a more dependable, quality supplier, and the long-term costs to both parties will be lower. There is a strong mutual interest in continuing the relationship.

Some partnerships also extend into joint planning activities for new product development. In some cases the buyer, or supplier, gains some access to technical expertise that it doesn't have to develop internally.

Suppliers gain by having a more predictable business future. Smaller suppliers benefit by obtaining the usually greater technical expertise of their larger customers and through them, better information on the world marketplace requirements.

This approach puts greater importance on supplier selection. Some important selection criteria are

1. They must be economically viable.
2. Their strengths and weaknesses must be accurately determined, and needed improvements targeted.
3. They must have appropriate facilities and equipment.
4. There must be related, current experience in similar products and processes.
5. There must be appropriate workforce skills and a willingness to continue training.
6. There must be commitment of management to continuous improvement.
7. There must be willingness to meet customer (or MBNQA) criteria.
8. They must be willing to develop or share quality history in order to evaluate trends.

Benefits to a Supplier

The purpose of the marketing research effort is to create and satisfy customers. A strategic resource is the customer base and the related marketing data. Continuing customer relationships have become the preferred way of doing business. Relationship marketing has been most common in business-to-business transactions but is becoming more common in consumer marketing because of the application of information technology, which allows interactive communication and data-based management. Catalog sales and financial service companies are examples.

Strategic Alliances

Another form of partnership is called a strategic alliance. It is a cooperative effort by two businesses in pursuit of their separate strategic objectives.[2] Such alliances have become more common in business-to-business relationships. The alliance involves the commitment and sharing of resources. Sometimes an alliance creates a joint venture, creating a new entity. The alliances also take the form of a just-in-time (JIT) agreement, usually as a sole source. This effectively makes the supplier a true extension of the buyer's internal processes.

Strategic alliances can be a valuable competitive tool. However, they have to be carefully negotiated and closely managed by both parties. Complacency could allow the product, price, or delivery to become noncompetitive.

The approach used in forward-looking, leading organizations is to create a strategic alliance, a partnership with important suppliers. La Torre, leader of the high-tech team at Coopers and Lybrand, management consultants, says, "I don't have a single technology driven company in my portfolio that isn't looking for a strategic partner. Investment bankers won't look at you unless you have two elements: a visible product and a strategic partner."[3] A partnership is strategic when two organizations find that, in examining their core competencies and future paths, they find a source of synergy and areas of complementary strength.

FACTORS IN A QUALITY AND PRODUCTIVITY IMPROVEMENT APPROACH

Forming a partnership requires a well-planned approach. It can be very complex. The following should be taken into account when planning a supplier partnership.

- The suppliers of purchased products or services who affect the satisfaction of the buyer's customer are an extension of the buyer's processes and should be subject to the same management consideration as internal processes.

- A buyer with a CPI program cannot risk accepting products or service from supplier processes of unknown variation. This could introduce special causes of variation in the buyer processes. The buyer could not control its own variation, cycle time, or quality costs. Therefore, any buying organization should require that suppliers of important material implement a continuous process improvement activity. All partnership requirements should be included in the purchasing agreement.

- The number of suppliers used should be minimized based on an analysis of risk, supplier history in meeting requirements, their capability based on a buyer's quality audit/survey, and their willingness to implement a CPI program—or at a minimum, effective process control. This will reduce product variation and internal management costs. For all these reasons, an important supplier should be approached as a partnership, a strategic alliance, with a long-term commitment between buyer and supplier.

- A mutually beneficial objective of the buyer and supplier is to achieve a level of performance such that the buyer would be at very low risk of accepting supplier material or services without acceptance inspection. All plans, procedures, and requirements must be mutually agreed to in the buying process and be a part of the contract.

- Buying complex products or services should be managed by a purchasing-led team of people who will be involved with the use of the items. Purchasing leadership is necessary to manage the contractual aspects of procurement. Such a team might be composed of representatives of all or some of the following organizations, depending on what is purchased:

  Sales—Representing the customer

  Research, Technical Staff, Engineering, Software Development

  Internal Operations or Production

  Finance

  Facilities

  Quality/Process Engineering

  Customer Service

Multifunction teams should also be involved, as appropriate, in the evaluation and selection of important suppliers.

- Buying organizations should publish, for both internal and supplier use, the quality policies and procedures it will follow. The policies should reflect an organizationally integrated approach. These may include such elements as

  Assignment of prime responsibilities

  Chain of communication

  Methods of supplier evaluation and selection

  Methods of initial and ongoing surveillance

  Procedures for design control

  Procedures to settle disputes

  Maintenance of privacy and information control

  Methods and procedures for product or service acceptance

  Supplier quality certification

  Support to suppliers, including training

JUST IN TIME (JIT) AND IMPROVEMENT

Just in Time (JIT) is a manufacturing management technique of having suppliers deliver materials of production just as they are needed in the customer's process. Ideally the customer keeps no inventory, this is basically a manufacturing economic issue. It is a technique that saves the buyer money by reducing the cost of carrying inventory. The savings consists of reducing not only the nonvalue-added cost of inventory but also the related costs of space and labor. JIT is included as an element of improvement because establishing a successful JIT program requires, among other things, achieving and maintaining manufacturing process control, by the buyer and supplier. In this context, a supplier manufactures what his customer ordered and delivers it just in time for the customer to use it. There is no customer inspection, so if the customer is to maintain quality control over his products, the supplier's parts must all be within tolerance and essentially symmetrical around the nominal. Anything less than this can cause all kinds of customer problems—primarily, not having usable parts because some are defective; or if the parts are not mostly near the nominal target, creating an adverse effect on final product reliability.

Introducing JIT is typically approached in the strategic planning process. Many of the tools and techniques of quality improvement must also be part of the plan if JIT is to succeed. In fact, JIT can be used as a theme for introducing organization quality improvement. Industrial management is traditionally focused on production activities and is receptive to anything that reduces cost, cycle time, and waste. Management is comfortable with the production orientation of JIT. It speaks production management language even though it requires planning, operating, and measuring production

Table 8.1   JIT Success in North American companies.

Company	Reduced Inventory	Reduced Lead Times	Reduced Rework	Increased Inv. Turns	Reduced Space
Omark Industries	94%	95%	50%	—	40%
Hewlett-Packard	67–85%	80%	—	—	83%
Black and Decker	68%	65%	—	800%	65%
General Electric	82%	95%	51%	—	70%
Harley-Davidson	50%	—	52%	571%	62%
Westinghouse	75%	92%	—	372%	58%
Texas Instruments	60–94%	50–70%	75%	—	40%

Reprinted with permission of APICS–The Educational Society for Resource Management.

processes as in an improvement program. The need for implementing most elements becomes apparent when management realizes that JIT can succeed only if process quality control is achieved.

The first successes with JIT occurred in Japan. For example, it is not unusual for Toyota suppliers to deliver their products directly to the production line of their customer. The customer production line workers have no involvement in the action. The parts are ready for their use. It is also not unusual for a JIT supplier to deliver more than once a day.

JIT usage began in the US in the 1980s. Table 8.1 lists the benefits achieved by some companies.

JIT Themes and Concepts

In Figure 8.2, the themes and concepts of JIT are identified and oriented to illustrate their interrelationships. All are integral parts of JIT's application. The outer circle identifies the major elements. The inner circle notes the three areas of focus. There is a certain redundancy in identifying the elements of continuous improvement, people development, and total quality improvement since they are the basic principles of total quality improvement, but there is special focus on them for the production activities.

It is not the intention here to describe JIT fully, but there are a few observations that further the understanding of its relationship to quality improvement. Quality improvement is not only a JIT theme but also an equal partner in its achievement. Inventory reduction to the point of its elimination is another related, as well as the objective, theme. Inventory is considered an evil. It subtracts from business success and consumes resources. Business has depended on it as a safety valve, to provide material because the internal processes were undependable and suppliers were unreliable. Total process management and improvement reduce the need for inventory. They are the foundation needed to use JIT.

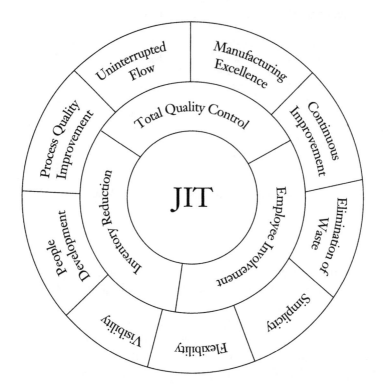

Figure 8.2   *Elements of JIT and their interrelationships.*

Some of the elements noted in Figure 8.2 are important because

- Lead time (cycle time) reduction provides a sales advantage as well as a cost reduction. It provides flexibility to meet customer changes at lower cost.

- Productivity improvement is a major goal. With JIT, however, the emphasis is on overall company productivity improvement. The objective is to lower the total cost per sales dollar.

- Suppliers play a large role in product cost, quality, and customer satisfaction. Without their full participation and adoption of continuous process improvement, JIT cannot be successful. Uncontrolled variations in their product quality or deliveries could result in costly problems to their customers' implementation. Even early supplier delivery could precipitate a costly problem to a company operating a JIT system. It would cause a change in storage, staffing, and cash flow requirements. Achieving the right balance requires good planning and careful implementation.

- Manufacturing excellence refers to searching constantly for improvement—seeking to be the best. (See Benchmarking, Chapter 11.)

- The elimination of waste applies to striving to eliminate variation constantly in all activities so that there is little wasted effort by anyone in the company and no wasted material or facilities. It means that nonvalue-added activities are reduced. It means total quality management.

- Simplification is an objective in product design, manufacturing processes, and all organizational activities.
- Flexibility is the capability to react quickly to changing situations without loss or waste. Short cycle times and as little inventory as possible are basic to becoming flexible. If there is a sizable investment in inventory it can result in delaying important changes or missing an opportunity.
- Visibility is a key ingredient of JIT. It means exposing waste and complexity so that it may be removed.
- People involvement is also a fundamental requirement. In its best form, the people involved in the tasks of a process also manage it. They set objectives, measure its performance, and solve the problems related to improving it.

REFERENCES

1. J. Windham. "Implementing Deming's Fourth Point." ASQ *Quality Progress.* (December 1995).
2. R. Maynard. "Striking the Right Match." *Nation's Business.* U.S. Chamber of Commerce (May 1996).

ADDITIONAL READINGS

Bossert, J.L. *Supplier Management Handbook.* Milwaukee: ASQC Quality Press, 1994.

Rackham, N., L. Friedman, and R. Ruff. *Getting Partnership Right: How Market Leaders Are Creating Long-Term Competitive Advantage.* New York: McGraw-Hill, 1995.

Van Mieghem, T. "Implementing Supplier Partnerships." *Quality Magazine* (1994).

STUDY QUESTIONS

1. What did Deming mean in saying that materials or services should be purchased based on total cost, not lowest price?
2. Why is it important to use suppliers that use statistical thinking and continuous process improvement in the operation of their organizations?
3. What is the value of supplier certification? What does it mean?
4. What are the advantages and disadvantages of supplier partnerships?
5. What is JIT and what are the advantages and disadvantages to the buyer?

Chapter 9

Quality Costs—Old and New

QUALITY COST DATA

One of the important precepts in improvement management and also one of Deming's 14 points is that decisions should be based on data, not on precedent or opinion. There are no data more fundamental in an organization—in management decision making—than cost information. Every organization uses it. It varies from simple, all-inclusive accumulated data that indicate the gross picture, to volumes of data measuring everything, much of which is history and of little use.

The output of a quality cost data system should be designed to report only what is important for decision making, and it must be in a useful form. Data collected should be a measurement or indicator of what management and improvement teams are trying to evaluate. A major shortcoming of most cost reporting systems is that the data are too general to be useful at the organization action level. For example, in multiple-product or service facilities the production cost of each product or service is not known with any reasonable accuracy. Moreover, in many cases, the reported costs distort the true costs and provide a poor basis for decision making. In particular, they don't and cannot report the cost of process activity in order for teams to analyze process operation.

THE BUSINESS COST MODEL

Figure 9.1 illustrates the traditional business cost categories. Also noted are the cost items of most interest in managing quality (some quality cost data can be identified for most organizations). The use of quality costs to determine what needs improvement is an important signal to everyone that the improvement process has a business basis.

The idea of a cost of quality has existed for many years. It was developed and fostered mainly by quality control specialists. Some or most of its elements can be found in industrial enterprises. Its content and limitations will be discussed later, but suffice to say at this point that cost data different from those traditionally collected are needed for process quality analysis and improvement.

THE QUALITY ECONOMIC MODEL

The historical economical quality cost model is shown in Figure 9.2. It shows the relationship among the basic quality costs of prevention, appraisal, and failure. It shows appraisal and prevention costs rising toward infinity as quality of conformance approaches 100 percent (perfection). Total quality costs are also higher as failure costs increase. Total costs are optimized at some point when the sum of the two costs is at a minimum.

This illustration is used to identify the relationship between the different quality costs. In the past it was common to find that appraisal costs were the largest factor in the appraisal-prevention combination. The problem has been that these relationships only appeared in quality control texts. Typically, general management considered appraisal (inspection/testing) cost as preventive. It relied on appraisal to prevent defects from reaching the customer. Preventing defects from occurring was not considered feasible; controlling and integrating all organization processes was an uncommon concept. The focus is now on prevention. Initially prevention costs will be high, but they will decline as control is reached and improvement becomes a part of everyone's job.

TRADITIONAL QUALITY COSTS

Measuring the cost of quality has been essentially an industry activity. It began as a measurement to determine the cost of quality control activities such as inspection and to determine the cost of product scrap, as well as the cost of reworking defective products and their parts.

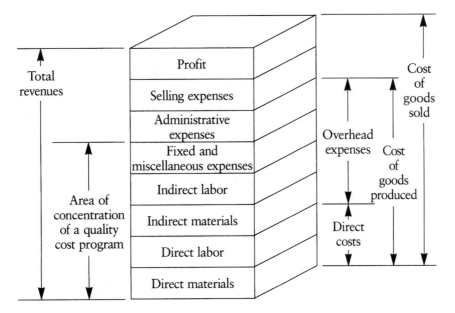

Figure 9.1 *Common product cost breakdown.*

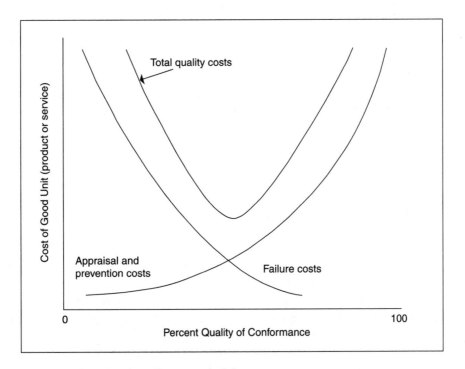

Figure 9.2 *The historical quality cost model.*

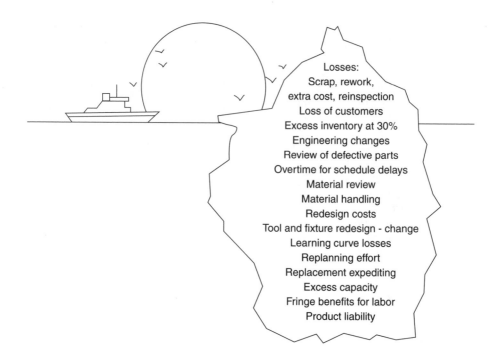

Figure 9.3 *The unrecognized costs of poor quality in industry. Some also apply to the service industry.*

These collected costs were the targets for reduction. However, as Figure 9.3 illustrates, those simple costs are merely the tip of the iceberg. Many other, and significant, costs are incurred when defective material is produced, but they are not collected. Some companies have done some work sampling and have derived an average cost factor to use, but it can be quite inaccurate. Companies didn't collect better quality costs because they didn't know how to reduce them. Further, manufacturing managed product cost reporting, and the collection system followed the traditional industrial engineering model of direct and indirect costs.. *Some* defective material was accepted as just part of the cost of production. Also, no one had any idea of how much was too much. They either didn't know the capability of their processes or lived with what they had. When the new total quality improvement movement began, some companies made a more concerted effort to measure their *total* cost of poor quality and were shocked to learn that it was as high as 30 percent of total sales. These hidden costs were major detractors from profit.

As the quality function evolved from inspection (quality control) to more preventive activities (quality assurance), quality cost collection was expanded into prevention, appraisal, and internal and external failure. These are defined in Table 9.1. This has been the standard categorization used by industry since the 1950s. However, few organizations had a cost collection system that could separate and collect all these costs, so the categorization remained an ideal. In most cases, any costs reported in many categories were limited to those of the quality organization.

Table 9.1   Quality cost definitions.

Prevention—Costs associated with quality planning, designing, implementing and managing the quality system, auditing the system, supplier surveys, and process improvements.
Appraisal—Costs associated with measuring, evaluating, or auditing products, and product materials to ensure conformance with quality standards and performance requirements.
Internal Failure—Costs associated with failures and defects (processes, equipment, products, and product materials) that fail to meet quality standards or requirements.
External Failure—Costs generated by defective products, services and, processes during customer use. They include warranties, complaints, replacements or recalls, repairs, poor packaging, handling, and customer returns.

The quality cost committee of the American Society for Quality (ASQ), an international organization with members in 163 countries, has published several volumes on quality cost collection and reporting using the standard categories. It has also established something of a standard for the cost elements within each category, as shown in Table 9.2. It illustrates how pervasive the costs of quality are and how comprehensive a cost collection system would have to be to report them. But even when many of the listed quality costs have been collected, success in using the data or reducing those costs has been limited, for the following reasons.[1]

- Business management has not been interested in the concept of quality costs. The categorizations, prevention, appraisal, and failure are too parochial, and they did not correlate with accounting practices.

- Management's attitude has been that reduction of quality costs was the responsibility of the quality organization, even though these costs were driven primarily by engineering designs, manufacturing methods, and suppliers' performance.

- The concept of prevention costs is intangible and ambiguous. The working relationships between prevention expenditures and resultant lower costs are too difficult to demonstrate most of the time. Appraisal costs—some inspection and testing—are considered a normal part of the production process.

- Quality costs have not been used as a factor in the measurement of management performance. Managers concentrate on the factors that do.

- The common definition of quality as "meeting requirements" has been fundamental in management's limited interest in quality costs. Meeting requirements means producing anywhere within the engineering tolerance. Dependence was placed on the appraisal of process output to ensure that only "within tolerance" products were accepted. It was expected that some production output would not meet requirements. This resulted in management's focus on quality costs of inspection, test, scrap, and rework. In practice, production and quality control management constantly wrestled with the question of what level of these costs was realistic and acceptable. The answer often depended on what

Table 9.2   The traditional quality cost categories and their elements as established by ASQ.

Detailed Quality Cost Description Summary	
Prevention Costs	**Appraisal Costs**
Marketing/customer/user	Purchasing appraisal costs
Marketing research	Receiving or incoming inspections and tests
Customer/user perception surveys/clinics	Measurement equipment
Contract/document review	Qualification of supplier product
Product/service/design development	Source inspection and control programs
Design quality progress reviews	Operations (manufacturing or service) appraisal costs
Design support activities	Planned operations inspections, tests, audits
Product design qualification test	Checking labor
Service design qualification	Product or service quality audits
Field trials	Inspection and test materials
Purchasing	Set-up inspections and tests
Supplier reviews	Special tests (manufacturing)
Supplier rating	Process control measurements
Purchase order tech data reviews	Laboratory support
Supplier quality planning	Measurement equipment
Operations (manufacturing or service)	Depreciation allowances
Operations process validation	Measurement equipment expenses
Operations quality planning	Maintenance and calibration labor
Design and development of quality measurement and control equipment	Outside endorsements and certifications
Operations support quality planning	External appraisal costs
Operator quality education	Field performance evaluation
Operator SPC/process control	Special product evaluations
Quality administration	Evaluation of field stock and spare parts
Administrative salaries	Review of test and inspection data
Administrative expenses	Miscellaneous quality evaluations
Quality program planning	
Quality performance reporting	
Quality education	
Quality improvement	
Quality audits	
Other prevention costs	

budget level the quality function could negotiate, not on what was needed to ensure that requirements were met. They were guesses, in any case, because no one knew what process variation was going to be.[1]

THE NEW QUALITY COSTS—
ACTIVITY BASED COSTING (ABC)

Traditional cost accounting systems are based on the concept that products and services consume resources. ABC is based on the concept that products and services consume activities, and that activities consume resources. Ideally in such a system it would be pos-

Table 9.2   continued.

Quality Costs—Old and New	
Internal Failure Costs	**External Failure Costs**
Product/service design failure costs (internal)	Complaint investigations/customer or user service
Design corrective action	Returned goods
Rework due to design changes	Retrofit costs
Scrap due to design changes	Recall costs
Production liaison costs	Warranty claims
Purchasing failure costs	Liability costs
Purchased material reject disposition costs	Penalties
Purchased material replacement costs	Customer/user goodwill
Supplier corrective action	Lost sales
Rework of supplier rejects	Other external failure costs
Uncontrolled material losses	
Operations (product or service) failure costs	
Material review and corrective action costs	
Disposition costs	
Troubleshooting or failure analysis costs (operations)	
Investigation support costs	
Operations corrective action	
Operations rework and repair costs	
Rework	
Repair	
Reinspection/retest costs	
Extra operations	
Scrap costs (operations)	
Downgraded end product or service	
Internal failure labor losses	
Other internal failure costs	

sible to measure, for example, the cost of all direct and indirect activities consumed by each product or its parts, or, the cost of activities in a service operation. This is very difficult to measure in most collection systems that allocate those factors proportionately to each product *equally*, associated to some basis like direct labor hours. In the allocation method, a piece of expensive equipment may be used on only a few products, but all the products carry its cost. As a result, inherently low-cost products may be made noncompetitive by having them carry the cost of other, undercosted products. This difference can be significant because the use of support labor, facilities, and equipment can vary widely among different products made in the same facility. Even in cases where management knows that one product is high cost and a low profit maker and keeps it because of competitive marketing strategies, it needs to know activity costs to make useful process improvements. Without process activity costs, improvement teams are handicapped in identifying the best improvement targets. Poor cost data can lead to counterproductive and even erroneous conclusions that process improvement methodology doesn't work. The best answer to this need is ABC.

ABC use is becoming worldwide. One Swedish engineering conglomerate has adopted it. For example, it takes the same amount of time, labor, and materials to make two different industrial robots. But if one must be tailored to a customer needs, it requires more engineering, greater purchasing activity, and more special inspection than a standard production model. If these costs were allocated equally to every item manufactured, the cost of the customized robot would be understated and the standard model overstated. The custom models were being underpriced and the standard models penalized, which could make them noncompetitive.

Installing ABC also provided the Swedish company with cost data it could use for activity analysis. It realized, for example, that it could save inspection costs on material from high-quality suppliers. It could also more accurately price custom work.

System Elements

The two basic elements of a simple ABC system are process value, and cost driver analysis.

Process Value Analysis

Process value analysis (PVA) is a method for identifying those activities that add value to the process output as well as those that add cost and little or no value. Value-added is the labor and material directly used in making a product. Process value analysis (PVA) is shown in Figure 9.4. Analyzing value, cost, and cycle time provides economic targets for improvement as well as the true cost for making improvements. The four activities involve

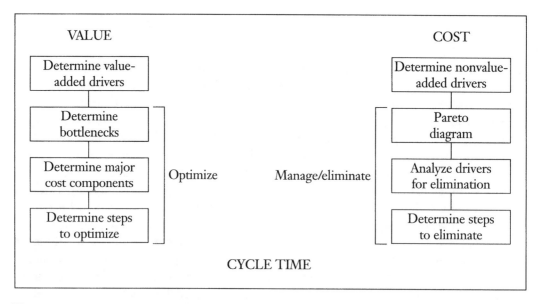

Figure 9.4 *Process value analysis.*

- Describing the process
- Analyzing the activity
- Analyzing the cost driver
- Identifying the improvement

Process description is identifying and describing the important business systems and functional processes in an organization. This is also one of the early steps in any process improvement. Figure 9.5 shows the common process model with the prime PVA activities noted. Activity analysis seeks to explain the process. It asks what each step is and why it exists. It requires the measurement of the cycle times and costs for each step and the separation of value-added from nonvalue-added activities. Analytical tools such as flow charts, process mapping, cause- and- effect charts, and Pareto diagrams are typical of those used in this analysis. (They are described in Part II.) Some elements of this analysis are shown in Table 9.3.

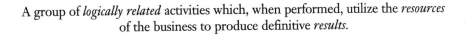

A group of *logically related* activities which, when performed, utilize the *resources* of the business to produce definitive *results*.

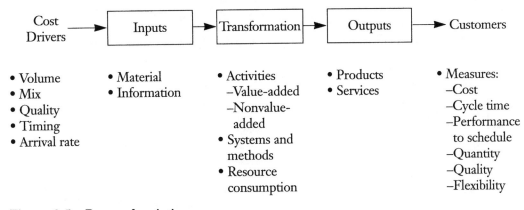

Cost Drivers	Inputs	Transformation	Outputs	Customers
• Volume • Mix • Quality • Timing • Arrival rate	• Material • Information	• Activities –Value-added –Nonvalue-added • Systems and methods • Resource consumption	• Products • Services	• Measures: –Cost –Cycle time –Performance to schedule –Quantity –Quality –Flexibility

Figure 9.5 *Process description.*

Table 9.3 Activities and cost drivers.

Activity	Cost Driver
Automatic machine	Machine cycles
Plastic molding	Machine hours
Purchasing	Purchased line items
Assembly	Direct labor hours
Process engineering	Hours
Product complexity	Material handling

This list reflects several different processes. There would be several activities and drivers within each.

Cost Driver Analysis

Cost driver analysis associates the value- and nonvalue-added activities with their costs. Obtaining these costs is the core of the ABC method. This is difficult when the accounting system is not designed to collect them in an appropriate, meaningful manner. Cost drivers in an industrial process may fall into one of the two categories noted in Table 9.4: primarily highly qualitative and volume based. Usually both are needed because of their different sources. The cost of volume-driven activities is usually available from the cost accounting system. The important primary costs are not. Each organization has to devise some informal method to obtain them. The improvement teams can play an important role in identifying what is needed. Improvement identification is conducted by the teams to optimize value-added activities, reduce nonvalue-added, and reduce lead time, cycle time, and waste.

Table 9.4　Examples of process cost drivers (Qualitative and Quantitative).

Primary	Volume
Coordination	Number of vendors/suppliers
Communication	Number of customers of process
Capability of staff	Number of supplier surveys/audits
Quality of material	Number of stocks
Quality/age of equipment	Number of material moves
Configuration	Number of tool orders
Availability of tools	Lost tool requests
Availability of material	Production rate
Availability of machines	Number of inspections
Availability of data	Dollar volume
Availability of people	Number of line items
Inspection requirements	Number of orders
Efficiency	Quantity per line item
Required documentation	Number of shipments
Complexity	Number of new materials/parts
Redundancies	Number of shortages
Accuracy of data	Number of rejects/defects
Change to requirements	Number of lost parts
Request for information/data	Number of approvals
Customer requirements	Number of requests for information/data
Schedule/timing	Number of setups
Priority	Number of part numbers
Safety/environmental requirements	Number of purchase requisitions
Location of resources	Number of changes to requirements
Timeliness	Number of delinquents
	Number of overshipments
	Number of minimum buys
	Number of receipts

Benefits of ABC

- Provides process improvement teams with cost details related to the process activities affecting variation and cycle time. The result is responsibility and accountability at the lowest organization levels.
- More accurately measures the results of improvement projects and actions.
- Integrates financial and quality performance, which gives recognition to their interdependence.
- Identifies the true sources of unacceptable variation.
- Allows the allocation of resources toward improvement.
- Provides visibility to management and the process members as to the performance, in business terms.

QUALITY AND TOTAL COST MANAGEMENT

Process quality costs ideally should be one element of a total cost management system—a system that allows a focus on the internal management needs and not just the financial accounting requirements for external reporting. Management should ask itself why it collects costs. What costs are needed in relation to the way the business is conducted? If it is an organization adopting or using a continuous improvement philosophy, it needs process activity costs. ABC provides such a management cost system. In this method, the important costs of product development/production activities are identified, with reasonable accuracy, to be used to measure what each product, service, and process actually costs. Management may decide to continue making some low-profit items to offer the market a complete line. They can then focus resources on where improvement efforts will pay off.

QUALITY COSTS AND QUALITY IMPROVEMENT

The difference between the traditional quality assurance and modern quality management (TQM) has been explained. To repeat briefly, higher quality is related to reduced process variation, both in and between all organization activities and functions. Therefore the kind of cost data needed in process improvement is different from the traditional quality costs (however, appraisal and failure costs may be indicators of where process improvement is needed).

A major difference between the old and new cost needs is that when the focus is on just meeting requirements, improvement efforts would stop when it was thought requirements were satisfied. The new quality objective, in comparison, is to eliminate or continuously reduce process variation and reduce cycle time. In this approach, the application of improvement techniques by teams requires process activity quality costs to aid in prioritizing improvement efforts and evaluating their effect. A different kind of quality cost system is needed to do so.

This need is supported by a study by Winchell and Hohner, sponsored by the ASQ and the National Association of Accountants. Some conclusions they reached include the following

1. Traditional quality costs were not a method for exercising control over costs in companies visited that supported continuous improvement. Flexibility is needed—not periodic reporting, as has been the common quality function practice.

2. The traditional quality cost systems were not used to support continuous improvement. They are excellent for implementing a structured information system that makes preplanned periodic reports. Such systems are useful if control is desired. Historically, however, quality cost reporting has not survived when used for this purpose.

3. Stand-alone quality cost systems, a common practice, were not effective and were short lived. They were perceived as nonvalue-added activities and not tied to improvement efforts. (The primary driver for the standard quality cost system was the DOD. MIL Q 9858 required that the contractor maintain a quality cost reporting system to be used for decision making. DOD quality system auditors insisted on contractors having one, but rarely asked how or if it was being used.)

4. The traditional quality cost categories did not fit the terminology of service organizations. As a result, quality cost was unfamiliar to them.

5. Quality improvement efforts drive the need for cost information. It is the other way around in traditional quality cost systems, where cost information precipitates a search for improvement.[2]

Item 5 reflects the important change in the nature of the quality cost information needed. Traditionally costs drove the problem corrective action. These costs are symptoms. Actions that remove symptoms usually don't remove the cause or improve the process. Using a process improvement approach will drive the need for process cost information.

QUALITY COSTS IN SERVICE ORGANIZATIONS

Gray reports an estimated 30% to 50% of service companies operating expenses are spent on quality costs, with about 70% of that, allocated to failure costs.[3] Yet few service companies pay attention to such costs. The basis for such costs is identified in Table 9.5. Related failure costs are such things as customer and employee turnover, lost productivity, and the various forms of rework.

Useful quality cost systems do not require exact cost measurements. Starting with good estimates as a basis, the cost effect of improvements can be indicated.

A before and after quality cost comparison would be interesting in organizations that are downsizing and restructuring. Many of these actions may well be counter-productive in achieving short-term savings.

Table 9.5   Quality costs: jobs, activities, and expenses.

Prevention	Detection	Correction
Market research	Internal auditors/ audits	Complaints
Customer/internal user sur-veys	Review of work	Worker's compensation
Training and education	Proofreaders	Error correction
Account reconciliation	Running spell check function	Service guarantees/warranties
Quality director, staff, and expenses	Fire alarm equipment	Interest penalties
Quality system audits	Inspectors	Disability payments
Quality planning	Appraisers	Equal Employment Oppor-tunity lawsuits
Supplier qualification pro-gram	Checkers	Returns
Preventive maintenance	Approvals	Replacements
Cross-functional design teams	Authorizations	Penalties
Customer service training	External appraisal costs	Rework
		Troubleshooting/repair
		Liability
		Hidden costs

LIFE CYCLE COSTS

The life cycle cost concept began in the Department of Defense in the 1950s, but was not effectively used until the mid 1990s. With maintenance costs in the billions of dollars, the DOD has required companies bidding for new work to include life cycle costs, and these costs are being used in the bid selection process.

Life cycle costs are little used in other parts of the economy. Several reasons for this can be identified:

- Lack of management interest
- Lack of a useful model
- Failure to understand the concept and its potential value
- Organization preoccupation with other activities
- Little customer demand

The life cycle cost concept can be applied to any product. It is the optimum cost that meets the needs of both supplier and customer. For example, there are light bulbs costing $12 that last ten times longer than a $1 bulb and use about $50 less electricity. People don't buy them. The consumer requires education before the bulb will sell well.

The life cycle costs of software, that is, development plus maintenance, are of growing concern. Many large and older programs in business and government are composed of a variety of interacting and interdependent programs. Their foundations, their initial programs, consist of program languages no longer used. For many, the original documentation has been lost. For some, documentation hasn't been maintained as changes have been made over the years. When changes need to be made or problems corrected, such as the year two thousand problem, the possible costs can be enormous.

Measuring software quality costs is very difficult, and there is no basis for doing it. Historical records have been poorly maintained. Some organizations have developed estimating factors to use when developing a budget for a new program effort, but they are just estimates, and since nearly every new program is unique, the risk of making a poor estimate is real and common.

REFERENCES

1. W.M., Baker. "Why Traditional Standard Cost Systems Are Not Effective in Today's Manufacturing Environment." *Industrial Management* (July/August, 1989).
2. W.O. Winchell, and G. Hohner. "Implementing Quality Cost Systems." ASQ, Annual Quality Congress Transactions, 1990.
3. J. Gray. "Quality Costs: A Report Card on Business," ASQ *Quality Progress* (April, 1995).

ADDITIONAL READINGS

Atkins, H., J. Hamburg, and C. Ittner. *"Linking Quality to Profits: Quality-Based Cost Management"* Milwaukee: Quality Press, 1994.

Campanella, J. *Principles of Quality Cost: Principles, Implementation and Use*, 2nd ed. Milwaukee: ASQC Quality Press, 1990.

STUDY QUESTIONS

1. If one objective of a business is to make a profit, why are quality costs important?
2. What are the traditional categories of quality costs?
3. What are the reasons that management has not used the traditionally classified quality costs to manage?
4. What is the basis of activity based costing? What are the benefits over the traditional quality cost method?
5. What is PVA? Cost driver analysis?
6. What is meant by life cycle costs?

PART II

Chapter 10

Tools for Continuous Improvement

- **The Seven Management Tools for Planning, Decision Making, and Control**
    - **Affinity Diagram**
    - **Relationship Diagram**
    - **Tree Diagram**
    - **Matrix Chart**
    - **Matrix Data Analysis**
    - **Arrow Diagram**
    - **Process Decision Program Chart**
- **Team Decision-Making Tools**
    - **Brainstorming**
    - **Multivoting**
    - **Crawford Slip Method**
    - **Nominal Group Technique**
    - **Delphi Method**
    - **Storyboarding**
- **The Seven Quality Control Tools**
    - **Team Use (?)**
    - **Qualitative Tools**
    - **Quantitative Tools**

- **Important Factors in Successful Process Control**
- **Process Capability**
- **Continuous Improvement**
- **Reducing Common Causes**

Tools for quality improvement have been developed over the years, beginning with the pioneer work of Shewhart at Bell Laboratories in the 1920s. His contribution was the concept of variation, special and common causes, and statistical control charts, which are the basis of SPC. The next major practical contribution to the QC tool kit was by Kaoru Ishikawa in the 1960s in combining Shewhart's work with some of his own and describing seven QC tools.[1] Their combined works represent the first practical scientific tools, usable by anyone, for analyzing and improving organization and process performance. Their first significant use in the West was in quality circles where the Ishikowa QC tools were used, and all are integral to the functioning of process improvement teams. The seven QC tools are a graphic means for process problem solving through group thinking and the analysis of data.

Also in the 1960s, the Union of Japanese Scientists and Engineers (JUSE) was fostering the development of the seven management tools for QC.[2] These are tools to qualitatively analyze problems of a complex nature that are not well defined. Both sets of tools are listed in Table 10.1.

THE SEVEN MANAGEMENT TOOLS FOR PLANNING, DECISION MAKING, AND CONTROL

The seven management tools are linguistic and graphic, for exploring problems, organizing ideas, and converting concepts into action plans, design criteria, and so forth. They have application in planning, research and development, designing, and selling products. They have been translated and modified to fit American application (Figure 10.1).

There are many situations in which there are little or no data to make decisions. New product planning is one such business situation. A customer need or market exists that may be broadly recognized but there isn't a clear path to define it, much less identify design criteria. Since we think linguistically rather than mathematically, there are often many ideas but no obvious way to distill them into actionable information. The seven management tools were developed for this kind of problem solving. There isn't a simple recipe to use these tools. The application situations are typically nebulous and abstract at the start. The tools require time to learn and apply, but they produce valuable results. They facilitate orderly, organized, and focused thinking from which you distill useful information from a variety of sources.

Affinity Diagram

The affinity diagram facilitates the definition of problems by organizing ideas according to a recognized relationship or affinity for each other. It is a method for building

Table 10.1   The Seven QC and Seven QC Management Tools.

Seven QC Tools	Seven QC Management Tools
Pareto diagram	Affinity diagram (K–J)
Cause-and-effect diagram	Relationship diagram
Flowchart	Tree diagram
Check sheet	Matrix chart
Histogram	Matrix data analysis chart
Scatter diagram	Arrow diagram
Graphs and control charts	Process decision program chart

Each set of tools has many applications for problem analysis and solution.

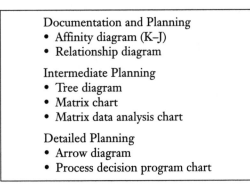

Documentation and Planning
- Affinity diagram (K–J)
- Relationship diagram

Intermediate Planning
- Tree diagram
- Matrix chart
- Matrix data analysis chart

Detailed Planning
- Arrow diagram
- Process decision program chart

Figure 10.1   *The Seven Management Tools.*

an overall hierarchical structure from a set of unstructured ideas. The genesis of this methodology is similar to that used by the Russian chemist, Dimitry Mendeleyev, who described the periodic table of elements in the nineteenth century. He wrote the characteristics of each element on a card. In arranging them, he recognized that they could be organized into families. These family members had a structural affinity for each other and could be so grouped. This reflects the idea of the affinity diagram, except that the elements in quality application are ideas.

The affinity technique fits well with the QFD methodology (discussed later), where the ideas are the "voice" of the customer. For example, a team trying to learn customer requirements with the intention of translating them into design requirements might begin by each member writing an idea on a file card. Then, laying the cards on a table, without conversation to influence them, the team members would arrange them into whatever logical groups they perceived. They would then reach a consensus as to which ideas had an affinity for each other. What had been several seemingly unconnected ideas actually had inherent organization relationships and patterns. The groups developed can then be prioritized and the same process repeated to connect the groups to the next level of information, such as goals and objectives or even design criteria.

Figure 10.2 is an example of an affinity diagram organizing the various factors involved in identifying key performance measures. This technique is a form of brainstorming for organizing creative thinking. As an alternate method, Post-its (adhesive-backed, note-sized paper) can be used in place of cards. They can then be stuck onto

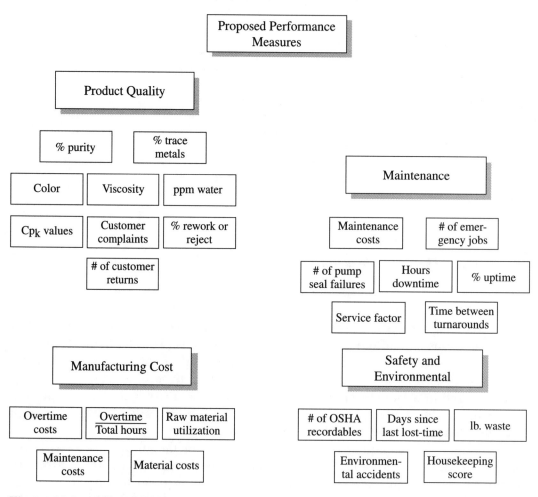

Figure 10.2 *Affinity diagram.*
Source: Nancy R. Tague, *The Quality Toolbox* (Milwaukee: ASQC Quality Press, 1995).

a wall and grouped by the team. It is often helpful to use another tool, the relationship diagram, in conjunction with the affinity diagram.[3]

Some benefits from using the affinity diagram are

- It encourages creative thinking.
- It suggests new connections between ideas and issues.
- It provides a climate for breakthrough thinking.
- It helps establish new communication links between organization elements. It assists in organization development and maturation.

Relationship Diagram

This diagram aids the problem-solving process by showing the relationship between problems and ideas in complex situations. It identifies meaningful categories from a mass of ideas. It is useful when relationships are difficult to determine. In using this tool, the team writes each idea in a circle and clusters the circles in proximity to each other. It then identifies which idea strongly influences another and uses arrows to indicate the direction of influence. The results are evaluated by identifying ideas that have the most arrows entering or exiting. Basic or key ideas are indicated by circles that have only exiting arrows. Figure 10.3 is pictorial of the tool; Figure 10.4

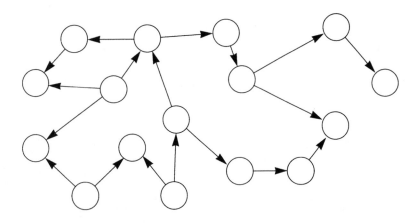

Logically Categorize Ideas

A pictorial of the result of assigning arrows to show cause and effect. Each circle represents a team's selection of the important problems. Assigning cause-and-effect arrows further clarifies relationships.

Figure 10.3   *Relationship diagram.*

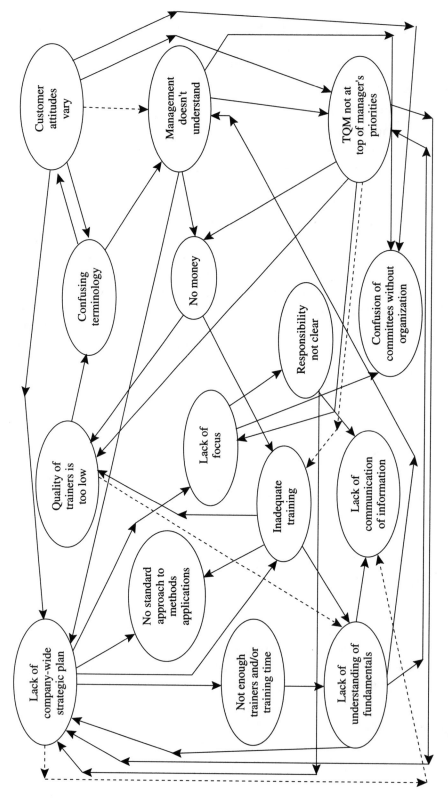

A solid line is counted as one point. A dashed line is counted as half a point. If only one team member strongly believes that an item is a major cause of another item, then an arrow is not shown on this chart but a quarter point is added to the total

The objective is to determine major cause (most arrows going out) issue that is most interrelated to other issues (most arrows in and out) and the issue that is both a major cause and has most interrelationships to other issues (most arrows going in and out). Results are tabulated in Figure 10.7.

Figure 10.4 *Relationship diagram—TQM problems and concerns.*

presents the results of a team brainstorming session that identified 15 major issues involved in developing a company improvement plan. Using this tool can

- Stimulate team members to think in multiple directions.
- Examine the cause-and-effect relationship between issues not normally examined.
- Maintain a balance within the team. Every member can offer ideas.

Tree Diagram

A tree diagram identifies the tasks and methods needed to solve a problem and reach a goal. It systematically traces the means and clarifies the problem to be solved by exposing its complete structure. From this analysis, the problem-solving method can be identified. The tree diagram can supplement the affinity and relationship diagrams and identify items that were missed. It's a simple structure, as shown in Figure 10.5. Figure 10.6 is an example of its application. This tool can be used to

- Keep team solutions tied to the original problem or objective.
- Provide assurance that all important links have been considered.

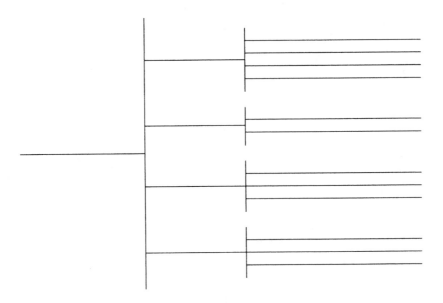

Identify ideas in greater and greater detail

Figure 10.5 *Tree diagram.*

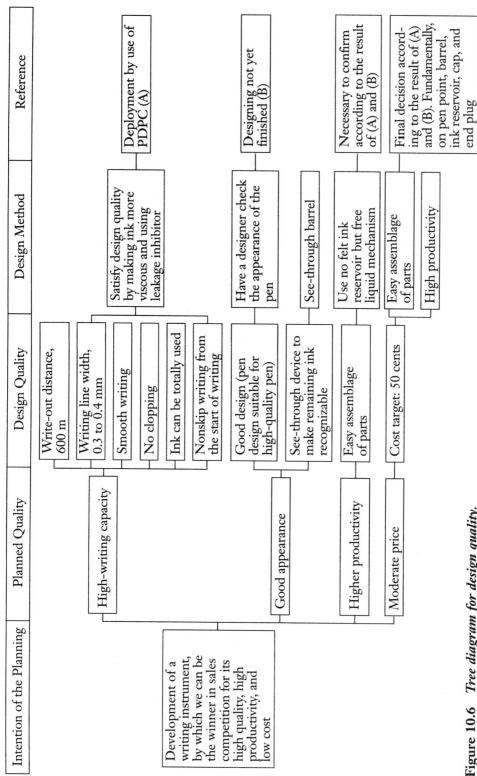

Figure 10.6 Tree diagram for design quality.

This example shows the systematic identification of tasks and means to develop a writing instrument.
Source: "The New Quality Technology," Hughes Aircraft Co. Reprinted with permission.

Matrix Chart

This type of chart yields information about the relationships and importance of task and method elements of the subjects concerned. It typically uses the information developed by the previously mentioned tools. Figure 10.7 shows the relationships among the issues identified in the relationship diagram (Figure 10.4), including a ranking technique to prioritize their importance.

Matrix Data Analysis

This tool shows all the key data clearly. It can be a rough, two-axis correlation picture. It is not always applicable, but it can provide a picture of such things as different product and market characteristics. It is typically used to weight and rank problem causes identified through other planning tools. Figure 10.8 gives an idea of what it can be used to display.

Arrow Diagram

An arrow diagram shows the time required to solve the problem and which items can be done in parallel. It is a simplified critical path method of planning and scheduling designed to show the optimum schedule for fulfilling a plan and tracking its progress. It incorporates many of the techniques used in the scheduling methods of program evaluation and review technique (PERT) and the critical path method (CPM). Figure 10.9 shows the type of diagram that results from this kind of planning.

Process Decision Program Chart

A chart for contingency planning, this focuses on possible sequences to help lead to a desirable result. It was developed to plan for the future while still in the development stage of problem solution planning. Figure 10.10 depicts a simple application.

TEAM DECISION-MAKING TOOLS

Teams need methods to identify problems and solutions in an orderly and efficient way as they progress. The following are those in most common use.

Brainstorming

Brainstorming is an organized or formalized method of soliciting the best ideas from team members for making decisions at any stage of operation. Without order and a methodology the best ideas will not always surface or problems will be poorly identified. Before making decisions, such as problem cause or solution, a team should examine all the options. One of the most effective ways to generate ideas or theories is by brainstorming. Properly managed and facilitated, it allows people to be as creative and free-thinking as possible.

This matrix is used to document the results of the relationship diagram (see Figure 10.4)

#	Item	TOTAL CAUSES (Total arrows going out)	TOTAL INTERRELATIONSHIPS (Total arrows going in and out)	RANK BY CAUSE	RANK BY COLUMN AND ROW TOTAL
1	Lack of company-wide strategic plan	7.5	12.5	4	4
2	Not enough trainers and/or training time	2.75	7.75	13	12
3	Lack of understanding of fundamentals	6	8.5	6	9
4	No standard approach to methods applications	2	8.5	14	10
5	Inadequate training	8	14.5	3	1
6	Lack of communication of information	4	8	8	11
7	Quality of trainers is too low	3.5	5.75	11	14
8	Lack of focus	6	14	5	2
9	Responsibility is unclear	3.5	11.5	9	6
10	Confusing terminology	3.5	7	10	13
11	No money	3	9	12	8
12	Profusion of committees without organization	1	4.5	15	13
13	Customer attitudes vary	8.5	9.5	2	7
14	Management doesn't understand	9.5	13	1	3
15	TQM not at top of manager's priority list	5.5	12.5	7	8

TOTAL EFFECTS (total arrows going in), by column 1–15:
5, 5, 2.5, 6.5, 6.5, 4, 2.25, 8, 8, 3.5, 6, 3.5, 1, 4.5, 7

LEGEND

An arrow placed in row 1 and column 2 indicates that item 1 is a major cause of item 2 ("Major" and "Cause" are the key words used when developing this matrix).

A double arrow was used to indicate a very strong (almost unanimous agreement) within the team and/or a very strong significant relationship but was still only counted as one point

A single arrow was used to indicate a majority agreement within the team and was counted as one point

A dashed line was used to indicate a major disagreement within the group (i.e., half felt that there was a major cause and half did not). A dashed line is counted as half a point

A dot was used when one team member had a strong belief that a major cause existed. This condition was counted as a quarter point

This symbol represents that this column and row relationship is not applicable

Figure 10.7 *The relationship matrix of problems, issues, and concerns from team findings.*
Source: "Using the 7-M Tools for Strategic Planning," Hughes Aircraft Co. Reprinted with permission.

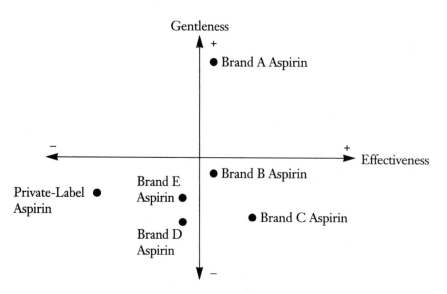

Figure 10.8 *Matrix data analysis comparing the relationship of different products to two main characteristics.*

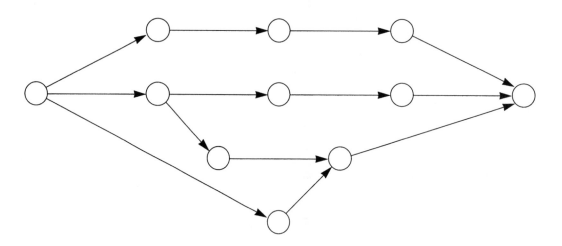

Equivalent to CPM (critical path method)/PERT (program evaluation and review technique), but kept simple. The completion of an event is shown by a circle with the arrows depicting the time for completion.

Figure 10.9 *Arrow diagram.*

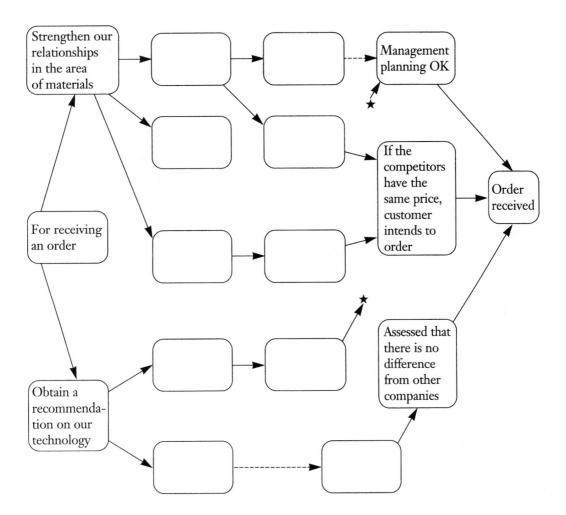

Note: Revise whenever situation changes.

The process decision program chart method was designed to help predict the future of an event while it is still in a developing stage and, thereby, help lead it to a desired result.

The process decision program chart method has two types of applications:

• Sequential extension: To design a plan to achieve a desirable objective, to deal with problems found while implementing the plan, and to make a correct decision and enhance the plan, thereby achieving the objective.

• Forced connection: To conceive countermeasures to avoid an undesirable situation by simulating a process of events leading to an undesirable result.

Figure 10.10 *Process decision program chart.*

The rules for conducting brainstorming sessions are key to its successful use.

1. Encourage everyone's contribution. The objective is to collect all the ideas members can think of. (It takes new teams several sessions before members are comfortable with this approach.) This is the essence of brainstorming.
2. No one is allowed to comment or show any negative reaction during the idea generation period.
3. Build on the ideas of others. This is one of brainstorming's sources of power. Quite often an impractical idea has the seed of a solution or directs thought in a new way that provides the answer. (This is also the reason for rule 2.)
4. Record and post all ideas as they are offered. If some ideas are irrelevant or negative, record them in a separate category to be reviewed later. Do not discard any idea.
5. Have members reduce the total list to one or a few key items and then select other tools to continue the problem-solving process.

There are several variations to this procedure that have been developed. The experience of the facilitator is very important in determining group dynamics and helping select the best way to operate.

Multivoting

1. Reduce the initial idea list to the key items and number each. This is done using a series of straw votes.
2. Have each member choose the item number he or she would like to discuss. Limit the team's selection to about a third of the total.
3. Tally and post the results, using a show of hands or a secret ballot.
4. Reduce the list further by dropping items with the fewest votes.
5. Continue to vote and cut, using discussion by the team, until one top-priority item is selected for action.

Crawford Slip Method

This is a method to gather and condense ideas in a structured but flexible way. Information is gathered anonymously and quickly, without group interaction. It is particularly useful in large groups. Briefly, it involves

1. Writing ideas on slips of paper (one idea per paper).
2. Collecting and sorting ideas into general categories.
3. Looking for patterns and similarities and consolidating ideas into a few main categories. (This is analogous to the affinity diagram, previously discussed.)

Nominal Group Technique

This is a structured approach. It involves limited (nominal) team interaction in generating a list of ideas or options and then narrowing it down. It's a good technique when handling new teams or controversial subjects, or when a team can't agree. Briefly, it includes the following steps.

1. Propose the task as a question to the group. The question is often proposed to members before the meeting.
2. At the first meeting, discuss the purpose of the subject selected and establish the operating rules to be followed.
3. Post the question and allow discussion only for clarification.
4. Have members, silently, write their ideas or questions on paper. Set a reasonable time limit. Have them prioritize their lists.
5. Have each member, in sequence, read his or her ideas in order of priority. List them on a flip chart. Continue the rotation until everyone has read his or her list (or just the top five ideas from each list). There is no discussion during this exercise.
6. Discuss and clarify ideas. An idea's wording can be changed if the originator agrees.
7. The facilitator or leader condenses the list to a minimum number of items.
8. Use the procedure in step 5 to reduce the list to the main items.
9. Give each member four to six cards. Have everyone write one item per card from the final list.
10. Have members mark each card by rank. If there are six cards per person, the highest rank is 6.
11. Collect cards and tally votes. The item with the most votes is the team selection.
12. If there are two or three items receiving a high number of votes, the group may elect to repeat the voting or investigate all the items.

Delphi Method

This is a method of collecting ideas from a group of experts, frequently geographically dispersed, using a leader to prepare questions and collect responses, they are received whether written, by phone, or by fax. It is a way to reach consensus without direct conversation. A common variation is to give the responses of each expert to the next one in line. This is a useful technique to avoid having strong personalities dominate. Except for its methodology, it is similar to other consensus-reaching techniques. It is often used to get a quick overview of the opinions of a group on some subject.

Storyboarding

A storyboard is a technique that visually displays thoughts and ideas. Thoughts and ideas are generated and grouped into categories. All aspects of a process become visible in one picture. The technique was developed by Walt Disney Studios as a way to develop cartoons. It is also somewhat similar to the Kepner-Trigoe method of problem solving.

Figure 10.11 shows an example of a storyboard. The common subject header cards are purpose, future state, who, what, when, cost, and miscellaneous. The headers used by a team depend on the topic. The better defined the topic statement is, the better the final result will be and the easier it will be to get there.

Storyboarding is a useful technique for group facilitators and teams in developing and communicating thoughts, ideas, project activities, and plans.

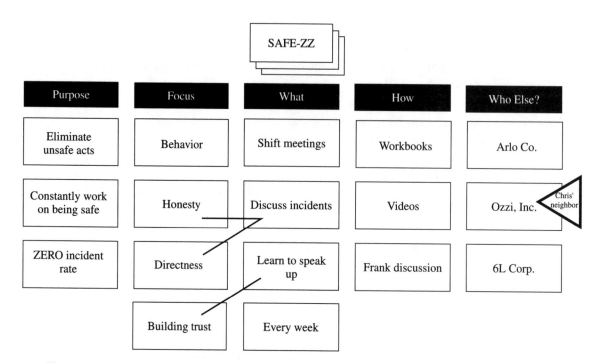

Figure 10.11 *Example of a storyboard.*
Source: Nancy R. Tague, *The Quality Toolbox* (Milwaukee: ASQC Quality Press, 1995).

THE SEVEN QUALITY CONTROL TOOLS

Hitoshi Kamikubo of JUSE, which has been instrumental in guiding the Japanese industrial success since their first discussions with Deming in 1950, stated in 1989 that he "believes that the main reason behind the astonishing growth and advance of the Japanese economy, based on industrial exports, is the effective and enthusiastic promotion of QC within companies. The largest contributing factor to this progress has been the many tools for quality control—the seven C tools."[4] These tools provide techniques for a structured approach to any problem analysis and solution. Maximum benefit is achieved when they are applied by a team or circle. This elicits the maximum amount of useful data that the tools are designed to manage. Figure 10.12 illustrates a common application of the tools and their relation to the Shewhart/Deming wheel for continuous improvement. The tools can be divided into two broad types, qualitative and quantitative. All use diagrams of some kind to organize and picture the analyses.

Qualitative
    Flowcharts/process maps (process maps may contain quantitative data)
    Cause-and-effect diagrams

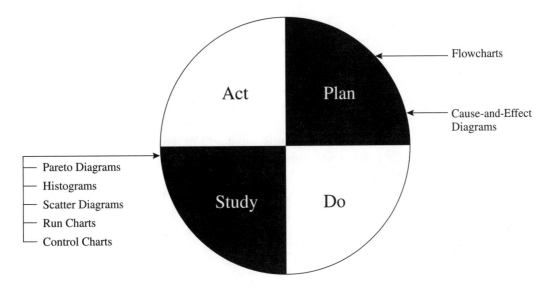

Figure 10.12   *Basic graphic methods.*

Quantitative

Scatter diagrams
Pareto diagrams
Run charts
Histograms
Control charts

The qualitative or nonquantitative tools are used primarily for problem analysis, although solutions or partial solutions are sometimes reached through their use. The quantitative tools require data—some measurement of characteristics or events. The two categories are most frequently used in various combinations, depending on the nature of the problem and the objective.

For example, in working to improve a business process, it is fundamental to first describe it in adequate detail. The flowchart and process map showing its elements are simple and powerful first tools. (One of the most straightforward ways to reduce cycle time is process simplification using flowcharts and process maps). Then, after the process has been accurately defined, the various problems in its operation are prioritized using the Pareto diagram. The cause-and-effect diagram would be the next logical tool to identify probable causes methodically from which the most likely are selected. Means for correction are determined and tried. The Pareto chart is then used to prioritize the problems that remain, and further corrective action is taken. A run chart may then be used to collect performance data over time to determine the trend and to get an idea of the extent of variation with respect to required limits or goals and to see the effect of corrective actions. Used repeatedly on some activity, particularly in nontechnical or mechanized processes, these tools invariably yield significant improvements.

Team Use

As can be seen in the tool descriptions that follow, ideas from the team's experience are captured and used. There may be some simple data taking. A knowledge of statistical theory is useful but not required. These tools require only organized thinking and simple arithmetic. The remaining tools—histograms and control charts—can add, where appropriate, a great deal more power to the analytical phase and are very important in improving process yield and customer satisfaction.

Sometimes more sophisticated statistical techniques are beneficial and require the assistance of an industrial statistician to provide guidance in their application and interpretation of results.

Qualitative Tools

Flowcharts

Making and using flowcharts are among the most important actions in bringing process control to both administrative and manufacturing processes. While it is obvious that to control a process one must first understand it, many companies are still trying to solve problems and improve processes without first describing how they are actually operating. The easiest and best way to understand a process is to draw a picture of its activities—that's basically what flowcharting is. There are many styles that can be used. Some people use pictures, some use engineering symbols, and others just use squares or rectangles for the whole diagram. There really is no right or wrong way to display the information. Flowcharts can vary from the elementary, identifying just the order of key process activities, to the complex, including information feedback paths and activity performance measures such as cycle time. The true test of a flowchart is how well those who create and use it can understand it and work with it.

Constructing Flow Diagrams

Every process is supplied with services/products from some supplier(s). Likewise, every process provides products/services to some other process - its customer(s). Figure 10.13 shows a generic process module. Using this figure as a guide, making a flowchart is simple as long as described by the following factors

1. It is most important that the right people be involved in making the chart. This includes those who actually do the work of the process, suppliers to the process, customers of the process, the supervisor of the area with which the process functions, and sometimes an independent facilitator. This is the team.
2. During team sessions, all data must be visible to all the people all the time. Using large sheets of paper and masking tape is imperative for a good flowcharting session. As one sheet is completed, it should be taped on the wall in sequence with previous work. Rarely should a session be completed without at least some rework of previous parts of the flowchart as the group members reflect on the information in front of them.

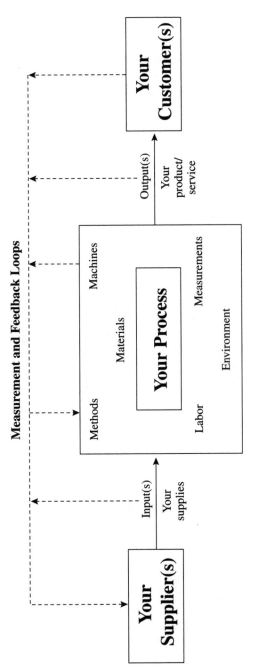

Figure 10.13 *Basic flowchart module.*

165

3. Enough time must be allotted. Experience shows that much more time is required to make a flowchart than is usually expected. More than one session might be required. Group members may need additional time to obtain more information on the functioning of the process. Frequently all members don't agree on how a process functions. It must be verified.

4. The more questions everyone asks, the better. Questions are the key to the flowcharting process. There are many questions that can be asked by both the facilitator and the group members. What is the first thing that happens? What is the next thing that happens? Questioning should continue throughout the process. Questions that will be helpful include (for manufacturing)

- Where does the service or material come from?
- How does the service or material get to the process?
- Who makes the decision if a service or material is needed?
- What happens if the decision is "yes"?
- What happens if the decision is "no"?
- Is there anything else that must be done at this point?
- Where does the product or service of this operation go?
- What tests are performed on the product at each part of the process?
- What tests are performed on the process?
- What happens if the test is out of tolerance?

Even more questions will arise during the session(s). Also, teams should not get bogged down on any one question. Keep moving. Questions can be researched and reported on later.

5. Finally, be sure that the final chart is verified against what is actually taking place.

The Benefits of Flowcharts

Organizations that use process flowcharting reap many benefits:

- The people who work in the process understand the process. They begin to control it instead of being its victim.

- Once the process can be seen objectively in a flowchart, improvement targets can be more easily identified.

- Employees realize how they fit into the overall process, and they visualize their suppliers and customers as a part of that overall process. This leads directly to improved communication between departments and work areas. It introduces system thinking.

- The people who participate in flowcharting sessions see all the activity interactions and become enthusiastic supporters of the entire quality effort. They will continue to provide suggestions for even further improvement.

- Process flowcharts are valuable tools in training programs for new employees.
- Work procedures written around current process flowcharts will be the most effective and are more likely to be followed.

Perhaps the most important benefit of using process flowcharts is that the people in the process will all understand it in the same terms. That understanding leads to employees who can better control their destinies, more economical processes, less waste in administrative functions, and better customer–supplier relationships between departments.

Process Mapping

A process map[5] is a comprehensive flowchart. It is the visual representation of a process, showing the sequence of tasks in detail. The purpose in mapping is to define the practices being used, then to look for better alternatives. Mapping, like flow-charting, is most useful when conducted by a team of people in, or closely associated with, the process under scrutiny.

Mapping, like flowcharting, is applicable to internal and external processes in any organization; for example, the selling process, order entry, and budgeting.

Types

Macro processes are identified from the top down. They are usually broad in scope and identify many smaller processes. An example would be the process from order entry to delivery of a product or service, with only the major steps noted. Even at the top level it can get complex, since important processes involve almost all internal organizations. Macro mapping is useful to identify key processes but difficult to analyze in detail. The usual methodology is to break down the macro map into manageable segments. If cycle time and costs can be established at the macro level, the results can be used to prioritize the use of resources.

Micro processes are the detailed elements of the macro processes. The real process analysis and improvement work is done at the micro level, and its effect measured at the higher level.

Application

Process mapping is a good place to begin work on the improvement process team activity. Often, even when team members have worked in the process under analysis, they encounter the fact that they all don't have the same perspective or conception of how the process works. Clarifying these differences opens the participants' minds to new improvement ideas.

An overview of the steps in process mapping, like flowcharting, includes

1. Defining the process. Identify suppliers and customers, the inputs and outputs, and the process owner (usually the first stopping point, because it is usually found that none exists—one reason the process needs improving). Identify process boundaries.
2. Mapping the process. Identify the major elements. Put the operations in sequence. Add arrows to show direction of work flow. Include parallel processes that occur simultaneously. Establish the cycle time from boundary to boundary.

3. Analyzing. Group tasks that are related, question and understand each step, rank frequency of doing each task, and separate tasks that must be done from those sometimes done.
4. Mapping alternatives. Add flexibility to process paths. Identify decision points. Choose between alternatives.
5. Mapping inspection points. Show pass-fail paths and rework loops.
6. Evaluating and improving the process. Reduce nonvalue-added steps.

There are no standardized rules for drawing a process map. As long as the participants agree, specific rules make little difference. For organizations with several improvement teams at work, however, some general standards should be set so that all the teams can understand every map. Figure 10.14 is an example of one approach. It identifies one process, the steps in getting a part from receiving to storage. One objective would be to reduce the number of steps and the nonvalue-added time.

Cause-and-Effect Diagrams

One unique and valuable tool for obtaining the maximum information is the cause-and-effect diagram. This tool was first developed in 1943 by Ishikawa at the University of Tokyo; he used it to explain to a group of engineers from the Kawasaki Steel Works how various factors acting in and on a process could be sorted and related.

The cause-and-effect diagram (also known as the fishbone diagram) is a method for analyzing process dispersion. The diagram's purpose is to relate causes and effects. Not only is this tool invaluable for virtually any issue requiring attention, but it can easily be learned by people at all levels of the organization and applied immediately. It can become a standard tool for communicating between groups. There are three basic types of cause-and-effect diagrams: dispersion analysis, process classification, and cause enumeration. Figure 10.15 depicts the basic format for the cause-and-effect diagram. Note the hierarchical relationship of the effect to the main causes and their subsequent relationship to the subcauses. For example, main cause A has a direct relationship to the effect. Each of the subcauses is related in terms of its level of influence on the main cause. While a cause-and-effect diagram can be developed by an individual, it is well suited for team applications. One of the most valuable attributes of this tool is that it provides an excellent means to facilitate a brainstorming session. It will enable the participants to focus on the issue at hand and immediately allow them to sort ideas into useful categories, especially when dispersion analysis or process classification methods are used.

Dispersion Analysis

Let's assume there are difficulties with customer complaints. Let us further assume that a team of about seven individuals from various functions throughout the organization is formed. Each of these individuals has sound knowledge of the overall business as well as an area of specific expertise. This team will provide a good example of

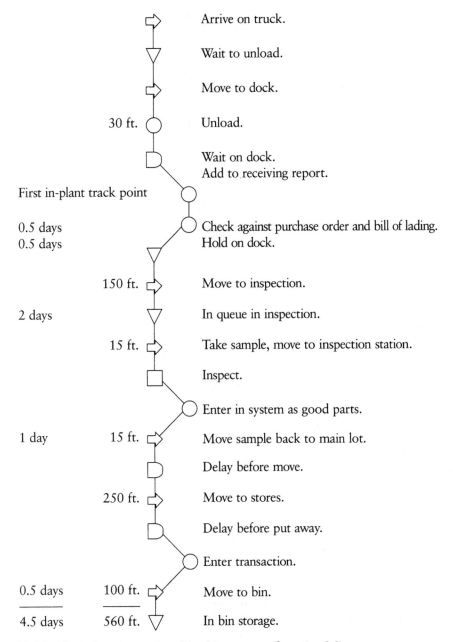

		Arrive on truck.
		Wait to unload.
		Move to dock.
30 ft.		Unload.
		Wait on dock. Add to receiving report.
First in-plant track point		
0.5 days		Check against purchase order and bill of lading.
0.5 days		Hold on dock.
	150 ft.	Move to inspection.
2 days		In queue in inspection.
	15 ft.	Take sample, move to inspection station.
		Inspect.
		Enter in system as good parts.
1 day	15 ft.	Move sample back to main lot.
		Delay before move.
	250 ft.	Move to stores.
		Delay before put away.
		Enter transaction.
0.5 days	100 ft.	Move to bin.
4.5 days	560 ft.	In bin storage.

Figure 10.14 *Sample process map. Tracking a part from its delivery to storeroom.*

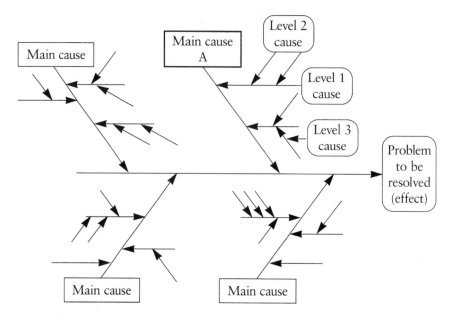

Figure 10.15 *Basic cause-and-effect diagram.*
Reprinted with permission of J. Stephen Sarazen, President, EXLGroup, Inc., exlinc@aol.com, from his article entitled, "The Tools of Quality" (from ASQ *Quality Progress*, July 1990).

the way to construct a cause-and-effect diagram using the dispersion analysis methods. There are three steps:

1. It is quite simple to construct the diagram. First determine the quality characteristic you wish to improve—perhaps customer satisfaction. There must be consensus when the problem statement is written. For example, "Customers are dissatisfied."

   In a manufacturing process, you might use a specific characteristic of a product as the effect, such as a problem with paste thickness in a surface mount line, poor paint coverage, or welding errors. In an administrative or service area, use customer complaints, decreased sales volume, or increased accounts receivables that are past due.

2. Now the team must generate ideas as to what is causing the effect and contributing to customer dissatisfaction. The causes are written as branches flowing to the main branch. Figure 10.16 shows the main cause headings resulting from an actual session in a service/distribution business. In this case, the team determined five areas—product quality, service, order processing system, distribution system, and order fulfillment—as the potential main causes of dissatisfied customers. If there is difficulty in determining the main branches or causes, use generic headings—such as methods, machines, people, materials, environment, or training—to help start the team.

3. The next step is to brainstorm all the possible causes of problems in each of the major cause categories. These ideas are captured and applied to the chart as subcauses. It is important to continually define and relate causes to each other.

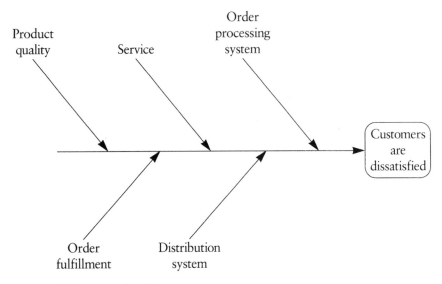

Figure 10.16 *Main cause headings.*
Reprinted with permission of J. Stephen Sarazen, President, EXLGroup, Inc., exlinc@aol.com, from his article
entitled, "The Tools of Quality" (from ASQ *Quality Progress*, July 1990).

It is acceptable to repeat subcauses in several places if the team feels there is a direct, multiple relationship. This effort will ensure a complete diagram and a more enlightened team.

Returning to Figure 10.16, it can be seen that the team identified five main causes of customer dissatisfaction. Now the team members must ask themselves, "What could contribute to each of these five main causes?" Once several subcauses have been identified, the team continues asking the same question until the lowest level causes are discovered. Figure 10.17 shows the completed portion of the diagram for one of the main causes: service. The team identified reliability issues, carrier issues (for example, a trucking company), poor communications, and lack of, or poor, training. The next level of causes is identified by asking the question, "What could cause a problem in these areas?" In the case of the poor communications, the team focused on functions and jobs—sales people, field representatives, and managers—as potential causes. It can be seen that a lack of knowledge of the customer can cause managers to communicate poorly. Subsequently, you can see that inexperience and training can be two key contributors to a manager's lack of customer knowledge. Thus, there are six levels of causes in this example.

Process Classification

Another type of diagram is known as the process classification diagram. This tool is as valuable in service-based businesses as it is in manufacturing companies, since every product or service is the result of a process. Although the basic process for constructing this type of diagram is similar to the one used for dispersion analysis, there are some differences. These differences are driven by the application. For the process

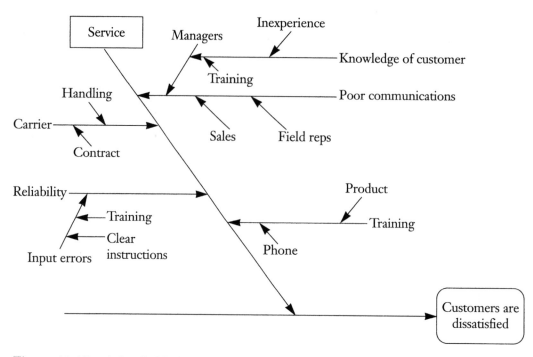

Figure 10.17 *A detailed look at one main cause.*
Reprinted with permission of J. Stephen Sarazen, President, EXLGroup, Inc., exlinc@aol.com, from his article entitled, "The Tools of Quality" (from ASQ *Quality Progress*, July 1990).

classification method, identify the flow of the process to be improved and then list key quality-influencing characteristics at each of the steps.

1. Identify the process and develop a flow diagram of the primary sequential steps. For example, in a generic selling process, the following steps might be identified: make initial customer contact, develop an understanding of customer needs, provide information to the customer, follow up, close the sale, and follow up on the sale.

2. Now add all the things that might influence the quality of each step. Use the method described in the previous section. Brainstorming with a team of knowledgeable people will make the finished diagram more like the actual process.

Team analysis results are converted to action by assigning responsibility to members to prepare a plan, implement the prioritized solutions, and report results to the team. Another approach is to quantify the key variables in the main causes and measure the effect of implementing solutions. This is a desirable but not always practicable approach.

Figure 10.18 shows an example of a completed process classification diagram. The intent is to take the cause and effect to the lowest level in order to understand all the contributing factors to improve the process. It is also advisable to consider the connecting steps from process step to process step. Everywhere there is a hand-off from one step to the next, there are likely to be possible causes of dispersion. Many opportunities for improvement can be found in these areas.

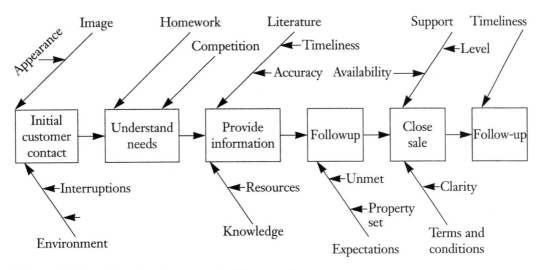

Figure 10.18 *Completed process classification diagram.*
Reprinted with permission of J. Stephen Sarazen, President, EXLGroup, Inc., exlinc@aol.com, from his article entitled, "The Tools of Quality" (from ASQ *Quality Progress*, July 1990).

Cause Enumeration

The cause enumeration method involves simply brainstorming all possible causes and listing them in the order they are offered. Once the brainstorm has exhausted itself, the team begins the process of grouping the causes as it did for the dispersion analysis diagram. The end result looks exactly the same.

This process can be enhanced dramatically using the affinity diagram process. It is a valuable method for gaining insight and organizing ideas.

Application

Understanding processes, using teams, and identifying areas of opportunity are excellent ways to move toward continuous improvement while solving some tough issues. But they are only the beginning. To obtain the full value from the cause-and-effect diagram, it must be turned into action. It is therefore wise to quantify the problem and as many of the potential causes as possible. Once this has been done, the teams can determine the priority areas to be addressed and can track improvements.

In the example of Figure 10.17 , the business was able to quantify the problem of customer dissatisfaction by measuring several key parameters, including the number of calls about problems, the number of requests to return material for specific reasons, and delays in customer payments. In the area where subcauses were identified, various parts of the organization were surveyed to determine the primary areas of opportunity for addressing the causes identified by the cause-and-effect diagram. For example, one need was for training in simple statistical problem-solving methods. This need was quantified not only by the number of people needing training, but also by the results of the training applications.

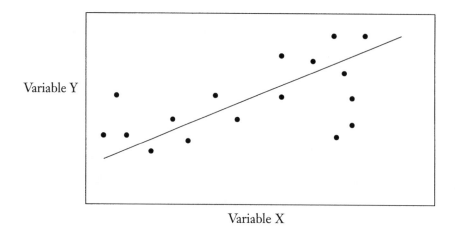

Figure 10.19 *Scatter diagram.*

As the team and organization move to quantify the causes, other tools play key roles. Pareto analysis, histograms, control charts, scatter plots, and multivari analysis might be particularly valuable. They are discussed in the following pages.

Quantitative Tools

Some statistical concepts were introduced in Chapter 1 in relation to managing variation and also in the Six Sigma goal. They are part of the general subject of quality control statistics. SPC and process capability (PC) also fall under that heading. Quantitative tools are based on data that are transformed into useful information.

Scatter Diagrams

The other tools in this study are all methods for handling one type of data at a time. Scatter diagrams show the relationship between paired data such as that encountered in analyzing a process using the other QC tools. For example, the cause-and-effect analysis identifies individual factors but does not provide a means to establish whether a measurable relationship exists between them. It doesn't describe which variables relate to each other, which vary at the same time, which is cause, and which is the effect. With a scatter diagram, several corresponding groups of data are collected and plotted with respect to each other. Figure 10.19 depicts the technique. Figure 10. 20 is an example of the relationship between viscosity of oil with respect to temperature. Drawing a trend line through the plots shows how strong a relationship is. The closer the points are to the line, the stronger and more interdependent the variables are— hence the stronger the cause and effect.

Correlation

The strength of the relationship between two variables can be expressed quantitatively in terms of a coefficient of correlation that varies from plus one (+1), to minus one (–1). Zero means no relationship:

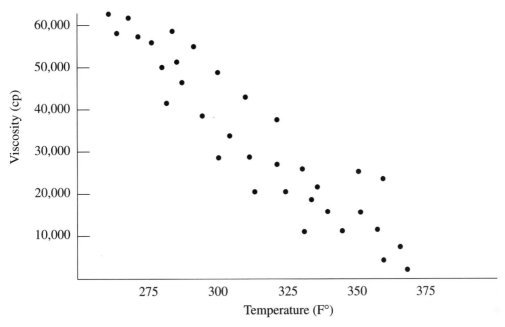

Temperature vs. Viscosity

Figure 10.20   *Scatter diagram showing the relationship between two variables with a dependent relationship and good (negative) correlation.*

- Interpretation. Figure 10.21 shows the basic scatter patterns and how correlation is expressed. The correlation can be calculated mathematically, but in most QC applications a visual analysis is sufficient.
- Application. The scatter diagram can be used for any two variables, but some knowledge has to be applied. Variables can be selected and a good correlation indicated when there is actually no relationship. For example, a good correlation might be seen in a diagram of oil viscosity versus the number of automobiles crossing the Golden Gate Bridge, but the result is meaningless.

Check Sheets

Checksheets are designed, structured formats for recording process data in a manner that can reveal underlying patterns. They can, for example, give a picture of the data distribution (a histogram), such as that shown in Figure 10.22.

Data collected on a properly designed checksheet can be a simple quick check on a process (without calculations) to determine

- Process distribution—how widely the process varies.
- Existence and proportion of output outside of requirements.
- Skew of the output distribution—an unbalanced distribution.
- Whether further process measurement and analysis are needed.

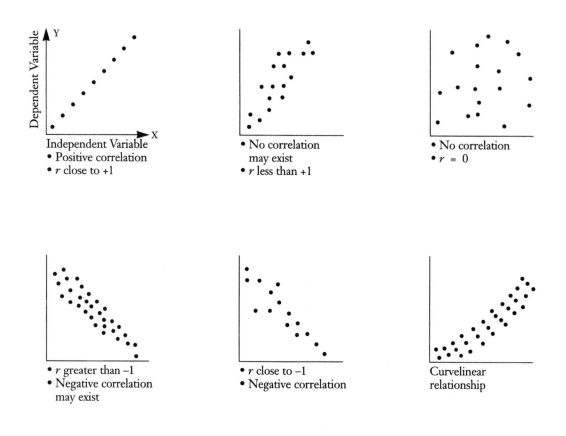

r = correlation coefficient

Figure 10.21   *The relationship between scatter diagrams and correlation.*

Histograms

Histograms are a graphic means of summarizing variation in a set of data. They are used when process variables can be measured (grams, millimeters, volts, dollars). The pictorial nature of a histogram exposes patterns of the data, such as its range (horizontal axis) and frequency of occurrence. Figure 10.23 shows a typical form.

The horizontal axis is in terms of the data metric. The vertical bars indicate the frequency of occurrence of the collected measurement. The pattern of a histogram provides a good indication of how a process was operating *at the time* samples were taken.

Different patterns illustrate how varied a process operation can be. A bell shape describes a process fairly balanced around some central average value. This would approximate a normal distribution (described later in this chapter), which is the most desirable. Further analysis is needed to determine whether this process operating range is adequate to meet specifications all the time. The other patterns suggest that further analysis is needed to determine the cause of their abnormality. The pictorial nature of the histogram lets you see patterns that are difficult to discern in a simple table of measures.

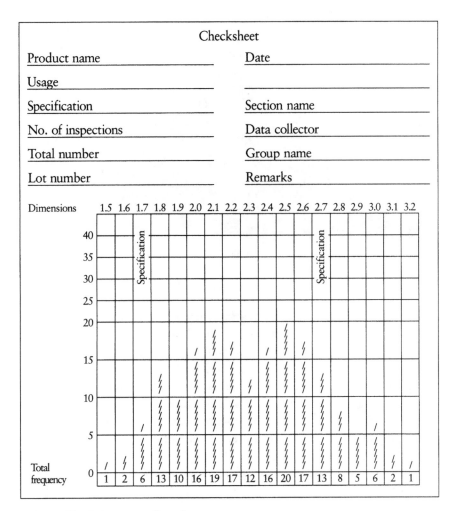

Figure 10.22 *Checksheet to collect data.*

Case Study

The importance of using data and facts is stressed in problem-solving and quality improvement efforts. But sometimes the data can seem overwhelming or of little value as the problem at hand is tackled. Consider the following example. A manufacturer of electronic telecommunications equipment was receiving complaints from the field about low signal volume on long-distance circuits. A string of amplifiers manufactured by the company was being used to boost the signal at various points along the way. The boosting ability of the amplifiers (engineers call it the "gain") was the prime suspect in the case. The design of the amplifiers had called for a gain of 10 decibels (dB). This means that the output from the amplifier should be about 10 times stronger than its input. Amplification is needed to make up for the weakening of the signal over the long-distance connection. Recognizing that it is impossible to make every amplifier with a gain of exactly 10 dB, the design allowed the amplifiers to be considered acceptable if the gain fell between 7.75 dB and 12.2 dB. These permissible minimum and maximum

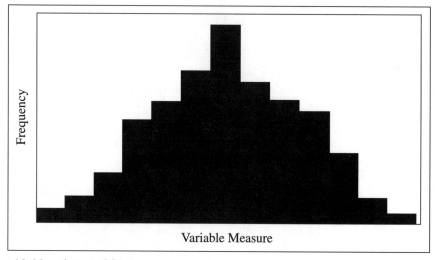

Figure 10.23   *A typical histogram.*

values are sometimes called the specification (or spec) tolerance limits. The expected value of 10 dB is the nominal (target) value. There were literally hundreds of amplifiers boosting the signal on a long connection. The average gain of the amplifiers should have provided adequate overall amplification to the signal over the wires—the assumption of the designer. The quality improvement team investigating the low volume condition arranged to test the gain of 120 amplifiers. The results of the tests are listed in Figure 10.24. This table of data contains 120 measurements to examine. The gain of all the amplifiers fell within the specification limits. This didn't seem to identify the problem. One could jump to the conclusion that a 10 dB gain is not enough. However, the data in the tables do not give a useful "picture" for analysis. The team members decided to construct a histogram to give them a better "picture" of the 120 data points. They divided the specification range into nine intervals of 0.5 dB each and counted the number of data points that fell in each interval. They found that there were 24 amplifiers whose gain reading was between 7.75 dB and 8.24 dB, 28 amplifiers between 8.25 dB and 8.74 dB, and so on. The histogram of the data is shown in Figure 10.25. The height of each bar on the histogram represents the number of amplifiers with gain readings that fell within the dB range that the bar covers on the horizontal axis. For example, the histogram indicates that 19 amplifiers had a gain reading between 9.25 dB and 9.74 dB. The histogram of the data gave the team a very different view of the situation. While all the amplifiers fell within the specification limits, the readings were certainly not evenly distributed around the nominal 10 dB value. Most of the amplifiers had a lower-than-nominal value of gain. This pattern was hard to see in the table of data, but the histogram clearly revealed it. If most of the amplifiers in the series on a long-distance connection boost the signal a little bit less than expected (less than the 10 dB expected), the result will be a low volume level. The histogram gave the team a clearer and more complete picture of the data. The team could now concentrate its investigation in the factory to find out why the manufacturing line was not producing amplifiers that were more evenly distributed around the nominal value.

Gain of 120 Tested Amplifiers in dB									
8.1	10.4	8.8	9.7	7.8	9.9	11.7	8.0	9.3	9.0
8.2	8.9	10.1	9.4	9.2	7.9	9.5	10.9	7.8	8.3
9.1	8.4	9.6	11.1	7.9	8.5	8.7	7.8	10.5	8.5
11.5	8.0	7.9	8.3	8.7	10.0	9.4	9.0	9.2	10.7
9.3	9.7	8.7	8.2	8.9	8.6	9.5	9.4	8.8	8.3
8.4	9.1	10.1	7.8	8.1	8.8	8.0	9.2	8.4	7.8
7.9	8.5	9.2	8.7	10.2	7.9	9.8	8.3	9.0	9.6
9.9	10.6	8.6	9.4	8.8	8.2	10.5	9.7	9.1	8.0
8.7	9.8	8.5	8.9	9.1	8.4	8.1	9.5	8.7	9.3
8.1	10.1	9.6	8.3	8.0	9.8	9.0	8.9	8.1	9.7
8.5	8.2	9.0	10.2	9.5	8.3	8.9	9.1	10.3	8.4
8.6	9.2	8.5	9.6	9.0	10.7	8.6	10.0	8.8	8.6

Figure 10.24   *Results of tests of 120 amplifiers.*
This material is contained in the in-house training package, "Quality Improvement Tools.®" Contact: Juran Institute, Inc., 11 River Road, P.O. Box 811, Wilton, CT 06897-0811.

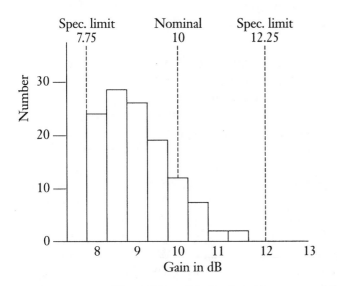

Part Number AN898   120 Units Tested

Figure 10.25   *A histogram clearly shows that most of the amplifiers had a lower-than-nominal value of gain.*
This material is contained in the in-house training package, "Quality Improvement Tools.®" Contact: Juran Institute, Inc., 11 River Road, P.O. Box 811, Wilton, CT 06897-0811.

Histograms in Problem Solving

As this example illustrates, the histogram is a simple but powerful tool for elementary analysis of data. Key concepts about data and the use of histograms in problem solving can be summarized as follows

1. Values in a set of data almost always show variation. Although the amplifiers were designed for a nominal value of 10 dB gain, very few of them actually had a measured gain of 10 dB. Furthermore, few amplifiers had exactly the same gain. This variation is due to small differences in literally hundreds of factors surrounding the manufacturing process—the exact values of the component parts, the nature of the handling that each amplifier receives, the accuracy and repeatability of the test equipment, even the humidity in the factory on the day the amplifier was made. Everything varies. It is inevitable in the output of any process: manufacturing, service, or administrative. It is impossible to keep all factors in a constant state all the time.

2. Variation displays a pattern. In the amplifier example, the pattern of variation shown in Figure 10.25 had a number of characteristics. For example

   - All values fell within the specification limits.
   - Most of the values fell between the nominal and the lower specification limit.
   - The values of gain tended to bunch up near the lower specification limit.
   - More values fell in the range of 8.25 dB to 8.75 dB than in any other 0.5 dB category.

   Different phenomena will have different variation, but there is always some pattern to the variation. For example, we know that the height of most 10-year-old boys will be close to some average value and that it would be relatively unusual to find an extremely tall or extremely short boy. If we gathered the data on the time required to repair an appliance for a customer or the time required to process paperwork or the time required to complete a transaction at a bank, we would expect to see some similar pattern in the numbers. These patterns of variation in data are called "distributions." The purpose of this discussion is to point out that there are usually discernible patterns in the variation, and that these patterns often tell a great deal about the cause of a problem. Identifying and interpreting these patterns are the most important topics discussed here. There are three important characteristics of a histogram: its center, width, and shape.

3. Patterns of variation are difficult to see in simple tables of numbers. Again, recall the amplifier example and the table of data in Figure 10.24. Looking at the table of numbers, we could see that no values fall outside the specification limits, but we cannot see much else. While there is a pattern in the data, it is difficult for our eyes and minds to see it. Unless it is exposed, the wrong conclusions may be reached and improper actions may be taken.

Patterns of Variation

Figure 10.26 shows common patterns of process variation. The following list contains general explanations of each type and provides suggestions for further analysis.

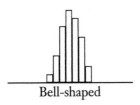
Bell-shaped

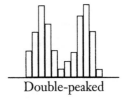
Double-peaked

Plateau

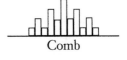
Comb

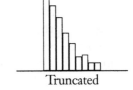
Skewed

Truncated

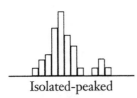
Isolated-peaked

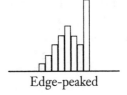
Edge-peaked

Figure 10.26   *Common histogram patterns.*
This material is contained in the in-house training package, "Quality Improvement Tools.®" Contact: Juran Institute, Inc., 11 River Road, P.O. Box 811, Wilton, CT 06897-0811.

- The bell-shaped distribution is a symmetrical shape with a peak in the middle of the range of data. This is the normal, natural distribution of data from a process. Deviations from this bell shape might indicate the presence of complicating factors or outside influences. While deviations from a bell shape should be investigated, such deviations are not necessarily bad. As we will see, some non–bell-shaped distributions are to be expected in certain cases.

- The double-peaked distribution is a distinct valley in the middle of the range of the data with peaks on either side. This pattern is usually a combination of two bell-shaped distributions and suggests that two distinct processes are at work, and two different sets of data have been tabulated.

- The plateau distribution is a flat top with no distinct peak and slight tails on either side. This pattern is likely to be the result of many different bell-shaped distributions with centers spread evenly throughout the range of data. Diagram the flow and observe the operation to identify the many different processes at work. An extreme case occurs in organizations that have no defined processes or training—each person does the job his or her own way. The wide variability in process leads to the wide variability observed in the data. Defining and implementing standard procedures will reduce this variability.

- The comb distribution reflects high and low values alternating in a regular fashion. This pattern typically indicates measurement error—errors in the way the data were grouped to construct the histogram—or a systematic bias in the way the data were rounded off. A less likely alternative is that this is a type of plateau distribution. Review the data collection procedures and the construction of the histogram before considering possible process characteristics that might cause the pattern.

- The skewed distribution is an asymmetrical shape in which the peak is off-center in the range of data and the distribution trails off sharply on one side and gently on the other. In a positively skewed distribution the long tail extends rightward, toward increasing values. A negatively skewed distribution would have a long tail extending leftward toward decreasing values. The skewed pattern typically occurs when a practical limit or a specification limit exists on one side and is relatively close to the nominal value. In these cases, there simply are not as many values available on one side as there are on the other. Practical limits occur frequently when the data consist of time measurements or counts of things. For example, tasks that take a very short time can never be completed in zero or less time. Those occasions when the task takes a little longer than average to complete create a positively skewed tail on this distribution of task time. For example, the number of weaving defects per 100 yards of fabric can never be less than zero. If the process averages about 0.7 defects per 100 yards, then sporadic occurrences of three or four defects per 100 yards will result in a positively skewed distribution. One-sided specification limits (a maximum or minimum value only) also frequently give rise to skewed distributions. Such skewed distributions are not inherently bad, but a team should question the impact of the values in the long tail. Could they cause customer dissatisfaction (for example, long waiting times)? Could they lead to higher costs (for example, overfilling containers)? Could the extreme values cause problems in downstream operations? If the long tail has a negative impact on quality, the team should investigate and determine the causes for those values.

- The truncated distribution is an asymmetrical shape in which the peak is at or near the edge of the range of the data, and the distribution ends very abruptly on one side and trails off gently on the other. One might also encounter truncation on the right side with a negatively skewed tail. Truncated distributions are often smooth, bell-shaped distributions with a part of the distribution removed, or truncated, by some external force such as screening, 100 percent inspection, or a review process. Note that these truncation efforts are an added cost and are, therefore, good candidates for removal.

- The isolated-peaked distribution is a small, separate group of data in addition to the larger distribution. Like the double-peaked distribution, this pattern is a combination and suggests that two distinct processes are at work. But the small size of the second peak indicates an abnormality, something that doesn't happen often or regularly. Look closely at the conditions surrounding the data in the small peak to see if you can isolate a particular time, machine, input source, procedure, operator, and so on. Such small isolated peaks in conjunction with a truncated distribution might result from the lack of complete effectiveness in screening out defective items. It is also possible that the small peak represents errors in measurements or in transcribing the data. Recheck measurements and calculations.

- The edge-peaked distribution is a large peak appended to an otherwise smooth distribution. This shape occurs when the extended tail of the smooth distribution has been cut off and lumped into a single category at the edge of the range of the data. This shape very frequently indicates inaccurate recording of the data (for example, values outside the "acceptable" range are reported as being just inside the range).

Pitfalls in Interpretation

There are four important pitfalls that a quality improvement team should be aware of when interpreting histograms:

1. Before stating a conclusion from the analysis of a histogram, make sure that the data are representative of typical and current conditions in the process. If the data are old (such as, the process has changed since the data were collected) or if there is any question about bias or incompleteness in the data, it is best to gather new data to confirm and enhance the conclusions.

2. Don't draw conclusions based on a small sample. As pointed out earlier, the larger the sample, the more confidence exists that the peaks, spread, and shape

of the histogram of the sample data are representative of the total process or group of products. As a rule of thumb, if the intent is to construct before-and-after or stratified histograms to examine differences in variability or the location of peaks, use a sample large enough to give you 40 or more observations for each histogram to be constructed. For example, if the plan is to stratify the data into three groups, the minimum sample size should be around 120 (3 × 40). If this is not practical, consult a statistical adviser to design an appropriate sampling and hypothesis testing scheme.

3. It is important to remember that the interpretation of the histogram is often merely a theory that must still be confirmed through additional analysis and direct observation of the process in question. The first conclusion and interpretation might not be correct—even if it sounds perfectly reasonable. Always take time to think of alternative explanations for the pattern seen in the histogram.

4. A histogram from an ongoing activity is a picture of only one instant in time. A series of such "snapshots" at fixed intervals may give additional and valuable information to an improvement team. A series of such histograms is the initial step in establishing control charts.

The key accomplishments of a histogram analysis are as follows

1. Some aspect of the process has been quantified by facts, not opinions.

2. There is a better understanding of the variability inherent in the process; there is a more realistic view of the ability of the process to produce acceptable results consistently.

3. There are new ideas and theories about how the process operates or about the causes of a problem. The stage is set for additional investigative efforts.

Pareto Diagrams

The Pareto principle is several things. It is a ranking system. It is also a way of managing project by prioritization. Finally, it is a process—an orderly way of thinking about problems that affect us.

The Pareto principle was first defined by Juran in 1950. During his early work, Juran found that there was a "maldistribution of quality losses." Not liking such a long name, he named the principle after Vilfredo Pareto, a nineteenth-century Italian economist. Pareto found that a large share of the wealth was owned by relatively few people—a maldistribution of wealth. Juran found this was true in many areas of life, including quality technologies.

In simplest terms, the Pareto principle suggests that most effects come from relatively few causes. In quantitative terms, 80 percent of the problems come from 20 percent of the machines, raw materials, or operators. Also, 80 percent of the wealth is controlled by 20 percent of the people. It is a well-used idea in inventory measurement that 80 percent of the dollars are represented by 20 percent of the items. Finally, 80 percent of scrap or rework quality costs come from 20 percent of the possible causes.

In the quality technologies, Juran calls the 20 percent of causes the "vital few." He originally called the rest of the causes the "trivial many." However, he and other quality professionals came to understand that there are no trivial problems on the manufacturing floor and that all problems deserve management's attention. Juran has since renamed the trivial many the "useful many." But no matter the labels, the Pareto principle is a powerful tool.

A Management Tool

Data can be collected on the state of scrap, rework, warranty claims, maintenance time, raw material usage, machine downtime, or any other cost associated with manufacturing a product or providing a service. In the case of providing a service, for example, data can be collected on wasted time, number of jobs that have to be redone, customer inquiries, and number of errors. The data should be organized as illustrated in Figure 10.27. The most frequent (highest cost) cause is placed on the left, and the other causes are added in descending order of occurrence.

Figures 10.28 and 10.29 are examples of Pareto diagrams. It is quite obvious which causes or problems have to be reduced or eliminated to have any real impact on the system. A double Pareto diagram, as in Figure 10.30, can be used to contrast two products, areas, or shifts, or it can be used to look at a system before and after improvement.

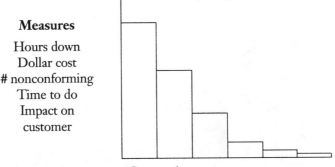

Figure 10.27 *Generalized Pareto diagram showing examples of the kinds of data that can be plotted.*

Reprinted with permission from ASQ *Quality Progress*, November 1990.

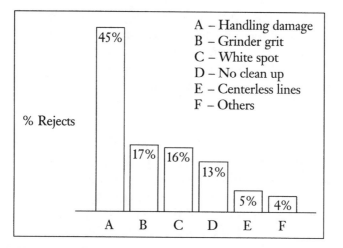

Figure 10.28   *Strut rod rejects.*
Reprinted with permission from ASQ *Quality Progress*, November 1990.

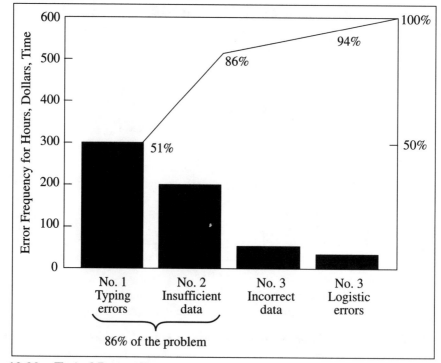

Figure 10.29   *Typical Pareto diagram.*

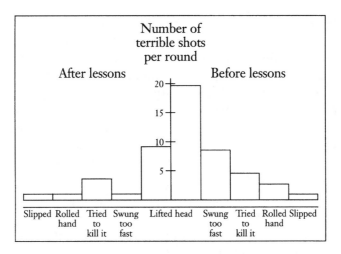

Figure 10.30 *Poor golf shots.*
Reprinted with permission from ASQ *Quality Progress*, November 1990.

Product	Problem					
	Labels	Liner	Glue	Score	Warp	
A	2		8			10
B	1		4			5
C		1		7	28	36
D		2			4	6
E	3		11			14
F	1				1	2
G	1					1
H				2		2
I	2					2
	10	3	23	9	33	

Figure 10.31 *Data collected on supplied boxes.*
Reprinted with permission from ASQ *Quality Progress*, November 1990.

A Way of Thinking

Figure 10.31 is not a Pareto diagram but a set of data on problems encountered with boxes used to package a number of different products. The most frequent problem is on only one of the box types. Talking to the supplier about the specific problem (warping on box style C) will solve almost half of the difficulties. This would also probably lead to less warping of box style D, particularly if the boxes are made on the same line.

The next most frequent problem is glue. The problem occurs over several box types. Are they made on a common line? Is the glue or glue lot the same among these?

If so, then a common cause has been identified and should be eliminated. The "mess" of incoming box supply problems will be reduced 80 percent by solving the two problems that have the most impact on quality. Of course, the improvement process is not stopped. The box manufacturing process should be continually analyzed using the Pareto diagram and the other tools of quality.

American industries—manufacturing or service—are some of the greatest collectors of data in the world. The trick is to recognize which data are useful. The Pareto principle describes the way causes occur in nature and human behavior. It can be a very powerful management tool for focusing personnel's effort on the problems and solutions that have the greatest potential payback.

Run Charts

The simplest picture of how a process is operating can be seen in a Run Chart. It is constructed by plotting a performance measurement with respect to time as in Figure 10.32 (also Figures 1.2, 1.3).

The most common use of run charts is to show trends—whether the measured data is increasing or decreasing. It also gives an indication of the range of process variation, but not in a manner that variation acceptability can be judged. Run charts also lack the ability to predict future process performance. To obtain these missing features requires the use of control charts.

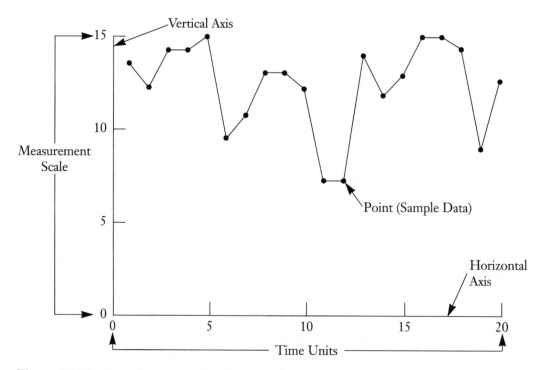

Figure 10.32 *Run chart example of sequential sample averages.*

Control Charts

Data Collection

Quality control has always emphasized measurement and data. One big QC activity has been product inspection and test. Both involve attributes or variables measurement and usually data recording. It is quite common for quality organizations to have a great deal of data collected and reported over a long period of time. The weakness has been that operating management didn't use it for process management, much less process improvement. Sometimes quality trend charts were prepared to indicate the direction of product quality. If poor, people were blamed and symptoms attacked. Or the collected data were used only to report performance (process yield) and weren't in a form useful for process analysis and improvement.

Planning

The purpose of process quality data is to use it to take action. Therefore, the data should be in a form and structure to facilitate action. Collecting the most useful data must be planned. Failure to collect the correct data is one of the most common reasons for not taking action or taking the wrong action. The basic tenet is to plan according to how and for what purpose the data will be used. The first requirement is to understand the process to be studied (flowchart). Identify key performance measures and where in the process they will be measured. In other words, identify what type of data is needed. What collection format will be the most useful in the subsequent analysis? The proper format could, for example, result in developing a histogram in the process of recording the data. Specifically tailored charts for a process operator to record data directly are another example. The result might be a run chart that can easily be converted to a control chart if properly designed.

Checklists are another format frequently used. They typically provide go/no-go data. An identified event either happened or didn't. This kind of data is very useful in cause-and-effect analysis. How to collect data can be summarized by following the steps listed in Table 10.2.[6]

Statistical Concepts for Process Control

The statistical tools for process control can be understood and used without mastering the underlying theory. However, setting up an SPC application for the operators of a process does require more understanding. When done properly, data collection and initial interpretation of the data for control actions are straightforward. Monitoring the SPC program for important anomalies and more sophisticated evaluations requires a greater knowledge of statistical theory. But the basic concepts, applications, and interpretations can be used by anyone who can do arithmetic.

The basis for SPC and the tool of interest, control charts, is a recognition of the fact that everything varies and a method is needed to measure and interpret the constant changes. Fortunately, most groups or populations of things occur in a common pattern, called the normal distribution. (For example, intelligence quotients (IQs) follow this pattern, as do the heights of males or females. If a small sequential sample of the process output is measured, it will almost always display this normal distribution pattern.

Table 10.2   How to collect data.

Data collection is a type of production process itself and, like any process, needs to be understood and improved. Generally speaking, 10 points must be addressed when collecting data:

1. Formulate good questions that relate to the specific information needs of the project. It is much easier to get others to help collect data if they believe those in charge know precisely what they are looking for and that they are going to do something with the collected information.
2. Use the appropriate data analysis tools and be certain the necessary data are being collected. Whenever practical, collect continuous variable data. A few minutes of thought before gathering data can often prevent having to recollect data because they are incomplete or answer the wrong question.
3. Define comprehensive data collection points. The ideal is to set the collection point where the job flow suffers minimum interruption. An accurate flowchart of the work process can help immensely.
4. Select an unbiased collector. The collector should have the easiest and most immediate access to the relevant facts.
5. Understand data collectors and their environment. The training and experience of the collectors determine whether they can handle this additional assignment.
6. Design data collection forms that are simple. Reduce opportunities for error and capture data for analysis, reference, and traceability. The forms should also be self-explanatory and look professional. The KISS (keep it simple, stupid) principle applies here.
7. Prepare the instructions for use. In some cases, a special training course might be necessary for data gatherers. In other cases, a simple sheet of instructions will suffice.
8. Test the forms and instructions. Try out the forms on a limited basis to make sure they are filled out properly. If they aren't, the forms or instructions might need revision.
9. Train the data collectors. Training should include the purpose of the study, what the data will be used for, a properly completed form, and a discussion about the importance of complete and unbiased information.
10. Audit the collection process and validate the results. Randomly check completed forms and observe data collection during the process. Look for missing or unusual data, and be wary of variations in the data that might result from biases in the data collection process.

This information is contained in the in-house training package, "Quality Improvement Tools.®" Contact: Juran Institute, Inc., 11 River Road, P.O. Box 811, Wilton, CT 06897-0811.

The normal distribution describes the pattern of the measured process output. For example, Figure 10.33 shows how sample pieces from a process may vary. When more samples are taken a pattern appears called a distribution as in Figure 10.33b (the vertical scale is the frequency of occurrences). The most common is a normal distribution represented by the symmetrical curve of the line shown to the extreme right in Figure 10.33b. This distribution has some useful characteristics that will be explained later. The next set of curves shows that distributions can differ as in Figure 10.33c. The fourth set, shown in Figure 10.33d, represents a series of sample histograms, over time, that represent, in this case, a stable process. Pictures taken of an unstable process are shown in Figure 10.33e.

Control charts use similar distribution pictures in a simpler format. If four or five samples are taken from a process periodically and sequentially, and the average of each sample measurement is plotted with respect to time, figure 10.34 shows the key elements of a control chart. All plotted data are calculated from sample measurements. Upper and lower process control limits can be calculated and the behavior of the sample data points can be interpreted to understand process stability.

a. Pieces vary from each other.

b. But they form a pattern that, if stable, is called a distribution.

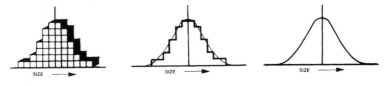

c. Distributions can differ in location, spread, or shape, or any combination of these.

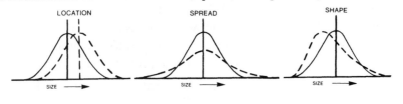

d. If only common causes of variation are present, the output of a process forms a distribution that is stable over time and is predictable.

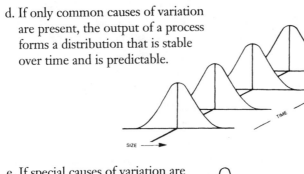

e. If special causes of variation are present, the process output is not stable over time and is not predictable.

Figure 10.33 *Variation—Common and special causes.*
Reprinted with permission from Ford Motor Company.

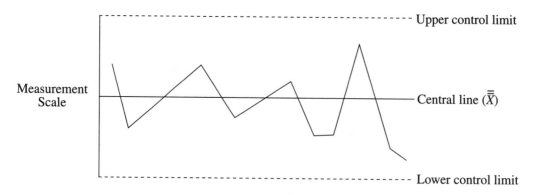

Figure 10.34 *Elements of a control chart.*

Common Types of Control Charts

Table 10.3 lists the types of control charts most commonly used. The nature of the process and measurement determines which is used. There are two categories: One is for processes where parameters of interest can be measured in terms of variables, that is, liters, pounds, dollars, percentage; the other category is for all other kinds of discrete measures for example, good-bad, errors per item, number of errors.

$\overline{X}$ *and R*　One common chart is known as an X bar chart ($\overline{X}$), because it is a chart of sample averages ($\overline{X}$).

A chart commonly used with the ($\overline{X}$) is the range chart (R) as in Figure 10.35. The range (highest minus lowest) chart is a plot of the range for each sample with calculated control limits. The range chart is sensitive to shifts in process width. The problem doesn't appear as quickly on the ($\overline{X}$) chart because of the effect of averaging averages. The $\overline{X}$ and R charts are basic to SPC. However, they can be used only when a characteristic, such as inches, pounds, volts, and so forth, can be measured. An $\overline{X}$ standard deviation chart combination is sometimes used for large-volume processes and large sample sizes.

Other charts have been developed for other applications where a process is measured in terms of events or counts, such as good-bad, defects per unit, errors per purchase order, sales per advertising dollar, and so on. They are all evaluated for statistical control the same as the ($\overline{X}$) chart using the tests shown in Figure 10.36a.

Construction

The following simplified procedure illustrates the relatively straightforward nature of constructing a common $\overline{X}$ bar ($\overline{X}$ and R) chart. (Other types are discussed in subsequent paragraphs.)

1. Select sequential samples of 4 or 5 items, at regular time intervals and measure the parameter of interest. Plot the average value of each sample.
2. Calculate the average of the plotted sample averages. This is the process operating center ($\overline{X}$).
3. Calculate and draw in the process control limits using at least 25 consecutive plotted points. These are also referred to as the plus or minus three sigma (±3s) limits. The formulas for calculating control limits for all the common control

Table 10.3   Types of control charts.

X (X bar)	Shows average outputs of a process
R	Shows the uniformity of a process
pn	Shows the number of defective products for sample subgroups of equal sizes
p	Shows the fraction of defective products for samples of unequal sizes
c	Shows the average number of defects within each product for sample subgroups of equal sizes
u	Shows the average number of defects within each product for sample subgroups of unequal sizes

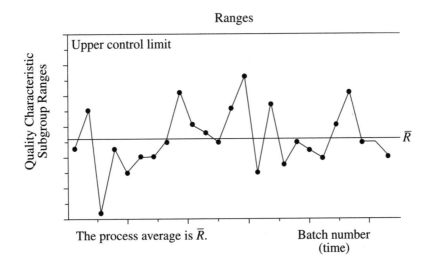

Figure 10.35   *Control chart for a sample measurement range.*

charts are shown in Figure 10.36a.* Test the chart for statistical control by also using the tests described in Figure 10.36b. These tests indicate whether the points are occurring in a random manner. If not, the process is not in control. Just because points are within control limits does not mean the process is in control. If it is not in control, special causes of variation are present and must be removed. Other problem-solving QC tools are used to identify the special causes.

4. After removing the special (assignable) causes of variation, recalculate the new control limits, based on new samples.

5. Continue to take samples periodically to assess the process performance.

The control chart is complete. The plotted points show the process variation. The control limits indicate what its performance variation limits should be.

---

*Note: There are other useful ways to set control limits but they are beyond the scope of this text.

Table of Constants for Variables Control Charts

$\overline{X}$ and R Control Charts				$\overline{X}$ and S Control Charts				
n	A_2	D_3	D_4	d_2	n	A_3	B_3	B_4	C_4
2	1.880	0	3.265	1.128	10	0.975	0.284	1.716	.9727
3	1.023	0	2.574	1.693	11	0.927	0.321	1.679	.9754
4	0.729	0	2.282	2.059	12	0.886	0.354	1.646	.9776
5	0.577	0	2.114	2.326	13	0.850	0.382	1.618	.9794
6	0.483	0	2.004	2.534	14	0.817	0.406	1.594	.9810
7	0.419	0.076	1.924	2.704	15	0.789	0.428	1.572	.9823
8	0.373	0.136	1.864	2.847	16	0.763	0.448	1.552	.9835
9	0.337	0.184	1.816	2.970	17	0.739	0.466	1.534	.9845
10	0.308	0.223	1.777	3.078	18	0.718	0.482	1.518	.9854
11	0.285	0.256	1.744	3.173	19	0.698	0.497	1.503	.9662
12	0.266	0.283	1.717	3.258	20	0.680	0.510	1.490	.9869
					21	0.663	0.523	1.477	.9876
					22	0.647	0.534	1.466	.9882
					23	0.633	0.545	1.455	.9887
					24	0.619	0.555	1.445	.9892
					25	0.606	0.565	1.435	.9896

Tests for Special Causes

1. These test are applicable to $\overline{X}$ charts and to individuals (X) charts. A normal distribution is assumed. Tests 1, 2, 5, and 6 are to be applied to the upper and lower halves of the chart separately. Tests 3 and 4 are to be applied to the whole chart.
2. The upper control limit and the lower control limit are set at 3σ above the center line and 3σ below the center line. For the purpose of applying the tests, the control chart is equally divided into six zones, each zone being 1σ wide. The upper half of the chart is referred to as A (outer third), B (middle third), and C (inner third). The lower half is taken as a mirror image.
3. The presence of a cross indicates that the process is not in statistical control. It means that the point is the last one of a sequence of points (a single point in Test 1) that is very unlikely to occur if the process is in statistical control.
4. Although this can be taken as a basic set of tests, analysts should be alert to any patterns of points that might indicate the influence of special causes in their process.

Figure 10.36 a–b *Formulae for calculating upper and lower control limits for all common control charts.*

Formulae for Upper and Lower Control Limits

Type of data	Control chart	Sample size n	What is to be controlled	Control lines: Central line	Control lines: Control limits	Process standard deviation
Variables	$\bar{X} - R$ control chart	Small normally < 10 usually 3 or 5	$\bar{X}$ – Variation of sample means	$\bar{\bar{X}}$	$UCL_X = \bar{\bar{X}} + A_2\bar{R}$ $\quad LCL_X = \bar{\bar{X}} - A_2\bar{R}$	$\hat{\sigma} = \bar{R}/d_2$
			R – Variation of sample ranges	$\bar{R}$	$UCL_R = D_4\bar{R}$ $\quad LCL_R = D_3\bar{R}$	
	$\bar{X} - S$ control chart	Large usually > 10	$\bar{X}$ – Variation of sample means	$\bar{\bar{X}}$	$UCL_X = \bar{\bar{X}} + A_3\bar{S}$ $\quad LCL_X = \bar{\bar{X}} - A_3\bar{S}$	$\hat{\sigma} = \bar{S}/c_4$
			S – Variation of sample standard deviation	$\bar{S}$	$UCL_S = B_4\bar{S}$ $\quad LCL_S = B_3\bar{S}$	
	X control chart (individuals with moving range)	1 When rational subgroups are impossible	X – Variation of individuals	$\bar{X}$	$UCL_X = \bar{X} + 3\,\bar{R}/d_2$ $\quad LCL_X = \bar{X} - 3\,\bar{R}/d_2$	$\hat{\sigma} = \bar{R}/d_2$
			R – Variation between individuals	$\bar{R}$	$UCL_R = D_4\bar{R}$ $\quad LCL_R = D_3\bar{R}$	
Attribute	p control chart	Large changeable	p: Fraction defective	$\bar{p}$	$UCL_p = \bar{p} + 3\sqrt{\bar{p}(1-\bar{p})/n}$ $\quad LCL_p = \bar{p} - 3\sqrt{\bar{p}(1-\bar{p})/n}$	$\sqrt{\dfrac{\bar{p}(1-\bar{p})}{n}}$
	np control chart	Large constant	np: Number of defects	$n\bar{p}$	$UCL_{np} = n\bar{p} + 3\sqrt{n\bar{p}(1-\bar{p})}$ $\quad LCL_{np} = n\bar{p} - 3\sqrt{n\bar{p}(1-\bar{p})}$	$\sqrt{n\bar{p}(1-\bar{p})}$
	c control chart	Constant unit	c: Number of defects per unit	$\bar{c}$	$UCL_c = \bar{c} + 3\sqrt{\bar{c}}$ $\quad LCL_c = \bar{c} - 3\sqrt{\bar{c}}$	$\sqrt{\bar{c}}$
	u control chart	Changeable unit	$u = \frac{c}{n}$: Average defects per unit	$\bar{u}$	$UCL_u = \bar{u} + 3\sqrt{\bar{u}/n}$ $\quad LCL_u = \bar{u} - 3\sqrt{\bar{u}/n}$	$\sqrt{\bar{u}/n}$

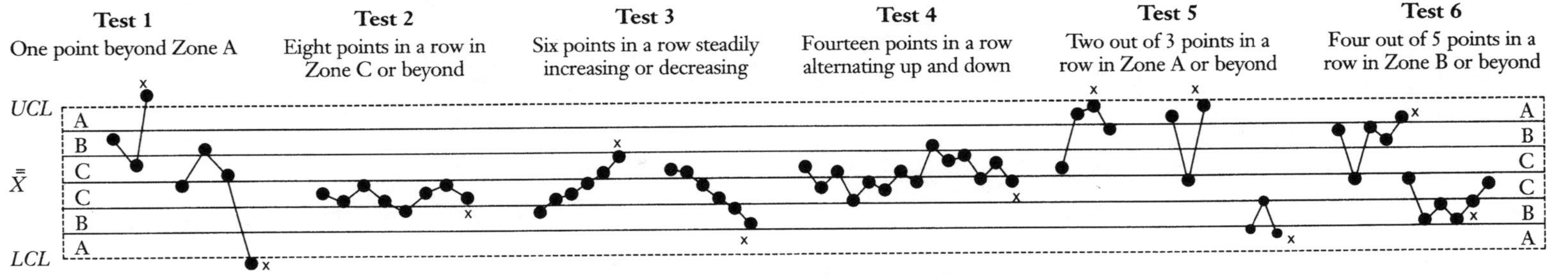

Test 1
One point beyond Zone A
Test 2
Eight points in a row in Zone C or beyond
Test 3
Six points in a row steadily increasing or decreasing
Test 4
Fourteen points in a row alternating up and down
Test 5
Two out of 3 points in a row in Zone A or beyond
Test 6
Four out of 5 points in a row in Zone B or beyond
UCL
X̿
LCL
A
B
C
C
B
A

Tests to Determine Control

Figure 10.36b ***Test patterns for analyzing control charts.***

In summary, Figure 10.37 depicts (conceptually) the sequence and result of getting a process in statistical control and then improving it. Figure 10.37 A shows the process varying widely; 10.37 B is the process after special causes are removed; and 10.37 C shows the process average changed after a change in the process is made. In 10.37 D, the variability has been reduced by identifying and reducing common causes.

Example

It is important for a sales agency to track the change in new accounts.[7] They tabulated the number of new accounts over 40 months. The result is shown in Table 10.4. Examining the data in the table provides little useful information other than that the number of new accounts varies from month to month.

It was then decided to see if a run chart, Figure 10.38, would provide any insights. It showed the range of variation for the average for each month, but not whether the selling process was a factor.

These data were then converted into a control chart. As previously discussed, control charts of different types can be used. In this case a moving range chart was selected. The moving range is more sensitive to month-to-month changes.

Converting the data into a moving range chart was done using the formula (from the chart, Figure 10.36) for individual $\overline{X}$ values and where R is the absolute value difference between successive monthly values. This is what makes it a moving range chart. For example, the absolute value between April and May of 93 is 287 − 397 = 110, the moving range that month.

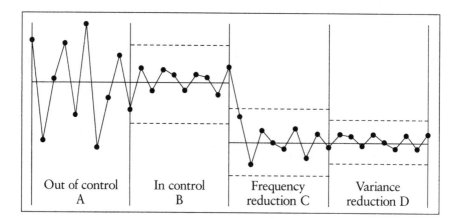

Figure 10.37   *Four stages of statistical quality control (SQC).*

The formula is

$$\text{CLx} = \frac{\overline{X} + / - \overline{MR}}{\text{d2 } (n = 2)}$$

Where: CLx = Control limit for $\overline{X}$

$\overline{MR}$ = Average moving range

d2 + Constant from Figure 10.36

Average $\overline{X}$ = 258 R = 117   d2 = 1.128, A2 = $\dfrac{3}{1.128}$

$$\text{UCL} = \overline{X} + \text{A2} \times R$$
$$= 258 + (2.66 \times 117) = 569$$
$$\text{LCL} = 258 - (2.66 \times 117) = 53$$

The tabular data, when plotted as a control chart, are shown in Figure 9.

Table 10.4   The number of new accounts per month.

Date	3/83	4/83	5/83	6/83	7/83	8/83	9/83	10/83	11/83	12/83
New Accounts	236	387	287	464	456	261	184	181	25	37
Moving Range		162	110	177	8	195	77	33	126	12

Date	1/94	2/94	3/94	4/94	5/94	6/94	7/94	8/94	9/94	10/94	11/94	12/94
New Accounts	155	277	380	347	278	494	384	403	182	307	18	219
Moving Range	118	122	113	43	69	216	110	19	221	125	289	201

Date	1/95	2/95	3/95	4/95	5/95	6/95	7/95	8/95	9/95	10/95	11/95	12/95
New Accounts	190	154	165	119	308	268	411	358	78	237	69	316
Moving Range	29	36	11	46	189	40	143	53	280	159	168	247

Date	1/96	2/96	3/96	4/96	5/96	6/96
New Accounts	336	133	243	319	260	415
Moving Range	20	203	110	76	59	155

Sample

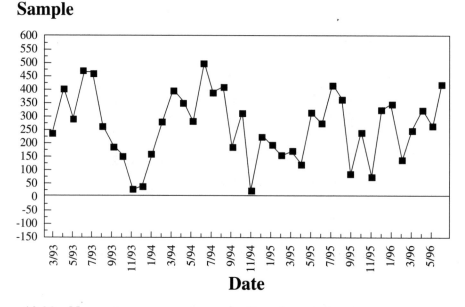

Figure 10.38 *New customer account growth—Run chart.*
Source: Dale P. Ragsdale, AQP 19th Annual Spring Conference, 1997 Proceedings. Reprinted with permission of the Association for Quality and Participation, 801B W. 8 St., Ste 501, Cincinnati, OH 45203-1607.

New information from the control chart is

- Sales activities are part of a process. This process is stable; it varies randomly within expected (calculated) limits (although these is some indication of a cycle effect present when sales peak in the summer). The variation is the inherent in the nature of the process used to acquire new accounts.

- If it is desirable to increase the average new accounts above the 258 level, some change in the product, service, or process would be needed, for example, getting better customer feedback, sales force training, and the like. Management now has information in a form to be able to make decisions.

Attributes Charts

Control charts for attributes are important for several reasons:

1. Attribute type situations exist in every process, in any kind of organization, for example, paperwork errors, deliveries per day, good-bad medical outcomes.
2. Attribute data are often already available where there are counts made, or defects identified, in management reports, but not converted to control charts.

---

†The Range ($\overline{R}$), is the difference between the highest and the lowest measurement, for each data point. for $\overline{R}$ is their average.

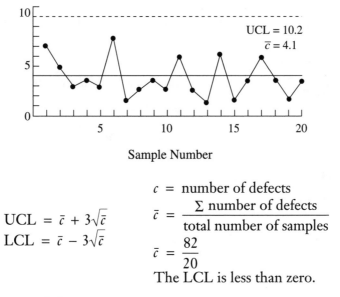

c = number of defects

$$\bar{c} = \frac{\Sigma \text{ number of defects}}{\text{total number of samples}}$$

$$\text{UCL} = \bar{c} + 3\sqrt{\bar{c}}$$
$$\text{LCL} = \bar{c} - 3\sqrt{\bar{c}}$$

$$\bar{c} = \frac{82}{20}$$

The LCL is less than zero.

Figure 10.39   *c control chart.*

3. When there is no data collection, attribute data are usually easier and less costly to collect.
4. In organizations introducing process quality management, attribute control charts are the easiest to use to demonstrate the principles and show quality improvements.

Attribute Chart Types

c Chart   This chart (Figure 10.39) shows defects/errors per sample, or unit, where each sample is the same size. If not, new limits would be needed. The *c* chart can also be used for such data as typo errors per page, or defects in a roll of cloth or metal. The measurement scale is discrete. The process capability is *c*.

u Chart   A variation of the *c* chart is the *u* chart. It depicts the number of defectives—items that contain defects. The measurement scale for *u* charts is continuous. Samples can vary in size (but should be kept to within 25 percent of the average sample size). The process average is *u*. The process capability is *u* when in control. Limits are calculated as shown in Figure 10.40. Different control limits would be needed for each different sample size *n*.

P Chart   This chart (Figure 10.41) depicts the proportion or fraction (*p*), of nonconforming items in a sample of varying size. Fraction defective *p* is the ratio of the number of nonconforming items to the total number checked. Percent defective is $p \times 100$.

• As the subgroup size varies, upper control limits (UCL) and lower control limits (LCL) vary:

$$UCL = \bar{u} + \frac{3\sqrt{\bar{u}}}{\sqrt{n}}$$

$u = $ *number of defects per sample*

$$\bar{u} = \Sigma \frac{c}{\Sigma n}$$

$$LCL = \bar{u} - \frac{3\sqrt{\bar{u}}}{\sqrt{n}}$$

$c = $ number of defects

Figure 10.40   *For a u chart.*

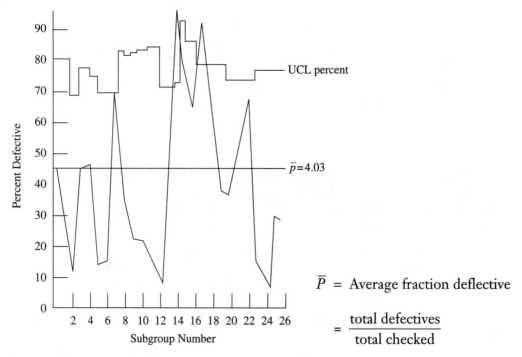

p Control chart reflow solder machine

UCL percent

$\bar{p} = 4.03$

$\bar{P} = $ Average fraction deflective

$= \dfrac{\text{total defectives}}{\text{total checked}}$

Figure 10.41   *p control charts.*

Computations
    Control limits are based on the binomial distribution (k = number of subgroups)
      Central line:

$$np = \frac{\Sigma\, n\bar{p}}{n}$$

$$UCL = np + 3\sqrt{n\bar{p}\,(1 - \bar{p})}$$

$$\text{where } \bar{p} = \frac{\Sigma\, np}{\Sigma\, n}$$

$$LCL = n\bar{p} - 3\sqrt{\bar{p}n\,(1 - \bar{p})}$$

Figure 10.42 *np control charts.*

np Chart   The *np* chart (Figure 10.42) is similar to the *p* chart except that it measures the number of defective items in the sample, when the sample size (*n*) is constant.

    Figure 10.43 is a diagram to aid in the selection of the correct control chart based on the nature of the data and samples.

Charts for Low–Volume, Short-Run Manufacturing

Many processes operate at a low output volume. In addition, the use of JIT production systems results in smaller lot sizes and more frequent runs. This means more setups, different parts, and different specifications moving through the same operation. The lot size requirements for using the control charts previously described (requiring 4 or 5 items in 25 or more continuous samples before control limits can be calculated) preclude their application to low-volume, short-run manufacturing. However, there are simple techniques to provide control charts by either operation (with different part numbers) or a small lot of the same part through different operations. They provide a picture of the process variation. Figure 10.44 illustrates an for $\bar{X}$ and R chart for the two different parts being cut on the same machine.[8] Control limits are calculated as shown in Table 10.5.

    The coded for $\bar{X}$ value is derived by using the deviation from the specification nominal value of the part being processed. The nominal (target) value becomes the zero point on the $\bar{X}$ chart. The sample size between parts is kept constant. The control limits are the 3s limits. The charts are interpreted the same as any control chart. Another form of short-run for $\bar{X}$ and R control charts, developed by D. R. Bothe, allows plotting multiple part numbers and different part characteristics on the same chart.[9] Figure 10.45 shows how material is followed through different operations with this chart. Examples of the for $\bar{X}$ and R charts of this type are shown in Figures 10.46

Control Chart Decision Tree

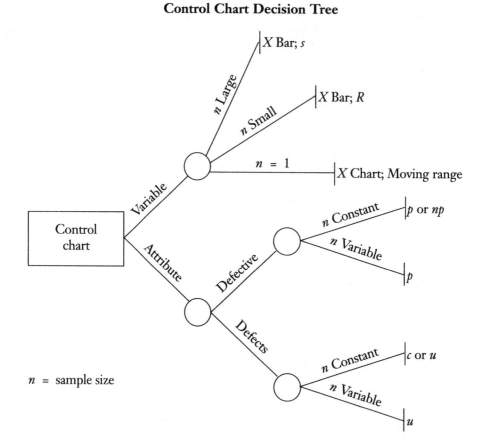

Figure 10.43 *Factors in the decision process to select the appropriate control chart.*

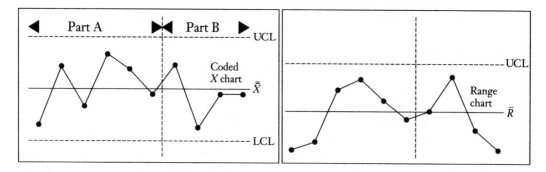

Figure 10.44 *The target $\overline{X}$ bar and R chart with control limits.*

Table 10.5   Formula to calculate control limits for low-volume short-run processes

$$D_3 = 0 \text{ for } n = 1 \text{ to } 5$$

n	D_4	A_2	d_2
1	3.27	2.66	1.13
2	3.27	1.86	1.13
3	2.57	1.02	1.69
4	2.28	0.73	2.05
5	2.11	0.58	2.33

Chart	Control Limits	Center Lines	Plot Point	Sample Size
$\bar{X}$	$\text{UCL} = \bar{\bar{X}} + A_2\bar{R}$ $\text{LCL} = \bar{\bar{X}} - A_2\bar{R}$	$\bar{\bar{X}} = \dfrac{\Sigma \text{ coded } \bar{X}}{k}$	Coded $\bar{X} =$ $\bar{X}$ – target value	3 to 5 and constant
R	$\text{UCL} = D_4\bar{R}$ $\text{LCL} = D_3\bar{R}$	$\bar{R} = \dfrac{\Sigma R}{k}$	R	

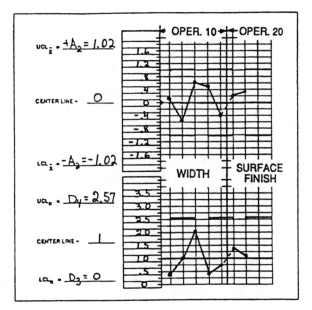

Since the plot points of a short-run chart are dimensionless numbers, one chart can follow an order for a part number through a job shop with all the data from different operations plotted on the same chart.

Figure 10.45   *Example of short-run control charts plotting multiple part numbers and different part characteristics on the same chart.*

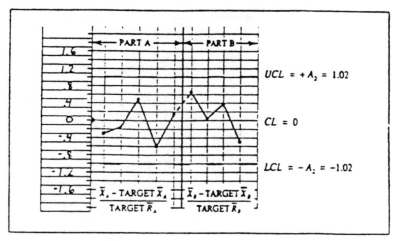

Figure 10.46 *The short-run $\overline{X}$ chart for n = 3.*

and 10.47. The short-run control limits of both for $\overline{X}$ and R charts are independent of both for $\overline{X}$ and R. If a constant subgroup size is maintained, only one chart is needed to monitor all part numbers run through an operation.

Multivari Charts

Another type of chart used to gain insight into the nature of process variations is called the multivari chart, developed by Dorian Shainan. It identifies the types of variation. Figure 10.48 illustrates how much is positioned in the manufacturing cycle and with respect to consecutive time periods. Vertical lines show variations within a piece or sample. Averages are connected to show the variation of those averages. The example shows little variation between averages (means) but a large variation within pieces. The time variation shows little variation within pieces and between means, but a large variation from batch to batch or period to period, or both. This information is useful in eliminating variables that could be candidates for further analysis or in planning designed experiments. In using this tool, it is important to collect data sequentially, collect it all, and use only current data.

Ratio Control Charts

A control chart for the ratio of two variables is particularly useful in nonmanufacturing (service and support) processes. Figure 10.49 shows its application in the U.S. Department of Labor Unemployment Insurance (UI) Quality Control (QC) program.[10] The objective is to estimate the rate and to identify the causes of errors in the payment of UI benefits. The figure shows the ratios of dollars of UI benefits overpaid to the total UI benefits paid. The chart shows the existence of spe-

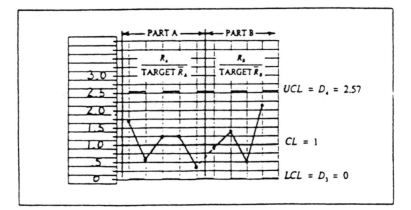

Figure 10.47   *The short-run range chart where the ratio R/Target R is plotted.*

cial causes when the overpayment ratios exceed upper and lower limits. The author of the referenced article suggests other applications for the ratio estimates to include

- The ratio of charges underbilled, or overbilled, to total billings in accounts receivable.
- The ratio of employee's time spent correcting errors or reworking defects to productive work time.
- The financial ratio, such as savings to disposable income, price to earnings, or debt to equity. Many of these and other ratios are used by business analysts and managers, but they are not treated as data from a process in which expected variation could be calculated and deviations used for rational decision making.

In Figure 10.49, the central line is the ratio (R) computed from all samples selected in consecutive weeks.

$$R = \frac{\text{Total Dollar Errors } (y)}{\text{Total Dollars Paid } (x)}$$

$$\text{UCL} = R + 3\sqrt{v}$$
$$\text{LCL} = R - 3\sqrt{v}$$

Where:

n = number of payments weeks
N = total number of payments in period

$$\text{where: } v = \frac{1}{x^2}\left[\frac{N^2(n-1)\left[(y-xR)^2\right]}{N}\right]$$

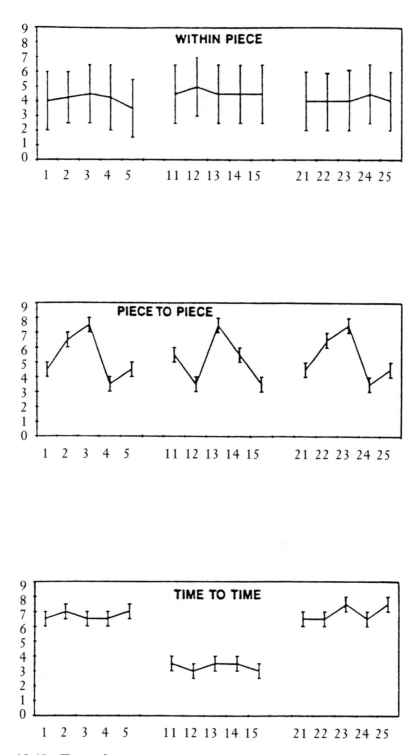

Figure 10.48   *Types of variation.*

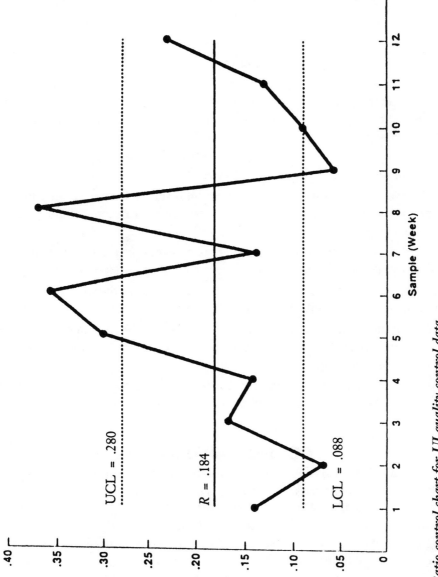

Figure 10.49 *Ratio control chart for UI quality control data.*

207

IMPORTANT FACTORS IN SUCCESSFUL STATISTICAL PROCESS CONTROL

SPC can't be installed; it's a part of process management. It must be designed to fit the process, people, and organization. Management must understand the concepts, value, as well as limitations of SPC. A successful SPC program has the following elements

- Management support of corrective actions.
- Participants with proper training both in the classroom followed by use on the job.
- Process operators, preferably in teams, must be involved in the application, development, implementation, and interpretation of results, as well as corrective action.
- Success involves some "unlearning." People must learn to respond to data and not to tamper (adjust) when it is in control.
- Don't have a quality functional organization install and operate the SPC program. Process operators will not take ownership or responsibility for performance.
- Don't try to chart all product characteristics. Select only those that are critical. Review results periodically to eliminate useless data collection.
- Organizations need to promulgate clear instructions as to what to do when an out-of-control process is recognized.
- Process improvement teams are typically multifunctional. It may be difficult to schedule meetings. Management must provide the time to show that improvement team meetings have a high priority.
- Senior management must regularly review the SPC program and its results. This is of critical value to the entire organization.

PROCESS CAPABILITY

The term *process capability* has been used in a general way in this chapter to refer to a process that meets requirements. For processes using variables measurements, process capability can be quantified as a calculated index.

Determining process capability is the action of studying the causes of variation, separating them into common and special causes and eliminating the latter. Capability cannot be improved until this is done.

There is a difference between having a capable process and being in statistical control—capable and highly capable. This is illustrated in Figure 10.50.

Process capability in administrative applications (processes) is essentially the same concept—eliminating defects and errors—except that when the process measurements are variables, capability cannot be quantified. Process *variation* can be measured and control established (control charts), and that is its capability. It will improve only

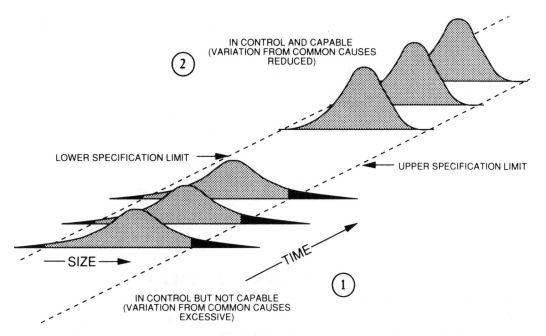

Both processes are in control. Process 1 is not capable of producing a product that is within limits. Some product (solid black) is defective. Process 2 is both in control and capable.

Figure 10.50 *Difference between process control and process capability.*

if the factors causing errors (complexity, poor training, and so on) are removed. The seven QC tools are particularly effective in doing this.

Measuring Process Capability Using Indices

A calculated process capability index is useful as an indicator of how a process, in control, is performing with respect to requirements—the specified tolerance. As discussed earlier, a process in control will produce product within its +/– 3s boundaries. This 6s spread is its capability. But, as Figure 10.50 illustrates, it can be capable and still produce outside the tolerance.

Capability can be expressed in terms of a number that is a ratio of the width of the engineering tolerance to the capability. For this case, the process average and tolerance center coincide. In this case it is called the *capability index* (Cp) and is (for variables)

$$Cp = \frac{\text{Upper Engineering Tolerance - Lower Tolerannce Limit}}{\text{Process}(6s)}$$

Process variation held to within the engineering tolerance provides a capable process. The terminology used is that, if the ratio is 1.0, it has a 3s capability. If the ratio is 2.0, it has a 6s capability. For quality assurance, the ratio should be greater than 1.0 because performance is dynamic. It does not remain exactly centered. (The process average is an approximation, as is any average).

Many companies are adopting a 6s capability as their long-range improvement goal. In the late 1980s the leading industries in Japan had an average 4s capability and are still improving.

Another index measure takes into account the effect of the process not coinciding with the tolerance center. It is called the C_{pk}.

$$C_{pk} = \text{the lesser of } \frac{(USL - u)}{3s} \text{ or } \frac{(u - USL)}{3s}$$

The measurement data used for capability determination are typically based on a small sample. This can provide a useful indicator, but it is still an estimate. When making short-term capability studies to get a rough idea where the process is, it is recommended that instead of using the +/– 3 process range a more conservative 8s (±4s) should be used.[11]

CONTINUOUS IMPROVEMENT

Perhaps the most profound difference in the new and other quality management philosophies is the concept of continuous improvement: Improve process quality forever (of course improvements must be economically achievable, but the search never ends). The value of continuous improvement can be illustrated using an industry process. Figure 10.51 show a series of histograms from a process, as it is improved. It begins with a process that, when measured, is not capable of producing all parts to specification. The process is not in statistical control; there are special, correctable causes of variation at work (Figure 10.51 a). Taking corrective action removes special causes and some of the variation (Figure 10.51 b). Now, the inherent capability of the process is known. Next, in Figure 10.51 c, action is taken to center the process on the specification center. There is no change in variation. It produces more good product with respect to the tolerance requirements. Then, the common causes (the inherent capability of the process) are improved. The result is shown in Figure 10.51d. Variation is reduced. However, any shift in the process would result in producing some defective product. So, further reductions of common causes are made (Figure 10.51e). This process is then highly capable. There is little probability that out-of-tolerance products will be made.

The continuous improvement concept is also shown in Figure 10.52 as time-based improvements. It can also be illustrated in terms of tracking the C_p improvement efforts (Figure 10.53).

REDUCING COMMON CAUSES

The preceding paragraphs describe the concepts and methodologies used in the adoption of SPC for process control and improvement. Reducing process variation after a process is in control requires other statistical tools, which might be referred to as

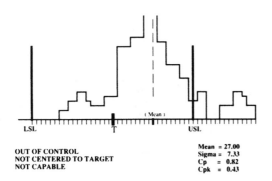

T   = Specification target
LSL = Lower specification limit
USL = Upper specification limit

The vertical scale is the frequency of occurrence of a sample measurement.

OUT OF CONTROL
NOT CENTERED TO TARGET
NOT CAPABLE

Mean = 27.00
Sigma = 7.33
Cp   = 0.82
Cpk = 0.43

a. Initial distribution

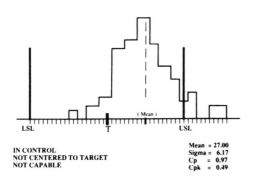

IN CONTROL
NOT CENTERED TO TARGET
NOT CAPABLE

Mean = 27.00
Sigma = 6.17
Cp   = 0.97
Cpk = 0.49

b. After removal of special cause

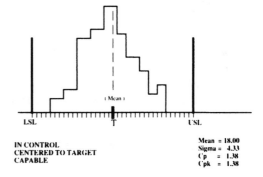

IN CONTROL
CENTERED TO TARGET
CAPABLE

Mean = 18.00
Sigma = 4.33
Cp   = 1.38
Cpk = 1.38

d. After reducing common cause

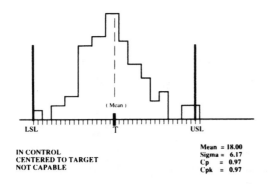

IN CONTROL
CENTERED TO TARGET
NOT CAPABLE

Mean = 18.00
Sigma = 6.17
Cp   = 0.97
Cpk = 0.97

c. After centering to target

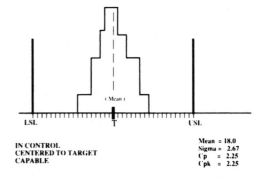

IN CONTROL
CENTERED TO TARGET
CAPABLE

Mean = 18.0
Sigma = 2.67
Cp   = 2.25
Cpk = 2.25

e. After further reduction of common cause

Figure 10.51 *Continuous improvement—Reduction of variations around the target value.*
Copyright of Motorola, Inc. Used with permission.

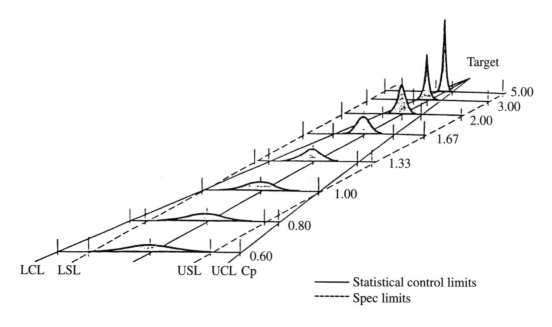

Continuous measurable improvement means reducing the variation of the process with respect to requirements (specification limits). The calculated indicator of improvement is the capability ratio (*Cp*).

Figure 10.52   *Continuous measurable improvement.*

advanced statistical methods. They are identified in Figure 10.54. These methods mainly involve experiments planned and designed to identify those process variables that most affect variation. Figure 10.54a compares experiments in which a process is operated holding one variable constant and noting the results. Then another is held constant, and so forth. Some important variables may be found this way but the one-fact-at-a-time technique can't identify the critical interactions that occur between some factors that actually can cause most of the variation. The two curves shown illustrate the different results that can be realized.

Figure 10.54b illustrates the usual relationship and common path for conventional versus experimental methods. The most commonly used is some form of Design of Experiments, which will be discussed in the next chapter. These kinds of improvements, the reduction of common causes, are done by changing the process or finding a way to better control critical process variables.

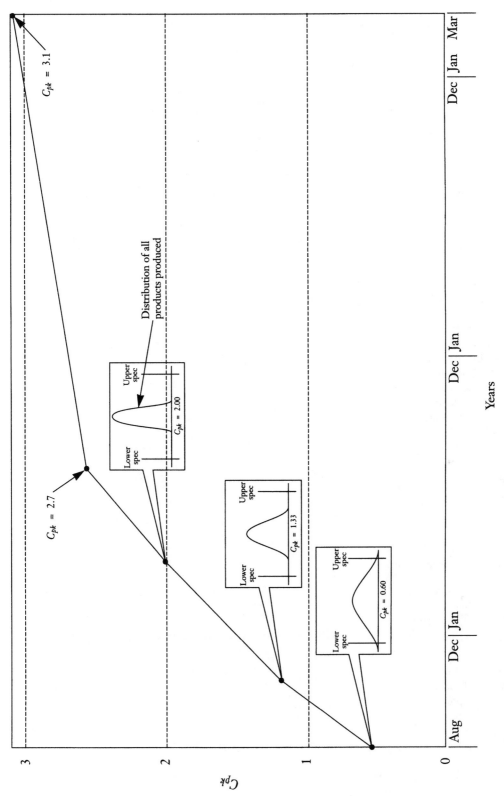

Figure 10.53 *Typical C_p or C_{pk} evolution.*

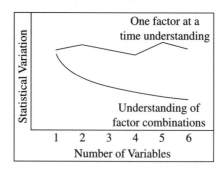

a. Reducing statistical variation through understanding variable combinations.

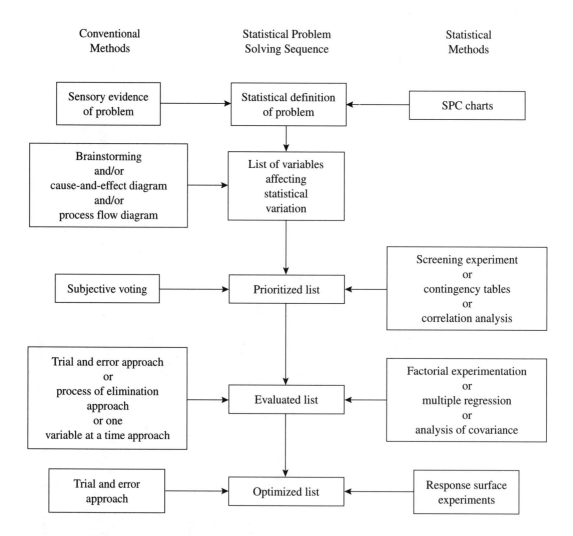

b. SPS sequence showing integration of conventional and statistical methods.

Figure 10.54 *Comprehensive depiction of all the statistical methods available to reduce process variation.*

REFERENCES

1. K. Ishikowa. Guide to Quality Control, Tokyo. *Asian Productivity Organization*. 1911. (Available from ASQ Quality Press, Milwaukee.)
2. H. Kamikubo. "New Way of Management Tools." ASQC Annual Quality Congress Transactions, Milwaukee 1989.
3. The affinity diagram originated from the KJ method developed by J. Karvaketa and H. Kamikubo in 1989.
4. Kamikubo. "New Way of Management Tools."
5. D. Galloway. *Mapping Work Processes* (Milwaukee: ASQC Quality Press, 1994).
6. "The Tools of Quality." *Quality Progress*, adapted from the *Quality Improvement Tools Workbook*, by Juran Institute, Inc., October 1990.
7. D.J. Wheeler, and D.S. Chambers. *Understanding SPC*, 2nd ed.
8. "The Quality Breakthrough." for Boeing Suppliers, 4th Qtr., 1989.
9. D.R. Bothe. "A Powerful New Control Chart for Job Shops." ASQC Annual Quality Congress Transactions, 1989.
10. A.W. Spisak. "A Control Chart for Ratios." ASQ *Journal of Quality Technology*, 1990.
11. J.C. Seigel. "Managing With Statistical Methods," Society of Automotive Engineers Technical Paper Series Number 820520, 1982.

ADDITIONAL READINGS

Juran, J.M. and F. Gryna. *Juran's Quality Control Handbook*. New York: McGraw-Hill, 1988.

ASQ Statistics Division. *Glossary and Tables for Statistical Quality Control*, 4th ed. Milwaukee: Author, 1996.

Besterfield, D.H. Quality Control, 4th ed., Milwaukee: ASQC Quality Press, 1994.

Kepner, C.H., and B.B. Trigoe. *The New Rational Manager*. Princeton, NJ: Princeton Research Press, 1981.

Memory Jogger II. Methuen, MA: GOAL/QPC, 1995.

Pyzdek, T., and R. Berger. *Quality Engineering Handbook*. Milwaukee: ASQC Quality Press, 1992.

Tague, N.R. *The Quality Tool Box*. Milwaukee: ASQC Quality Press, 1995.

Zaciewski, R.D., and L. Nemeth. "The Multi-Vari Chart: An Underutilized Quality Tool." ASQ *Quality Progress* (October 1995).

Chapter 11

Benchmarking

- **Purpose**
- **Benefits**
- **Principles**
- **A Way of Managing**
- **Types**
- **Steps in Benchmarking**
- **Training**
- **Communicating Results**
- **Pitfalls in Benchmarking**
- **Case Study**

Benchmarking is a comparative analytical tool to improve organizations, processes, products, and services. It can be defined as comparing products, processes, methods, and services with the best practices found in other organizations and adapting or adopting them as quality improvement projects.

Benchmarking is considered by many as the most valuable method for achieving improvement. Companies such as Xerox, AT&T, Mary-Kay Cosmetics, and all Malcolm Baldrige National Quality Award winners found that it provided the greatest improvements and was the most effective change agent of all their improvement activities. It is now being conducted by some organizations on a global scale.

Edward Tracy, AT&T vice president, stated, "If AT&T had not been into quality, I'm not sure we could have pulled off benchmarking because of the culture that is needed. You need to understand that benchmarking is a vital piece of the quality process. You need to understand quality principles and you must have the necessary quality skills, structure, and environment in place." He also said that "AT&T's benchmarking process has been not just mildly successful, but enormously successful."[1]

U.S. business has always measured success by profit, growth, and return on investment. At the same time, management always believed that improvement was possible. It annually prepared plans to improve. The basis of its plans was mostly an extrapolation of its latest (one-year) performance data. To improve the odds, management often put its most aggressive people in charge of the plan elements. "Make it happen" was the battle cry. Sometimes management was successful, sometimes not. Typically, no one was sure why the outcome was as it was. If successful, those leaders were rewarded. If not, replacements were found or they tried again. Various fads were adopted, such as MBO, but they fell out of use because they didn't prove consistently beneficial.

The Japanese have not used extrapolation planning as their fundamental policy. They spent many years analyzing in detail how the rest of the world's businesses worked. They identified how the successful companies worked, then adopted the best there was, often improving on it. They also exchanged this information with each other. This process has now been somewhat systematized and identified in the United States as benchmarking.

American companies did occasionally use benchmarking, but on an incremental basis. The most common use was in making detailed comparisons of competitive products to look for new features and lower-cost methods. Some companies made occasional use of it in determining competitive manufacturing costs and salaries. However, the practice was not widespread or systematic. Comparisons were not made for *all* the important activities in all functions, as they are in benchmarking today. Noncompetitive processes were rarely benchmarked even if they were similar. American business management has not been process management oriented. Typically, it also believed that only another business in the same market was worth evaluating.

Benchmarking is a comparison process. It is continuously identifying the best business practices anywhere and adopting or adapting them to your organization. It's a renewal process; it's not based on an evolutionary or extrapolation change rate, but on rapidly stepping into a higher order of effectiveness and efficiency. It's leapfrogging into the highest competitive position, process by process.

For example; Figure 11.1 lists "the best of the best" in a variety of companies that can be used to investigate (benchmark) best practices. The list is not static. Companies not listed improve to be included in the "best," at least in some activities; companies currently listed fall behind.

PURPOSE

Using benchmarking has some specific focus:

- Analyze operations to assess strengths and weaknesses of existing work processes.
- Know the competitive and economic sector leaders. Who is the best of the best?
- Discover what the leaders' best practices are and adopt or adapt them into your organization.
- Become the best of the best.

Allied Signal
Health care management
American Express
Billing and collection
Apple Computer
Inventory control
Ben & Jerry's
Environment management
Canon
Product development
Cap Gemini
Quality systems, technology transfer
Citibank
Technology management
Coors
Health care management
Corning
Manufacturing, technology management
Dow Chemical
Enivorment management, technology
  transfer
Edison
Health care management
Federal Express
Inventory control
Florida Power & Light
Quality systems
Ford
Training
Fujitsu
Technology transfer
General Electric
Robotics, training
Goldstar
Concurrent engineering
Helene Curtis
Marketing
Hershey Foods
Warehousing, distribution
Hewlett-Packard
Manufacturing

Honda Motor
Purchasing
IBM
Sales management
L. L. Bean
Customer service, warehousing, distribution
MCI
Inventory control
Merck
Sales management
Microsoft
Marketing, software development
Monsanto
Technology management
Motorola
Product development, quality systems, manufacturing
NCR
Purchasing, concurrent engineering
NEC Corporation
Quality systems
Nordstrom
Customer service
Philip Morris
Manufacturing
Polaroid
Training
Procter & Gamble
Sales management, technology management
Sharp
Product Planning
Sony
Product development
Square D
Technology transfer
3M
Environment management, technology transfer,
  product development
Westinghouse
Inventory control
Xerox
Customer service, quality systems, purchasing

Subject	Company	Says who . . .
Benchmarking	AT&T, Digital Equipment Corporation, IBM, Motorola, Texas Instruments, Xerox	Port and Smith
Benchmarking	Digital Equipment Corporation, Florida Power & Light, Ford, IBM/Rochester, Motorola, Xerox	Altany
Billing/collection	American Express, Fidelity Investments, MCI	Port and Smith
Billing/collection	American Express, MCI	Altany
Customer focus	General Electric (plastics), Wallace Company, Westinghouse (furniture systems), Xerox	Altany
Customer satisfaction	Federal Express, General Electric (plastics), L. L. Bean, Xerox	Port and Smith
Customer service	American Express, L. L. Bean, The Limited, Marriott, Procter & Gamble	Foster
Design for manufacturing assembly	Digital Equipment Corporation, NCR	Altany
Distribution and logistics	L. L. Bean, Wal-Mart	Port and Smith

Figure 11.1 *The best of the best.*

Source: R. C. Camp, *Business Process Benchmarking: Finding and Implementing Best Practices* (Milwaukee: ASQC Quality Press, 1995).

BENEFITS

As has been demonstrated now by several U.S. companies, such as Xerox, IBM, and Motorola, benchmarking has several valuable benefits:

- It is highly motivating for an organization to know that it is performing as well or better than the best. It frequently stimulates creativity for even greater improvement.

- A business with all its functions performing equal to, or better than, the competitors is in an advantageous market position.

- An organization that has experienced the benefits of benchmarking tends to want to continue the activity and remain the best.

- The benchmarking process fosters a new in-depth understanding by managers and employees of how organizations truly function. This makes the members more interested and motivated.

- Focusing on outside competition avoids nonconstructive internal competition. Need for improvement is more acceptable if it's recognized that someone outside is measurably better.

- It wakens management and employees to the need for change.

- It can be used as a means to introduce quality/process improvement into an organization, or as a way to restart a failed program.

Benchmarking has some additional advantages that make it even more important than relying just on self-improvement and innovation:

- It identifies strategic goals and objectives related to what the marketplace (competition) is now achieving (which may determine what customers expect).

- It can provide reduced cycle times. Small or big tasks get done faster. This has a positive effect on all business performance measurements.

- It identifies a new standard that must be achieved and exceeded to remain competitive.

Benchmarking can be illustrated by a simple example shown in Figure 11.2. The Street Maintenance Department of Los Angeles made a breakdown of its operating costs and compared them to those of private industry. It found that its costs were only 89 percent of private industry's costs. However, in its analysis it found that its transportation costs for hauling debris was higher. In investigating, it discovered that private industry used local sites where such fill material was needed, while the city used outlying designated dump sites. When the city also adopted this practice, its costs dropped to 78 percent of private industry, thus increasing its competitive advantage.

PRINCIPLES

Benchmarking involves measurement. Measurement, however, is not the objective. The objective is adopting the best practices, although measurement is necessary to know what is better or best.

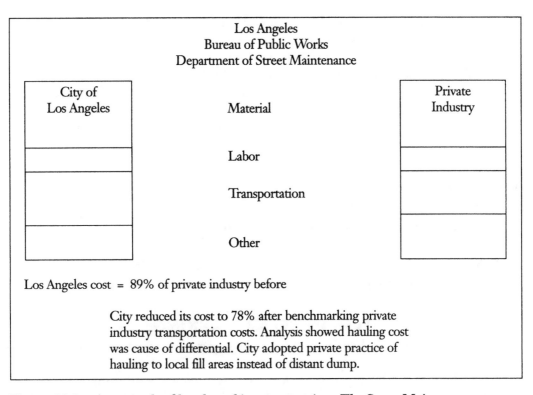

Figure 11.2   *An example of benchmarking a competitor: The Street Maintenance Department of Los Angeles found one process in which private industry was more competitive, adopted it, and became the most competitive.*

The measurement can be qualitative or quantitative. It can be a description of the better practice or it can describe differences in quantitative terms such as dollars, hours, or elapsed time. The best results are obtained by using both measures.

Since benchmarking can be applied to any organization, it is an appropriate technique for improving any activity, function, or process. Many functions within an organization are common to many other outside organizations, even in different kinds of business. For example, most companies make purchases, pay bills, and train employees. Which company or organization is the best at performing the same activities that you do? Which has the best process and best satisfies its customers?

Benchmarking may also include comparisons between intercompany activities as well as those of competitors. There is no limit in the search for the best practices anywhere.

A WAY OF MANAGING

Benchmarking represents a tool, methodology, and policy for managing. Therefore, it requires involvement and support by upper management. In addition, since implementing benchmarking findings requires acceptance and change by the people in the organization affected, those people must be convinced that management actively supports it.

Lip service or delegation to a staff function won't result in acceptance. The benchmarking activity requires resources: the time of people to investigate, evaluate, and implement competitive processes. Providing the funding and resources is management's most visible and tangible evidence of its support. One of the difficult resource decisions management must make is to assign their most experienced and knowledgeable people to the benchmark team. Such people are the best equipped to recognize the valuable processes, practices, and methods to copy. They will provide the biggest return on the effort.

TYPES

The two general types of benchmarking are

- Problem Based—Benchmarking used as a tool to solve specific problems proving difficult to solve by other improvement techniques. This can provide not only "a solution" but a major improvement.

- Processed Based—Benchmarking used as a continuous pursuit of quality improvement throughout an organization.

STEPS IN BENCHMARKING

From a broad perspective, benchmarking can be depicted as a continuous process represented by the plan, do, study, act sequence of a modified Deming wheel, shown in Figure 11.3. In more detail it can be described as a sequence or a process as represented by the flowchart in Figure 11. 4. Depicted is an eleven-step process based on implementation of benchmarking as generally described by Robert Camp.[2,3]

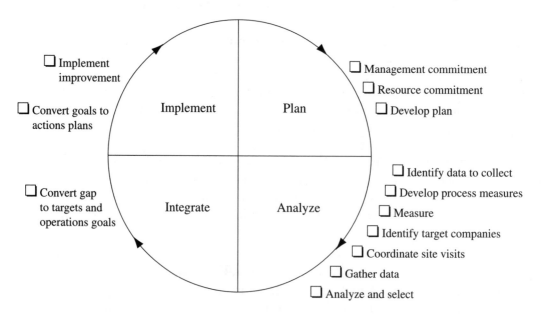

Figure 11.3 *The Deming wheel approach applied to the benchmarking process.*

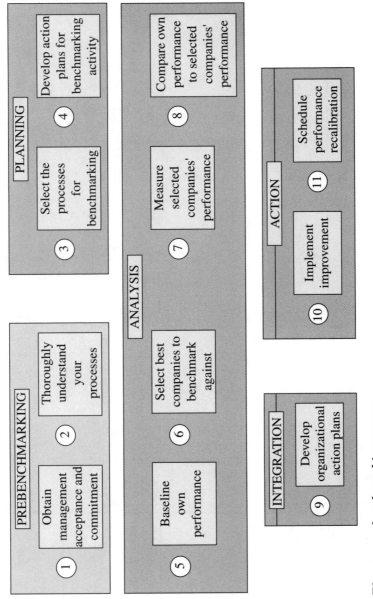

Figure 11.4 *Eleven-step benchmarking process.*

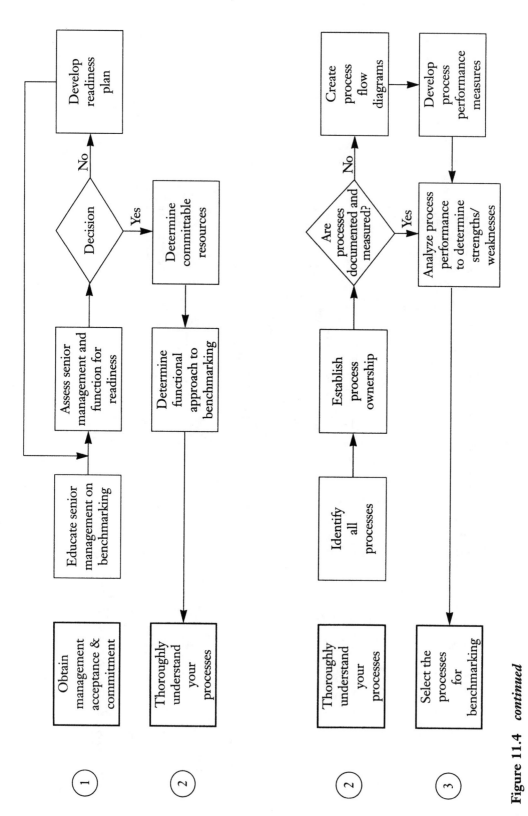

Figure 11.4 *continued*

224

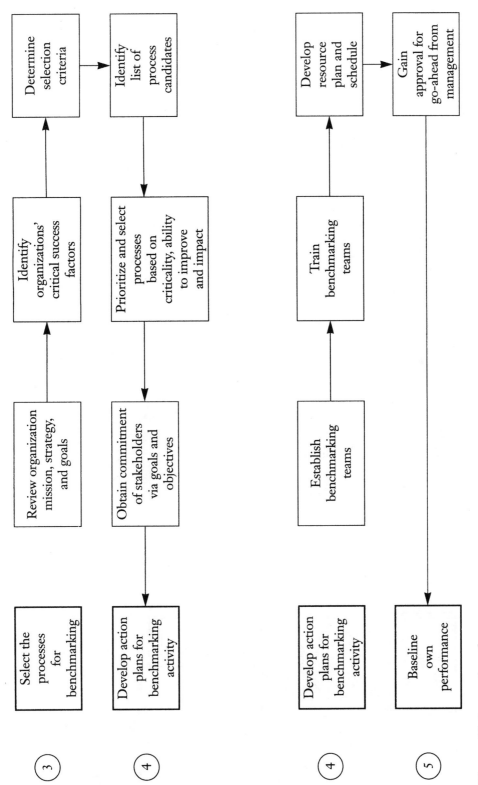

Figure 11.4 *continued*

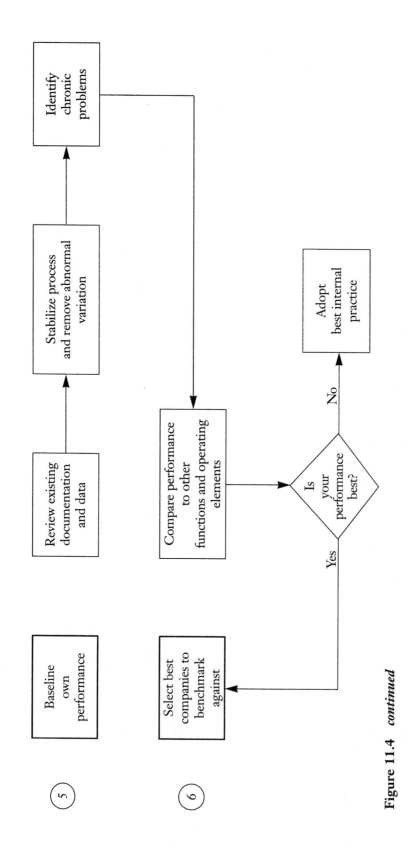

Figure 11.4 *continued*

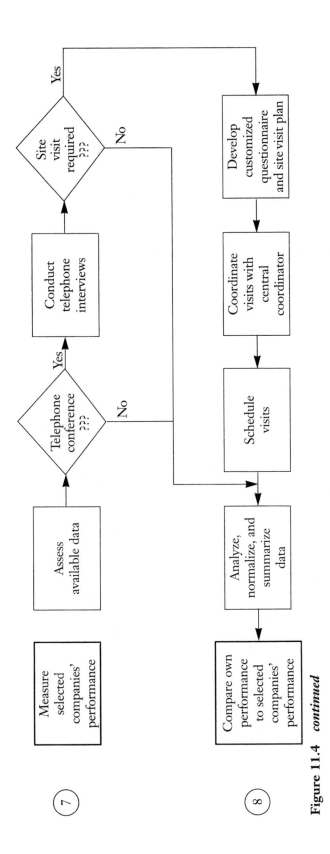

Figure 11.4 *continued*

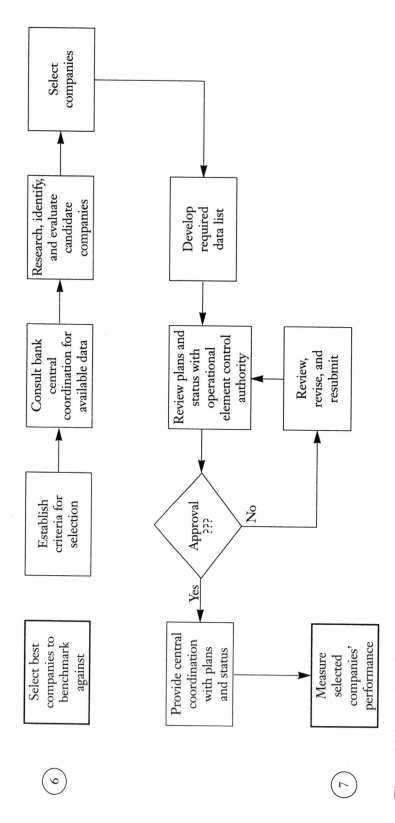

Figure 11.4 *continued*

228

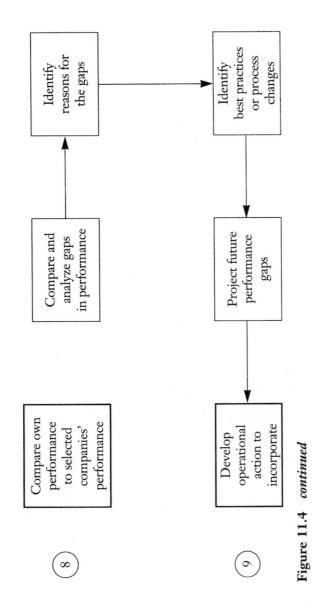

Figure 11.4 *continued*

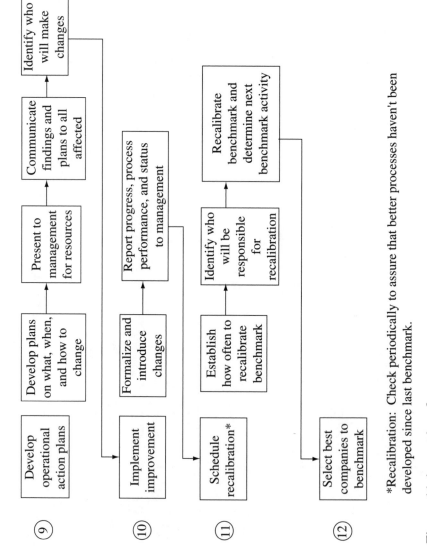

⑨ Develop operational action plans → Develop plans on what, when, and how to change → Present to management for resources → Communicate findings and plans to all affected → Identify who will make changes

⑩ Implement improvement → Formalize and introduce changes → Report progress, process performance, and status to management

⑪ Schedule recalibration* → Establish how often to recalibrate benchmark → Identify who will be responsible for recalibration → Recalibrate benchmark and determine next benchmark activity

⑫ Select best companies to benchmark

*Recalibration: Check periodically to assure that better processes haven't been developed since last benchmark.

Figure 11.4 *continued*

230

A common concern when initiating benchmarking is where and how the information about outside organization processes is obtained. There are several good sources:

1. Libraries. Access to a good business library with the capability to use the voluminous data available is a major asset and the place to begin. Business organizations publish a great deal of useful information.
2. Direct contact. The orientation in benchmarking is processes performance measurement and methodology. Companies in competition are traditionally fearful of providing data, but the issue can be made of interest to both parties if it is presented on a process information sharing/exchange basis. That is the reason it is necessary to define and measure the key processes first. Only then do you have something of interest to exchange. Exchanges with noncompetitors who have a similar process are usually much easier. The initial contact between competitors of interest should be made by upper management.
3. Data centers. These are voluntary groups of like businesses formed to share benchmark information. There are independent centers at some universities and there are consultant businesses with process information to sell.
4. Trade and professional associations. Members can find books on benchmark contacts.

TRAINING

The benchmarking methodology is frequently considered simple enough for anyone to master. This attitude has resulted in poor results and failures. As Figure 11.4 illustrated, benchmarking requires considerable preparation in-house before any outside contacts are made. Success depends on a team's fully understanding the methodology. Benchmarking training programs and seminars are available. They provide both the what to do and what not to do to maximize the effort. One good strategy is to plan to train a specialist or two who can then train other employees.

COMMUNICATING RESULTS

One of the benefits of using benchmarking is its ability to motivate people to look outside for ideas. One way to foster this reaction is to communicate benchmark findings to employees. Let them know how their activities compared to the best. It stimulates a constructive competitive attitude. Various means can be employed, but one technique that can present a quick overall picture is the so-called spider chart, as shown in Figure 11.5.

Key process measures and comparisons can be seen at a glance. Figure 11.6 is an example related to processes in a materials organization.

PITFALLS IN BENCHMARKING

Benchmarking is a simple concept but can be quite complex in application.[4] Not all benchmark attempts have been successful, mainly because management did not understand the need for a disciplined, planned approach, or the resources needed.

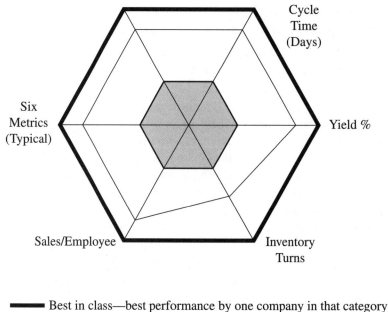

Best in class—best performance by one company in that category
Benchmark—the average of the top best companies in each category
Status of your performance

Figure 11.5   *Spider chart example—Communicate findings. (A more comprehensive example is included in appendix B.)*

Management authorizes it and sits back to wait for results. Or, upper managers scream when they see the costs the process is accruing.

Some other factors that can limit success are

- Lack of sponsorship by a senior manager. Benchmark team members should be the most knowledgeable of the process to be benchmarked. Usually these same people play an important role in the day-to-day functioning of the process. It takes upper management clout to get such people reassigned in such a manner that they don't also have to carry their normal workloads. During the benchmark activity, team members must work at it full time. This assignment conflict will exist unless management, from the top down, understands the benchmark process and is willing to sacrifice for the potential benefits.

- Failure of a team to thoroughly plan, describe, analyze, and document its own candidate process before examining outside process for comparison. This can result in the team's failing to understand the targeted processes, and thereby waste the effort. Target organizations experienced in benchmarking (and thousands now are) will quickly recognize the poor preparation and reject the exchange.

- Failure to clearly define the scope of its planned project. A team must do this before any analysis. Objectives must be kept simple so that the tasks don't become unmanageable.

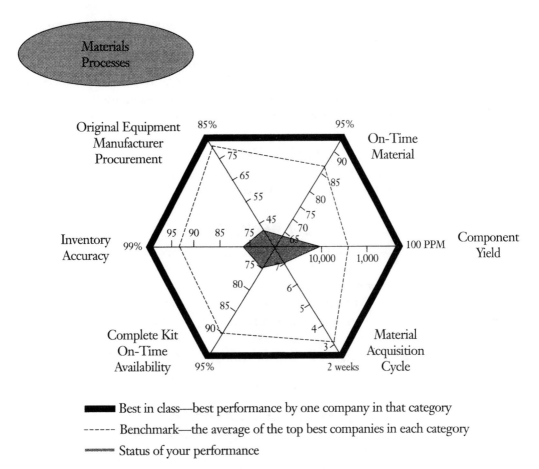

Figure 11.6   *Spider. Chart example—Benchmarking analysis.*

- Not positioning benchmarking within a larger strategy. Benchmarking is not an activity that should be conducted just to close all performance gaps with competitors. It should be an integral part of the organization's strategic quality objectives and within the organization's mission and goals.

- Emphasizing measurement rather than process. The objective is process improvement, although metrics are needed to make comparisons and measure gaps in performance. All the key measurements should initially be made so that some commonality will be found with the measures used by the target process. But understanding process differences is the objective. A simple universal metric such as cycle time will lead to all kinds of improvement ideas.

- Mismanagement of the target site visit factor. Management and teams frequently want to jump to making site visits before detailed preparations are made. Actually, there is often sufficient information available in the public domain to make site visits unnecessary. Moreover, visits take the time of the site organization. They also want to benefit by exchanging information in return.

- Failure to follow up on benchmarked process changes. The benchmark team must work with the normal process stakeholders to ensure that they understand and support the changes identified. Without this close cooperation, benchmarking will appear as a threat to the other process employees.

CASE STUDY

Appendix B is a case study of benchmarking by the Ritz Carlton Hotels Co. in order to reduce cycle time in their housekeeping system.

REFERENCES

1. K. Bemowski. "The Benchmarking Bandwagon." ASQ *Quality Progress* (January 1991).
2. R. C. Camp. *Benchmarking: The Search for Industry Best Practices That Lead to Superior Performance* (Milwaukee: ASQC Quality Press, 1989).
3. R. C. Camp. *Business Process Benchmarking: Finding and Implementing Best Practices* (Milwaukee: ASQC Quality Press, 1995).
4. I. DeToro. "The 10 Pitfalls of Benchmarking." ASQ *Quality Progress* (January 1995).

ADDITIONAL READINGS

Bureau of Business Practices. *Benchmarking: Action Plans and Legal Issues.* Waterford, CT: Simon and Schuster, 1997.

Camp, R. C. *Global Cases in Benchmarking: Best Practices from Organizations Around the World.* Milwaukee: ASQ Quality Press, 1998.

Harrington, H. J. *The Complete Benchmarking Implementation Guide: Total Benchmarking Management.* Milwaukee: ASQC Quality Press/Ernst and Young, L.L.P., 1996.

Micklewright, M. J. "Competitive Benchmarking: Large Gains for Small Companies." ASQ *Quality Progress* (June 1993).

Swanson, R. "Quality Benchmark Deployment." ASQ *Quality Progress* (December 1993).

Vaziri, H.K. "Using Competitive Benchmarking to Set Goals." ASQ *Quality Progress* (October 1992).

Chapter 12

Quality Awards and Standards

- **Standards**
- **Documented Standards**
- **Good Manufacturing Practices (GMP)**
- **Quality Awards**
  Communications
  Comparisons

With the growth in importance of quality in business, industry, government, and education there has been an emphasis on national and international standards and awards. Awards for quality achievement began with the Japanese, the Deming Prize. In the 1980s, the United States developed the Baldrige National Quality Award. A similar award is also granted to selected companies by the senators for each state. In the 1990s, the European Quality Award was established. All the awards are for high achievement in raising quality/productivity even though the criteria vary somewhat between awards.

Quality standards for organizations are written policies/procedures/specifications to be followed to reach some level of organization quality certification or acceptance. Many have become world standards through the actions of the International Standards Organization (ISO).

STANDARDS

There are some fundamental differences between the criteria and objectives of standards and awards. Standards are requirements that must be met to be approved or certified by some agency. Awards are a recognition of achievement in meeting award criteria. Both are periodically revised.

The first quality standards were physical standards for measurement. For the United States they are maintained at the National Institute of Standards and Technology for such things as the meter, pound, kilogram, time, and the like. These standards are the national primary references for measurement accuracy. All other laboratory standards are secondary, measured against the primaries.

DOCUMENTED STANDARDS

Quality standards set by government documentation began in the 1930s with the publication of sampling inspection tables (sampling plans). These tables became military standard MIL STD 105, "Sampling Procedures and Tables for Inspection by Attributes." This was followed by MIL STD 414, "Sampling Procedures and Tables for Inspection by Variables for Percent Defective." These statistical procedures developed from the works of Dodge and Romig. Inspection sampling is an economic method to determine an estimate of the quality of a lot or population. Statistical sampling is used in industry and also for public opinion polls.

The next important quality standards were documents that described requirements for a quality system to be maintained by organizations doing business with the federal government, mainly the Department of Defense (DOD). The important early standards were MIL I 45208, "Inspection System Requirements," and MIL Q 9858, "Quality Program Requirements." The first described the requirements an organization must meet to have an inspection system that satisfies DOD procurement. The MIL Q specification described the quality program (system) a contractor had to maintain. The Inspection specification was usually applied to the procurement of relatively noncomplex products. The MIL Q was applied to larger businesses making more complex equipment. It required the involvement of more functional organizations than just manufacturing/quality control and to some degree procurement, that is, engineering, finance, procurement, and suppliers. It led to the development of comprehensive quality control/quality assurance organizations containing various quality specialists. There are many other quality standards for various activities in a comprehensive quality system.

In the 1980s, the International Organization for Standardization (ISO) began to publish a variety of quality standards, particularly the 9000 series, for organization quality requirements.

ISO 9000 is a set of international standards designed to give buyers assurance that suppliers are using recognized effective management methods to control the quality of their products. They are used to certify that an organization meets the minimum criteria for a quality system as defined by the standards. They include a procedure to follow to become "Registered." Registration is not, however, a certification of product quality. Companies are allowed to advertise their certification achievement but may not stamp their product with the ISO 9000 registration logo.

The standards require that a manufacturer document and maintain a system for ensuring the quality of a process output. They also require that a company control its nonmanufacturing functions, such as engineering, purchasing, and service. The management system as a whole is reviewed, and ISO registration is granted. Recertification is required every three years for many certification bodies, with semiannual visits to review corrective actions. If a company has multiple sites, certification is achieved separately by each facility. These standards are not process oriented and don't require continuous improvement.

The three standards and their supporting documents are as follows

1. ANSI/ISO/ASQC Q9000-1-1994, Quality Management and Quality Assurance Standards-Guidelines for Selection and Use.
2. ANSI/ISO/ASQC Q9002-1994, Quality Systems-Model for Quality Assurance in Production, Installation, and Servicing.
3. ANSI/ISO/ASQC Q9003-1994, Quality Systems-Model for Quality Assurance in Final Inspection and Test.

Supporting documents include the following

ISO 9000-2:1993, Quality management and quality assurance standards-Part 2: Generic Guidelines for the application of ISO 9001, ISO 9002, and ISO 9003.

ISO 9000-3:1993, Quality management and quality assurance standards-Part 3: Guidelines for the application of ISO 9001 to the development, supply, and maintenance of software.

ISO 9000-4:1993, Quality management and quality assurance standards-Part 4: Guide to dependability program management.

ISO 9004-2:1991, Quality management and quality system elements-Part 2: Guidelines for services.

ISO 9004-3:1993, Quality management and quality system elements-Part 3: Guidelines for processed materials.

ISO 9004-4:1993, Quality management and quality system elements-Part 4: Guidelines for quality improvement.

ANSI/ISO/ASQC Q10011-1-1994, Guidelines for Auditing Quality Systems-Auditing.

ANSI/ISO/ASQC Q10011-2-1994, Guidelines for Auditing Quality Systems-Qualification Criteria for Quality Systems Auditors.

ANSI/ISO/ASQC Q10011-3-1994, Guidelines for Auditing Quality Systems-Management of Audit Programs.

ISO 10012-1:1992, Quality assurance requirements for measuring equipment-Part I: Metrological confirmation system for measuring equipment.

ISO 10013:1995, Guidelines for developing quality manuals.

ISO Handbook 3:1989, Statistical methods.

The requirements of ISO-9000 are depicted in Figure 12.1, and an overview of the ISO standards is shown in Figure 12.2. Copies of the standards can be purchased from ASQ, Milwaukee, WI.

ISO 9001	ISO 9002	ISO 9003
1. Management responsibility	■	●
2. Quality system	■	●
3. Contract review	■	■
4. Design control	▲	▲
5. Document control	■	■
6. Purchasing	■	▲
7. Purchaser-supplied product	■	■
8. Product identification and traceability	■	●
9. Process control	■	▲
10. Inspection and testing	■	■
11. Inspection, measuring, and test equipment	■	■
12. Inspection and test status	■	●
13. Control of nonconforming product	■	●
14. Corrective action	■	●
15. Handling, storage, packaging, and delivery	■	■
16. Quality records	■	●
17. Internal quality audits	■	●
18. Training	■	●
19. Servicing	■	▲
20. Statistical techniques	■	●

■ Full requirement   ● Minimal   ▲ Not required

Figure 12.1 *Requirements of ISO 9000.*

The Standards at a Glance

The standards explosion started with ISO 9000, and now there are ISO 14000, QS-9000, and TE-9000. With the number of standards that continue to be developed, there might be some confusion regarding their content. So, before another one is introduced, here are brief descriptions of the existing major standards.

ISO 9000

ISO 9000 is a series of three informational standards and supplementary guidelines on quality management and quality assurance, which were first published in 1987 and revised in 1994. The standards are not specific to any particular products and can be used by both manufacturing and service industries. These standards are nonprescriptive; they do not specify how a firm's quality assurance processes must occur, but they do mandate that a company define appropriate quality standards, document its processes, and prove that it consistently adheres to both. The standards require that a basic quality system be in place to ensure that the company has the capabilities and systems to provide its customers with quality products and services.

The ISO 9000 series includes:

* ISO 9000. A set of guidelines that helps users select and use the appropriate (ISO 9001, ISO 9002, or ISO 9003) standard.
* ISO 9001. The most comprehensive standard, covering design, manufacturing, installation, and servicing systems.
* ISO 9002. A standard that covers production and installation.
* ISO 9003. A standard that covers final product inspection and testing.
* ISO 9004. A set of guidelines for internal use by a producer developing its own quality system to meet business needs and take advantage of competitive opportunities.

To become registered to ISO 9001, ISO 9002, or ISO 9003, a company must have an accredited, independent third party conduct an on-site audit of the company's operations to verify that it is in compliance with the requirements of the appropriate standard.

Figure 12.2 *Overview of ISO 9000.*

238

ISO 14000

The ISO 14000 series of generic environmental management standards, which are currently under development by the International Organization for Standardization, will provide structure and systems for managing environmental compliance with legislative and regulatory requirements and will affect every aspect of a company's environmental operations.

The components of ISO 14000 include the general categories of environmental management systems, environmental auditing, environmental labeling, environmental performance evaluation, and life-cycle assessments.

These universal standards, which can be used by all countries and organizations, don't require a start-up performance test or audit, a final performance goal, or a single manual for documentation. They also don't have a prescribed performance improvement rate or mandated governmental or organizational policy.

The foreseen benefits of the ISO 14000 standards are that they will provide a worldwide focus on environemntal management; promote a voluntary consensus standards approach; harmonize national rules, labels, and methods by minimizing trade barriers and complications and by promoting predictability and consistency; and demonstrate commitment to maintaining and moving beyond regulatory environmental performance compliance.

ISO 14001 is the standard used for third-party registration. Registration to the ISO 14000 standards will require evidence of implementation of an environment management system, procedures that maintain compliance to applicable laws, commitment to continuous improvement, and commitment to pollution prevention (e.g., recycling, process changes, energy efficiency, and materials substitution).

With the precedent that has been established with the ISO 9000 series, it is likely that companies will need to be certified to those standards to compete globally—especially in Europe.

QS-9000

QS-9000 was developed in September 1994 by the Big Three's—Chrysler, Ford, and General Motors (GM)—Supplier Quality Requirements Task Force to define their fundamental quality system expectations, those of several heavy truck manufacturers, and other subscribing companies for internal and external suppliers of production and service parts and materials.

QS-9000 applies to all internal and external suppliers that provide production materials, production or service parts, or heat treating and other finishing services directly to the Big Three or other original equipment manufacturers subscribing to QS-9000.

QS-9000 uses the ISO 9001 standard as its foundation. QS-9000 is not a standard, but it contains the ISO 9001 standard; its requirements are much broader than ISO 9001.

While some say that QS-9000 doesn't really go beyond the ISO 9001 requirements, a comparison of the two shows that QS-9000 requirements are much more rigorous. There are 137 'shalls' [requirements] in the ISO 9001 document and 300 'shalls' in the QS-9000 document.

QS-9000 is divided into three sections:

- Common requirements, which include the exact text of ISO 9001 with the addition of automotive/heavy trucking requirements
- Additional requirements, which include requirements beyond the scope of ISO 9001 that are common to all three manufacturers
- Customer-specific sections, which contain requirements unique to Ford, GM, or Chrysler

TE-9000

TE-9000 is a supplement to the Big Three's QS-9000 requirement. As many as 50,000 tooling and equipment suppliers of nonproduction parts (items that are used in making parts for cars or trucks, such as tools, production equipment, dies, and molds) and even suppliers of some production items such as coolants could be affected by TE-9000.

TE-9000 includes ISO 9001 in its entirety, along with additional industry-specific requirements. Since the Big Three are requiring third-party registration from approved ISO 9000 registrars, TE-9000 is treated in a similar fashion.

Figure 12.2   *continued*

DuPont Corporation prepared a step-by-step road map for its ISO 9000 registration preparation (see Figure 12.3). Thorough planning of this kind is needed if registration is to be achieved and resources minimized. Becoming ISO registered is a minimum requirement to do business in some countries.

GOOD MANUFACTURING PRACTICES (GMP)

The U.S. Food and Drug Administration is authorized to regulate the medical device industry.[1] The device GMP14 regulation is designed to prevent the manufacture of poor-quality medical devices. It requires all device manufacturers to design, implement, and continually monitor a comprehensive quality assurance program. The program includes the application of good quality assurance principles. Special provisions are

- Preproduction design validation to assess device performance
- Recall authority without notice or hearing for probability of death, serious injury, or illness

QUALITY AWARDS

Quality awards are a recognition of achieving quality improvement objectives. They can be an effective motivational tool, and action taken in their pursuit can lead to valuable improvements. Awards can be internal or external. Many quality improvement programs include monetary incentives to reach quality goals. Others are entirely ceremonial, with recognition as the reward.

External awards can be earned from customers, trade or professional associations, and government agencies. Internal awards are valuable because they provide some satisfaction of the human need for work to have value other than pay. Combining the use of teams in pursuing quality awards fosters group efforts and a feeling of participating and contributing to the goals of the organization.

Some of the most prestigious external quality awards include

- The Deming Prize. Awarded by Japan to companies achieving high and challenging quality improvements by applying companywide quality concepts, particularly statistical techniques. It uses 10 criteria, all with equal scoring weights. Open to international applicants, it was won by an American company, Florida Power and Light, in 1991.
- The Malcolm Baldrige National Quality Award (MBNQA). This award was established in 1987 by the U.S. Congress to encourage organizations to commit to quality improvement, raise productivity, and improve competitiveness. It is intended to recognize significant, sustained performance improvement. The criteria no longer include the word "quality," but it is still a significant measure of success in the examination. The criteria evaluate the way companies manage in the current world marketplace. Some aspects of the design of the award are listed in Figure 12.4.

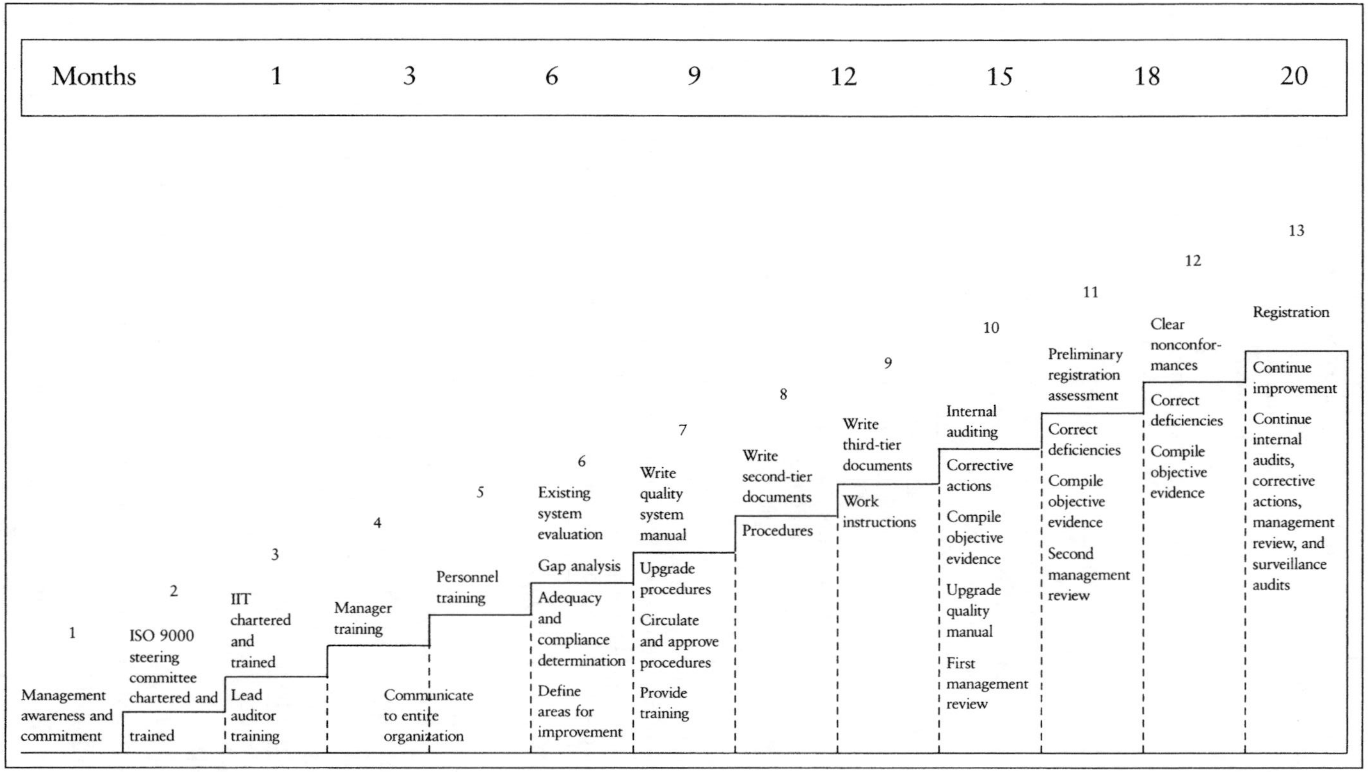

Months   1   3   6   9   12   15   18   20

1 — Management awareness and commitment

2 — ISO 9000 steering committee chartered and trained

3 — IIT chartered and trained | Lead auditor training

4 — Manager training | Communicate to entire organization

5 — Personnel training

6 — Existing system evaluation | Gap analysis | Adequacy and compliance determination | Define areas for improvement

7 — Write quality system manual | Upgrade procedures | Circulate and approve procedures | Provide training

8 — Write second-tier documents | Procedures

9 — Write third-tier documents | Work instructions

10 — Internal auditing | Corrective actions | Compile objective evidence | Upgrade quality manual | First management review

11 — Preliminary registration assessment | Correct deficiencies | Compile objective evidence | Second management review

12 — Clear nonconformances | Correct deficiencies | Compile objective evidence

13 — Registration | Continue improvement | Continue internal audits, corrective actions, management review, and surveillance audits

Figure 12.3 *DuPont's road map to ISO 9000 registration.*

241

P.L. 100-107 sets a number of key requirements for the U.S. National Quality Award, but nevertheless affords considerable latitude in Award criteria and processes.

To ensure a broad base of input to the design of the Award, many quality leaders—manufacturing, service, academic, consultants, and retired—were contacted regarding characteristics that should be incorporated into the award. In addition to stressing total quality, quality improvement, CEO-level quality leadership, statistical process control, and human resource utilization, several other features were mentioned repeatedly as highly desirable for inclusion in the Award. Those features most frequently mentioned were

1. **Performance.** The Award should be heavily performance based. That is, it should give considerable weight to quality improvement results, in preference to specific techniques or processes for achieving results.
2. **Innovation.** Award application should permit firms to highlight and get credit for unique approaches to achieving higher quality.
3. **"Measurables."** Award criteria and application evaluation should focus on quantitative results and positive trends, rather than on narrative descriptions of processes and anecdotal information. To be in a position to respond convincingly, firms would have to have in place a good quality measurement system, along with associated analytical capabilities.
4. **Customer Satisfaction.** Award consideration should consider not only customers' view of products and services, but also the entire functioning of the customer interface in planning products and services.
5. **World-class Quality.** Award evaluations should, where appropriate, explore the degree to which firms recognize the quality requirements of international markets, their systems for assessing where they stand, and their plans for establishing a leadership position.
6. **Quality Early in the Process.** Award criteria should reflect the need to address quality early in the design phase, both to reduce delays in bringing products to market and to enter markets with higher-quality products.
7. **External Leadership.** Award evaluations should give some weight to applicants' efforts to lead and support national and local activities in support of quality and its related infrastructure. This includes assisting suppliers, supporting quality standards, creating community councils, etc.

Figure 12.4 *Design of the Baldridge Award program.*

A board of examiners reviews the written applications for the MBNQA and conducts site reviews. Each of the categories is divided into 24 examination items. The criteria have continued to evolve over the years. Two awards can be given each year in each category: manufacturing, service, or small business. The award is presented annually by the president or the secretary of commerce. Organizations winning the award are permitted to use their achievement as a bragging point in their advertising.

Award applicant review is based on the following categories and criteria

- **Leadership**

  Focal point: How a company's senior leaders set directions and build and sustain a leadership system conducive to high performance.

- **Strategic Planning**

  Focal point: Strategic and business planning and deployment of plans.

- **Customer and Market Focus**

  Focal point: How the company seeks to understand the voices of customers and of the marketplace.

- **Information and Analysis**

  Focal point: The management and effective use of data and information to support key company processes and performance management systems.

- **Human Resource Develeopment and Management**

  Focal point: All key human resource practices—directed toward the development of a high-performance workplace and the development of employees.

- **Process Management**

  Focal point: All key work processes.

- **Business Results**

  Focal point: The company's performance and improvement in key business areas.

Organizations applying for or winning the award have reported that the most valuable aspect of their resource investment was the significant improvement in all operations and in customer satisfaction. The award has been motivational in that respect.

Communications

The MBNQA has had an impact on American business, directly on those who have applied/won, and indirectly on others. For those who have not paid attention or understood the implications, they are not aware of how much they are drifting outside the mainstream of the successful business community. Thier emphasis on short-term financial results may prove to be very costly in the long run.

Every year a Quest for Excellence conference is held to provide a forum for the previous year's award winners to discuss their experiences and lessons learned. The conference gives attending business leaders the opportunity to listen and question the winning companies' management teams. Audiotapes of past conferences are available. According to Dr. C. Reiman, former director of the Baldrige Award Office, speaking at the 1998 conference, the award has created significant change:

- The performance gap between the Baldrige winners and typical companies was getting larger. This causes problems in the supply chain.

- The award criteria have changed from a focus on quality improvement to one of overall performance excellence and the constant transformation of the workplace.

Other awards are:

- U.S. Senate Award. The U.S. Senate provides an annual award to organizations in each state that have demonstrated to an examining board that they have achieved significant quality improvement. Each state has developed its own criteria, and winners are chosen by the state's senators.

- The European Economic Community (EEC) has established a European Quality Award.

- *Quality Digest* magazine publishes a yearly listing of U.S. states that administer quality awards.

Comparisons

There are some differences between the awards, primarily a matter of emphasis:

- Deming Prize. Requires organization-wide involvement and improvement. The wide application of statistical methods is emphasized. Methods and results are evaluated.

- Baldrige Award. Similar to the Deming Prize, with emphasis on improvements over time and objective evidence of customer satisfaction. Applies to industry, service, and small business.

- Senate Awards. Most are similar to the Baldrige Award.

- ISO 9000. Requires systems and procedures to plan, implement, manage, and control quality. It is currently not performance oriented.

REFERENCES

1. K. A. Trautman. *The FDA and Worldwide Quality System Requirements Guidebook for Medical Practices* (Milwaukee: ASQC Quality Press, 1996.)

ADDITIONAL READINGS

Bemowski, K., and B. Stratton. "How Do People Use the Baldrige Award Criteria?" ASQ *Quality Progress* (May 1995).

Benson, R. S., and R. W. Sherman. "ISO 9000: A Practical, Step-By-Step Approach." ASQ *Quality Progress* (October 1995).

Kessler, S. *Total Quality Services: A Simplified Approach to Using the Baldrige Award Criteria*. ASQ Quality Press, 1995.

Malcolm Baldrige National Quality Award Business Case Study Packages. Available from ASQ Quality Press, Milwaukee.

Memory Jogger 9000. Methuen, MA, GOAL/QPC, 1996.

Nakhai, B., and J. J. Never. "The Deming, Baldrige, and European Quality Awards." ASQ *Quality Progress* (April 1994).

Struebing, L. "9000 Standards." ASQ *Quality Progress* (January 1996).

Chapter 13

Quality Function Deployment (QFD)

- **Purpose and Applications**

The purpose of QFD is to ensure that the initially required quality is rpoduced in every stage of product and process development. The objective, in every step, is to ensure that customer requirements are accurately identified and then maintained in every decision and activity involved in product delivery. Thus, quality is methodically deployed to ensure that the customer receives the product or service exactly as initially identified. Using QFD is a recognition that quality is produced by a sequence of planned and controlled events, that is, the concept, design, production, and quality system. QFD also recognizes that a product usually consists of a system of assembled parts. Achieving quality requires the control of the decisions in the assembly system and of the processes that affect it. This is the quality function that is deployed to achieve customer satisfaction. In some form, QFD is useful in any business or nonbusiness process to assure that requirements initially established are actually maintained.

QFD is a planning methodology, used most effectively by teams, particularly knowledgeable teams that have a clear understanding of organization practices and processes. The inputs to the plan are multifunctional. QFD can vary in its application from a one-step product definition (one matrix) to a complex detailed plan of all the steps in the design, production, and control process, through to delivery. The determinate of its complexity is dependent on the extent of the resources that management commits to this planning and definition activity and the complexity of the products and process. It is also an iterative methodology. It isn't likely that the first plan will satisfactorily yield all of the final answers. But that is one of its strengths; QFD will yield the best answer. Comprehensively applied, it forces answers to important design, process, and control issues before committing to production, that otherwise would not be faced until later in time. Without this planning, issues faced in production stages have to be settled with shortsighted compromises. This often results in a product with the original requirements compromised and less than the customer expected.

The time spent using QFD, beginning at the period of concept, has proved to reduce time to market by forcing all functions to make detailed decisions together, which results in product and process integration. This avoids most later design changes, with their attendant costly delays and product quality compromises. Using QFD can surface the lack of information needed to make good design decisions—that is, function, tolerances, materials, and manufacturing capabilities. Making this known early supports the need for such activities as building evaluation models and experimentation. Without this advanced disclosure, it is easier to postpone or avoid these valuable steps and face them later at higher cost.

QFD is a major improvement tool because it is system and process oriented. Traditional organization functions are secondary to planning the integration of their activities in technical detail. In this respect, QFD can even be classified as an organization development tool. Not only do functions have to become process oriented, but QFD demands useful information from the cost and information systems and support functions. QFD also benefits from the application of the problem-solving tools used in continuous process improvement. The initial steps, defining a concept in terms of customer requirements and design characteristics, can be very abstract. This is an ideal application of the seven management tools, the affinity diagram in particular (see Chapter 10).

The QFD technique is to thoroughly explore, define, and convert customer requirements into design characteristics, through to the part level, and then into the required manufacturing processes and controls. The mechanism to achieve and display the results is by matrix diagram that presents one set of ideas or data type against those of another, thereby providing a means to evaluate their relationships.

A completed plan to present a description of all the design features and manufacturing processes would be a series of interlinked matrices (decisions on one matrix drive the next, as depicted in Figure 13.1). After defining customer requirements— that is, the voice of the customer—the next step is to translate those requirements into technical requirements. Figure 13.2 illustrates this translation for a clothespin and a coffee cup. Figure 13.3 is an example for a service organization.[1]

In QFD, the simple matrix format is expanded to extract more information, as shown in Figures 13.4 and 13.5. Figure 13.6 shows a completed house of quality for the initial step in a car door design. This matrix would likely be completed by a team composed of marketing and engineering specialists. The matrix depth of detail is determined by the team. The matrix features are, briefly

1. Design characteristics. These are related to and affect several customer requirements. Those characteristics are measurable and affect customer perceptions. Their integrity must be maintained throughout the production process to ensure customer acceptance.

2. Customer perception. This is an evaluation collected from customer comments comparing the company's car to others' cars. This provides a basis for deciding priorities for design changes.

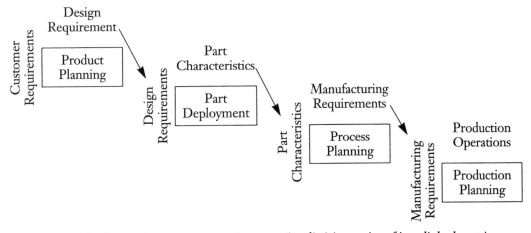

The result of deploying the customer requirements (quality) is a series of interlinked matrices defining all the important design decisions, production process descriptions, and controls. Sub-matrices for any of the four can provide detail to the degree desired. All entries on a matrix are tied to the original customer requirements.

Figure 13.1 *Depiction of matrix relationships.*

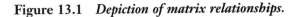

The Customers' Requirements	Examples of Translations into Technical Support

Clothespin

Grips things tightly ——————————— Gripping force
Easy to push/clamp on/off ———————— Force to load
                                   Force to unload

Don't mar/stain items ———————————— Stain absorption/transfer ratio
Resists weather damage—————————— Ultraviolet exposure hours
                                   Environmental test hours

Lasts a long time————————————————— Cycle life hours
Doesn't break/come apart ————————— Break force
Doesn't tangle ——————————————————— Time to grasp and apply
Can write on for record ——————————— Surface friction
                                   Absorption rate
                                   Square inches of surface

Coffee cup

Cup stays cool ——————————————————— Temperature at hand
Coffee stays hot ————————————————— Fluid temperature loss over time
Won't spill/tip ——————————————————— Tip force at top
                                   Fluid loss vertical impact
                                   Fluid loss horizontal impact

Resists squeeze—————————————————— Indent/force relation
                                   Force/set relation rule

Doesn't leak ————————————————————— Porosity

Figure 13.2 *Translating customer requirements into technical requirements.*
Source: Ronald G. Day, *Quality Function Deployment: Linking a Company with It's Customers* (Milwaukee: ASQC Quality Press, 1993).

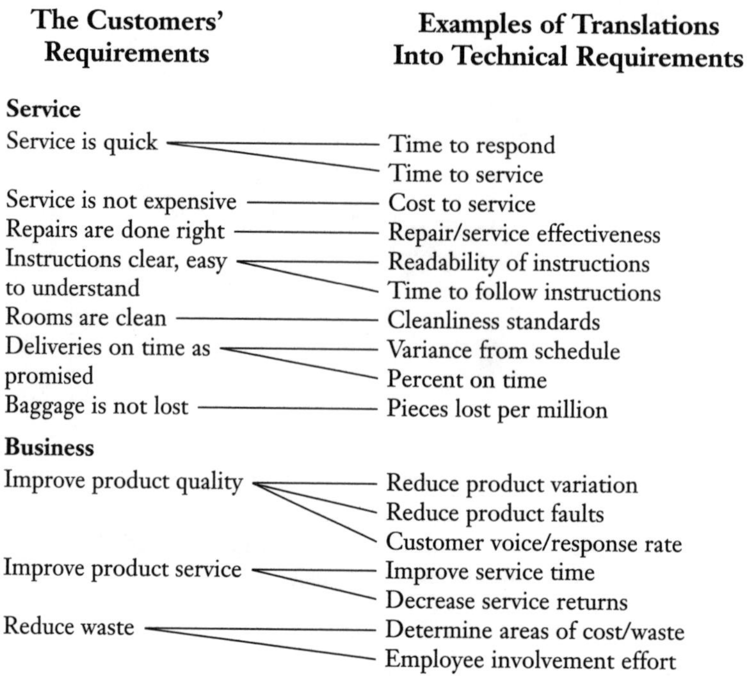

The Customers' Requirements	Examples of Translations Into Technical Requirements

Service

Service is quick ——————— Time to respond
———————— Time to service

Service is not expensive ——————— Cost to service
Repairs are done right ——————— Repair/service effectiveness
Instructions clear, easy ——————— Readability of instructions
to understand ——————— Time to follow instructions
Rooms are clean ——————— Cleanliness standards
Deliveries on time as ——————— Variance from schedule
promised ——————— Percent on time
Baggage is not lost ——————— Pieces lost per million

Business

Improve product quality ——————— Reduce product variation
——————— Reduce product faults
——————— Customer voice/response rate
Improve product service ——————— Improve service time
——————— Decrease service returns
Reduce waste ——————— Determine areas of cost/waste
——————— Employee involvement effort

Figure 13.3   *Translating customer requirements into technical requirements in non-product applications*

Source: Ronald G. Day, *Quality Function Deployment: Linking a Company with It's Customers* (Milwaukee: ASQC Quality Press, 1993).

3. Relationships. The strengths between attributes and characteristics (no symbols or too many weak relationships) are an indication that some customer requirements are inadequately addressed. Conflicting requirements are also identified and resolved.

4. Objective measures. These are a comparison of in-house evaluations of design characteristics against the customer's competitive perceptions. A lack of correlation would suggest that a different characteristic is needed to satisfy the requirement.

Targets are the design characteristics to be attained on the final product. They are established based on customer importance, difficulty, and cost.

The roof matrix is for correlation between characteristics. The objective is to determine the effect of one feature on the others. High correlation indicates product features that must be given consistent attention.

Figure 13.7 is an example of a completed matrix for the good operation and use requirement for a car door. To carry this first customer design evaluation in the direction of production of an actual door, all the customer design characteristics would have to be evaluated. Then the design characteristics would have to be

QFD "House of Quality"

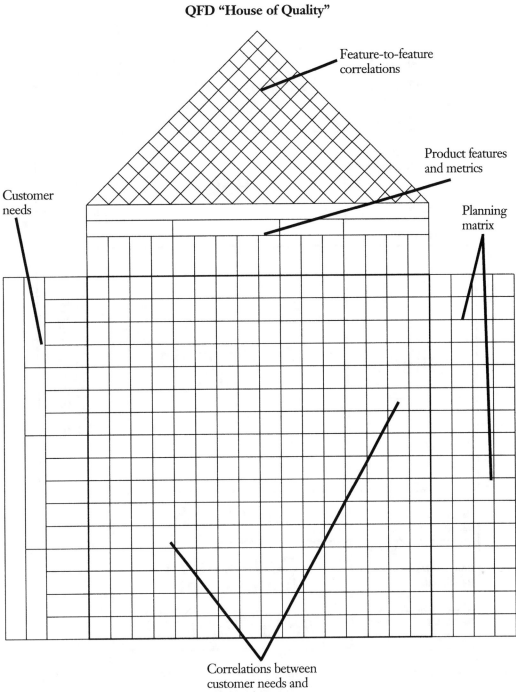

Figure 13.4 *The QFD matrix expanded to evaluate/compare other relationships.*

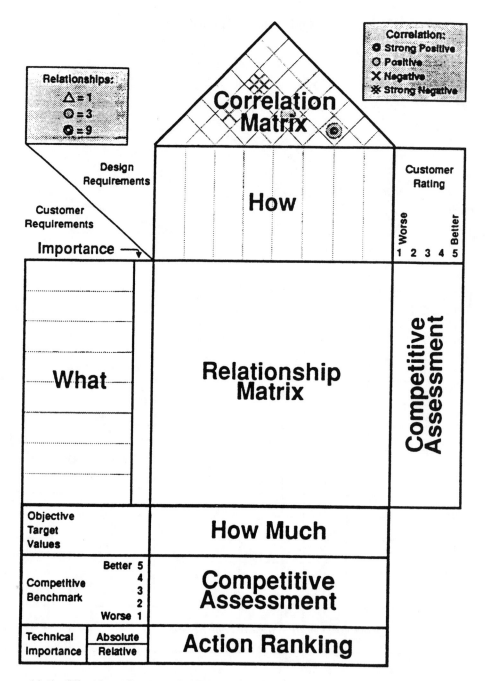

Figure 13.5   *The identification of all the types of evaluations that can be made by QFD teams, from the initial what and how elements.*

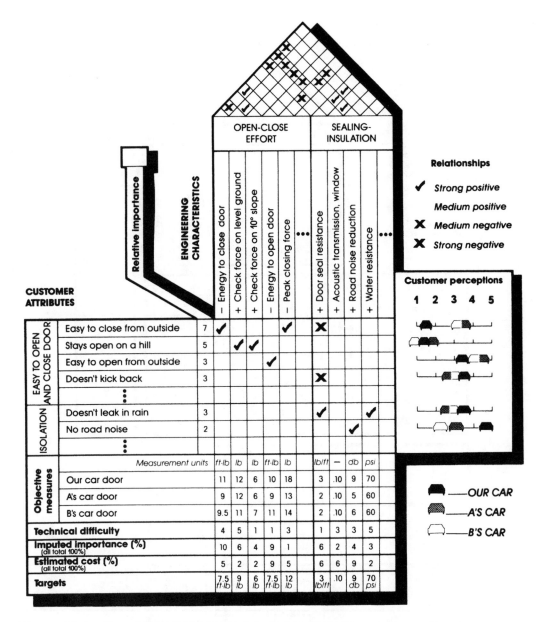

Figure 13.6 *Completed QFD matrix for car door design.*
Reprinted by permission of *Harvard Business Review.* An exhibit from "The House of Quality" by John R. Houser and Don Clausing, May/June 1988. Copyright © 1988 by the President and Fellows of Harvard College, all rights reserved.

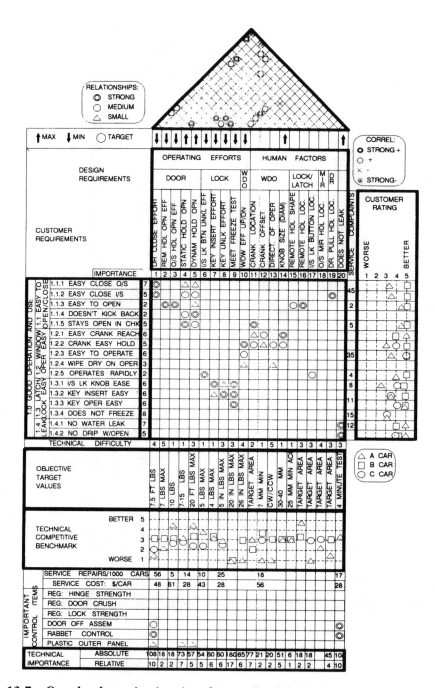

Figure 13.7 *Completed matrix picturing the completed decision process for the good operation and use requirement for a car door.*

Reprinted with permission of American Supplier Institute, Inc., of Dearborn, Michigan (U.S.A.).

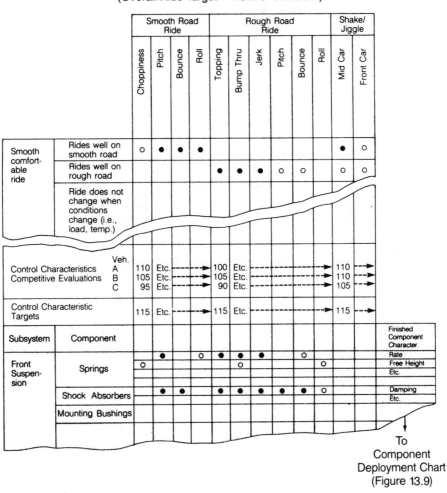

Finished component characteristic deployment matrix
From Planning Matrix
(Overall Ride Target—115% of Vehicle Z)

Figure 13.8   *Deployment matrix of one characteristic—Smooth ride.*
Reprinted with permission from ASQ *Quality Progress*, June 1986.

developed into a specific door part definition and then into the manufacturing processes for each part as well as the finished doors, using the interrelated matrices depicted in Figure 13.2

Figure 13.8 is an example of another matrix series that shows a component traced from a customer requirement for a smooth ride through several submatrices. The component "spring" is selected to display further quality deployment.

One characteristic, shown in Figure 13.9 is spring length. The process plan, shown in Figure 13.10, indicates that the spring wire is to be drawn and cut to length. It also notes the process controls to be used. Figure 13.11 shows the quality control plan for the process.

Component Deployment Chart

From Component Deployment Matrix (Figure 13.8)

Component	Finished Component Characteristic	Critical Component Part Characteristic
Spring	Rate	Wire Diameter Hardness Etc.
	Free Height	Wire Length Etc.
	Etc.	

To
Process Plan and
Control Charts
(Figure 13.10)

Figure 13.9   *Deployment matrix of one characteristic—Spring lengths.*
Reprinted with permission from ASQ *Quality Progress*, June 1986.

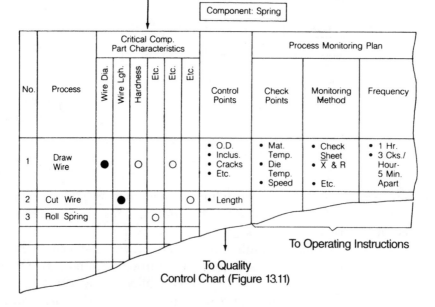

From Component Deployment Matrix (Figure 13.9)

Component: Spring

No.	Process	Wire Dia.	Wire Lgh.	Hardness	Etc.	Etc.	Etc.	Control Points	Check Points	Monitoring Method	Frequency
1	Draw Wire	●		O		O		• O.D. • Inclus. • Cracks • Etc.	• Mat. Temp. • Die Temp. • Speed	• Check Sheet • X̄ & R • Etc.	• 1 Hr. • 3 Cks./ Hour- 5 Min. Apart
2	Cut Wire		●			O		• Length			
3	Roll Spring			O							

Critical Comp. Part Characteristics — Process Monitoring Plan

To Operating Instructions

To Quality
Control Chart (Figure 13.11)

Figure 13.10   *Process plan and control chart.*
Reprinted with permission from ASQ *Quality Progress*, June 1986.

Quality Control Plan Chart

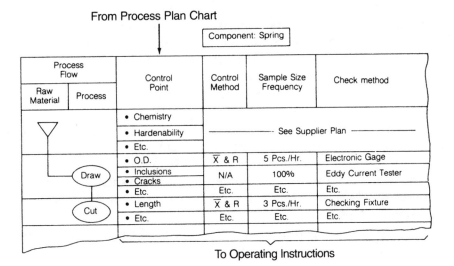

Figure 13.11 *Quality control plan for the process.*
Reprinted with permission from ASQ *Quality Progress,* June 1986.

This overview of QFD illustrates its comprehensive and unique capabilities, beginning with an accurate definition of customer requirements, comparison with competing products, and linking the connection even down to manufacturing work instructions. This structured planning process is bidirectional. If a production process isn't available or can't meet tolerance requirements, this is addressed in the planning stage. Questions that may require a change in design decisions are resolved before production. When a product completes production, it is the product the customer wants.

HINTS FOR SUCCESS

1. Recognize that the use of QFD requires a significant effort in planning new product design, development, and production processes before release to manufacturing. The size of the effort and the effect of the production start are related to the participants' experience with QFD methodology, among the other factors.
2. Begin with a simple pilot program.
3. The initial direction should not be charts for every activity. The GOAL/QPC's approach identifies 30 charts that will adequately plan a complex product.[2]
4. Adapt QFD to fit the organization, product, and process.

QFD is a basic planning methodology that is used for product and service development. It is useful in software development since the initial requirements planning is critical to program success.[3]

The use of QFD faces barriers in initial acceptance because it is labor intensive and typically delays the start of production, when compared to the common practice of independent sequential activities of marketing, design, and then production. Its proved value is that it results in a much smoother introduction into production, or delivery of a service, with many fewer problems, thereby reducing costs and overall cycle time.

QFD also provides valuable documentation of the product concept, requirements, design, and production history. The basis for decisions can be traced for the entire decision-making process. Subsequent product variations can also be better planned and implemented when the original model details are available. Moreover, QFD record is useful as a learning resource for new employees. It might also provide critical information in a product liability law suit.

QFD and Design of Experiments (DOE) are natural partners. This is illustrated in the example in Appendix A.

REFERENCES

1. R.G. Day. *Quality Function Deployment: Linking a Company with Its Customers* (Milwaukee: ASQC Quality Press, 1993).

2. B. King. *Better Designs in Half the Time* (Meuthen, MA: GOAL/QPC, 1989).

3. R.E. Zultner. "Software Quality Function Deployment: Applying QFD to Software." ASQ, Rocky Mountain Quality Conference, Denver, CO, 1989.

ADDITIONAL READINGS

Bossert, J. L. *Quality Function Deployment: A Practicioner's Approach*. Milwaukee: ASQC Quality Press, 1990.

Cohen, L. *Quality Function Deployment: How to Make QFD Work for You*. Milwaukee: ASQC Quality Press, 1995.

Chapter 14

Concurrent Engineering (CE)

- **Getting Started**
- **Factors in Success**
- **Examples of Using CE**

Concurrent/simultaneous engineering and the factors in product design were mentioned in Chapter 6. This chapter discusses more of the factors involved in performing CE.

CE is a methodology for the design, development, and manufacture of products that meet the market/customer demand for high quality, low cost, and fast delivery. From the design standpoint, higher quality includes satisfactory functional performance, reliability, and maintainability. The internal customer (of a design) is the manufacturing process, whether internal to the company or as subcontractors and suppliers. Manufacturing requirements are completeness, low cost, producibility, and, in the case of many products, what is called testability—that is, that product that can be thoroughly and economically evaluated for performance during the production cycle.

Lower costs result primarily from design simplicity, ease of manufacture, and the avoidance of design changes once the production begins. They are also dependent on understanding and preparing for the important product control parameters and levels to be maintained during manufacturing.

Faster deliveries—the time from concept to shipment—are a result of optimizing the requirements just discussed. They have become an important competitive factor. The highest profits for new products are realized in the initial periods after introduction—that is, until competition arrives and drives prices down. A rapid development-production cycle will ensure high profits and product leadership.

CE is the integration of improvement philosophy, tools, and techniques to the design-manufacturing process in combination with the tools and techniques of computer-aided design and manufacturing. It provides a methodology for managing and conducting the activity.

The most important CE management method is the use of multifunctional teams from product concept to manufacturing stability. It supersedes the traditional serial method of design and manufacturing whereby marketing gave engineering the general requirements for a product, engineering gave manufacturing a product design specification to meet the requirements, and manufacturing then figured out how to make the product and what it would cost. Suppliers, who typically provide a large percentage of the final product content, were in the same boat. Frequently, engineering had also already determined, through discussions and prototype building, which suppliers would be used. Organizational functional barriers were at their strongest. The marketplace got whatever came out of this sequence. It didn't exceed the competition.

What was missing was a systematic integrated approach to fully utilize all the untapped knowledge and skills of the people in an organization in a timely and effective manner. Timely does not refer to schedule but to getting the proper type of inputs to the design-manufacturing process at the time they can be most effective in decision making. It involves asking the important questions about function, complexity, materials, tolerances, processes, and so on in the early design phases by specialists who can contribute to the answer and by using techniques such as DOE to obtain the correct answers. Clearly, this all also involves effective communication and useful information systems. It is also a different way to manage. The various organization functional elements have to cooperate more intimately.

GETTING STARTED

Initiating a CE methodology isn't easy. A significant portion of this book describes the difficulties in converting to a continuous improvement philosophy. It involves changing the independent practices people have been taught and practiced. Achieving this with a highly intelligent and educated group that was accustomed to being in control and who were educated to solve difficult problems and make independent decisions may be the most difficult of all.

1. The first step is to expose top key managers and technical decision makers to the CE concept, elements, process, and benefits. Companies already on the improvement path find this easier to do since CE is a special and comprehensive application of the improvement philosophy. If a company has not adopted the improvement model, implementing CE is more difficult. In this setting it may yield useful results but will not near its total potential.

2. The top-level group should identify an important new product to be developed using CE. Boeing Commercial Aircraft Company, for example, successfully used it to develop its new 777 aircraft, a product using millions of parts. Years of work on team development preceded this application.

3. A team of key decision makers and specialists should be formed to plan the CE application. The team should represent marketing, engineering, manufacturing, procurement/subcontracting, finance, and quality engineering.

4. The team must be given fundamental training in all the improvement principles and techniques. These are the foundation for CE application. A CE team is not just a group of specialists who are assigned to bring their technical skills and traditional way of operating to design a new product. They must understand the proper tools and techniques. The subjects of the training include

- Improvement principles and practices
- Team training
- Seven QC tools
- QFD
- Design for manufacture and assembly
- DOE

5. The team should identify specialized knowledge that may be required and identify the individual(s) who will be on call to supply it.

6. The team should develop a design plan and target schedules. The cost of the effort will be difficult to determine with accuracy because the organizations have no previous experience to use as reference. However, using CE requires extra effort and normally takes longer than the serial approach. This will create some management anxiety, but management must accept the proved fact that the manufacturing cycle will be shorter and cheaper since there will be few engineering changes and few surprises. The final product will also exhibit few problems in the hands of the customer. For example, Hewlett-Packard found that, on a small project that might require from two to five full-time design engineers, it needed only half the time of a production engineer, one-third of a quality engineer's, one-tenth of a buyer's, 20 to 40 percent of a materials engineer's, 10 percent of an accountant's, and 10 percent of the time of an electromagnetic compatibility engineer's.[1] There were others who used even less time. Their contributions are more valuable in design and cost less than the expense of fixing mistakes later.

7. Other working teams required to work on the different facets of the development must be organized and trained to apply improvement tools.

8. The team should follow the general concept represented by Figure 6.5.

9. Key suppliers should be identified and made members of the appropriate teams when the time is right.

FACTORS IN SUCCESS

1. Train all team members in the objectives, methodologies, and tools being used.

2. Communicate with all affected functional organizations as to what the team is doing and how it will operate. If the company or element is not accustomed to this independent method, without preparation, managers will not likely welcome unplanned interference in the operation of their organizations.

3. Collocation of at least the key team members is almost a requirement for successful communication and cooperation. Organizations and even company-wide electronic communications would support communication.

4. Develop adequate database networking and implement the latest design automation.*

5. Include and use supplier knowledge and expertise.

6. Encourage the disclosure of serious problems or limitations.

7. Don't delay developing a CE capability because of limited capital for modern tools. Great benefits can be realized by training and organizing the teams to work together. It's a natural part of the continuous process improvement activities. "The integration of design and manufacturing software, coupled with the aggressive use of digital prototypes and virtual reality, is already helping auto makers cut costs as well as time-to-market."[2]

In 1988, manufacturers of the Lexus automobile broke all records by providing a high quality luxury car three years from design through production. The Ford Motor Co. in 1997 set a goal to complete that same cycle in two years, the Toyota Motor Co. in 18 months. Other auto companies have similar plans.

The goal is to produce a car from concept to delivery without producing a drawing and by having engineering and manufacturing use the same integrated software. (It has been common practice for each function to use its own software, with frequent incompatibilities causing problems.)

This integrated approach will

- Minimize and then eliminate the need for physical prototypes by using digital prototypes.(A digital prototype is a computer digital representation of the vehicle's physical design.)

- Use virtual reality for everything from ergonomic design for all aspects of the car design as well as the design of manufacturing assembly work, for both the production robotics and human work stations.

- Use three-dimensional computers to allow engineers to see and test new concepts, all from computer-aided design data.

This digital technology increasingly allows design and manufacturing engineers to communicate in real time—internally or with subcontractors anywhere in the world. It could be called computer-aided concurrent engineering.

EXAMPLES OF USING CE

1. ITEK Optical Systems Division of Litton Systems, Inc., found that Litton's adoption of TQM and CE created the changed atmosphere to greatly ensure

---

Note: CE has reached a new dimension with the application of even higher-powered computers and software.

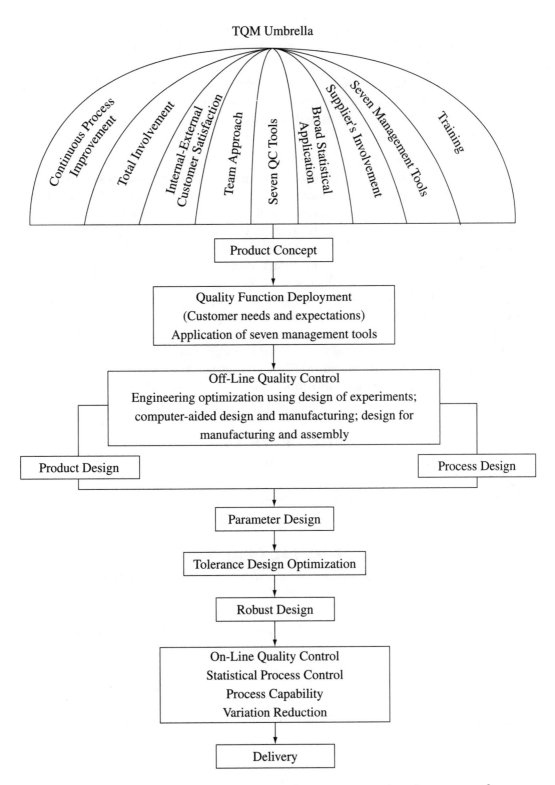

Figure 14.1 *The total quality management and concurrent engineering process of product and process design.*

that all the design and manufacturing factors were considered for one large project (astronomical telescopic glass segments) before beginning manufacturing.

2. John Deere and Co. used CE to cut 30 percent off the cost of developing new construction equipment and 60 percent off development time.

3. AT&T adopted CE and cut in half the time to make an electronic switching system.

CE is an expansion of the Taguchi "off-line and on-line quality control" methodology. Taguchi's particular emphasis was the introduction of a design step he called "parameter design," to identify the nominal values of those parameters that determine product performance during manufacture and customer use. These are also the parameter values that manufacturing must meet to ensure both product performance and high-process yield. The key tool in this methodology is DOE. Its place is illustrated in Figure 14.1. The role of SPC in manufacturing is to indicate how well the important parameters are controlled. All tools and techniques noted are described in various chapters of this book. An example of the use of QFD and DOE, as a CE activity, is described in Appendix A. CE is an obvious reflection of the continuous improvement philosophy applied to the product design manufacturing cycle. It is a different way to manage, in that new products are not the sole domain of engineering. It is a joint venture of the total organization. For it to succeed, teamwork must be valued as highly as technical competence and innovation. The design goal must be not just superior performance but the best total quality.

REFERENCES

1. A. Rosenblatt, and G. Watson. "Concurrent Engineering." IEEE *Spectrum* (July 1991).

2. G. Kaplan. "Auto Manufacturers Digitize in Depth." IEEE *Spectrum* (November 1997).

ADDITIONAL READINGS

Ranky, P.G. *An Introduction to Concurrent/Simultaneous Engineering*. CD ROM. Ridgewood, NJ: CIMware Ltd., 1997. Information at web site http"//www.cimwareukandusa.com

Turing, J. *Concurrent Engineering*. Campbell, CA: Logical Solutions Technology, 1991.

Chapter 15

Design of Experiments

- **The Taguchi Method**
- **The Experimental Process**
- **Methodology**

In the design of products and processes, the common approach has been for engineers to consider one characteristic, or factor, at a time and establish its value and tolerance. The basis for these decisions usually is the designer's knowledge and experience. Sometimes engineering standard practices are followed. The results were acceptable until recently, when higher quality at lower cost became a competitive imperative. This required a new approach to establishing characteristic performance values and more scientific process operating levels.

The most exacting way to do this is to use an experimental technique called design of experiment (DOE). It is a statistically formulated testing technique (based on the analysis of variance) that Fisher developed in England in the mid-1920s. Fisher sought to determine single effects and interactions when he developed DOE. The application was agricultural. The question was the effect that variations in sun, water, temperature, fertilizer, location, and so on had on growth. The tests were run in the field. A "one-variable-at-a-time" procedure could be followed in laboratory experiments, but it would not replicate what is intuitively known—that those variables don't stay constant. They interact, and that interaction can have a major effect on the outcome. The more complex the process, the greater value of DOE. It has been available but seldom used by industry. As the name implies, it is a structure to perform tests (experiments) that are specifically designed to provide information of product performance in its use environment, before production begins. In simple terms, it involves measuring combinations of different product characteristics in the stressful environments a product will encounter during production and final customer use. The significant difference between this and other stress testing is in the application of statistical techniques in the design of the test to disclose performance information not attainable any other way.

One definition of DOE is: "The planned, structured, and organized observation of two or more process input variables and their effect on the output variable(s) under study." The inputs are the independent variables, termed factors; the outputs are the dependent variables.

DOE provides such things as the best product characteristic values (parameters) and process variables settings (factors) that produce the best product performance, with minimum variation. This results in higher production yields and higher reliability to the customer.

The Japanese brought this powerful technique to bear on product and process development through the work of Taguchi. Its application is rapidly growing in the West. Thousands of experiments are conducted in many industries. The statistical theory and a detailed explanation of the design and conduct of experiments are beyond the intent or scope of this book. However, the following is an overview of what DOE is, how it is used, and how it fits with the other improvement tools and practices.

Figure 15.1 identifies typical variables in a manufacturing process. An additional input is the product design in the form of the product configuration (dimensions and materials). The problem is to determine the design tolerances *and* process variables settings, concurrently, that will yield the best product. (The best is one that functions reliably and meets customer needs and expectations.)

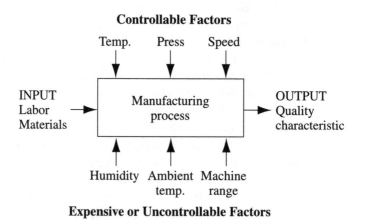

1. Which inputs affect the output parameters? Which process variables?
2. What is the relationship between the important inputs and the output parameters?
3. How can the output be controlled?

Figure 15.1 *Identification of controllable and uncontrollable (actually or financially) variables. A designed experiment can provide answers to the questions.*

The approach is to organize factors and level combinations into test matrices (arrays), and perform the tests. For example, factors could be three casting alloy ingredients, and the levels could be two different mixtures. The different combinations of factors and levels would be set up in a matrix according to a plan. Castings would be poured and the results would indicate which combination of ingredients and mixture produced the best castings. The technique requires a greater test effort in the product development cycle, but it shortens the overall design-to-delivery cycle and minimizes the costly, typical stream of design changes to debug the new product after it starts production.

THE TAGUCHI METHOD

The name Taguchi has become synonymous with DOE and its use in Japan and to a great extent in the United States. Taguchi's contribution made the technique more practicable and affordable compared to the classical, purely statistical approach. In brief, he developed some fixed arrays (experiment matrices) that significantly reduced the number of experiments required for various combinations of factors and levels. The trade-off was an increased risk of not detecting some important interactions. He developed some other supportive analysis techniques, however, referred to as the signal-to-noise ratio to reduce this risk. The risk is also reduced by using knowledgeable process specialists to assist in designing the experiment by selecting the controllable factors that most likely affect variation. Some statisticians have found some difficulty with this short-cut approach to DOE. Taguchi's position is that it is better to do this level of experimentation than none at all. This practical approach was acceptable to engineers who had often taken greater risks in estimating factors using previously acceptable design methods. However, significant progress has been achieved in developing experimental methods for design that maximize the amount of reliable information and minimize the number of tests required. This requires a thorough understanding of the design method before it is attempted, beginning with simple experiments to learn the methodology.

THE EXPERIMENTAL PROCESS

Each process and experiment is unique. There are some basic steps that need to be performed when designing and conducting experiments, and they are included to give some insight to the method. They are shown in Figure 15.2 and summarized briefly as follows.

- Preparation. The main objective of this step is to identify key sources of variation, identify the problem and objectives, and select a team that represents all the skills required to understand the problem and process thoroughly. As a minimum, team members should be trained in problem-solving techniques and the seven QC tools. The team identifies process inputs, measurable process characteristics, and outputs. It must identify the impact of each input factor on the output. If any factors appear difficult to change, they should be held constant during the experiment.

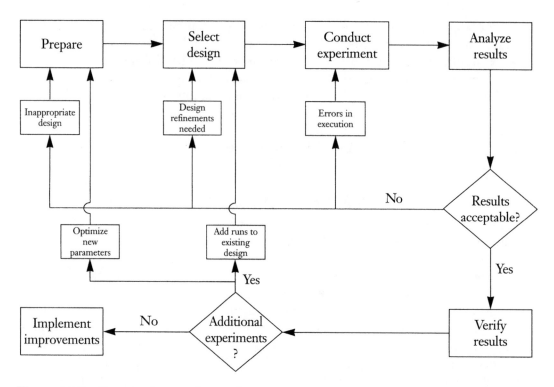

Figure 15.2 *Steps in the experimental process.*

- Selection of design. Engineers trained in the fundamentals of DOE do not usually have difficulty selecting an adequate design (number runs, order, levels, and so forth), but the team should have access to someone with a comprehensive theoretical knowledge of DOE. Major contributors to process variation can usually be isolated, using one or several common designs, with a surprisingly small number of runs.

- Conduct of the experiment. The first step is to recognize the objectives of the experiment. Data interpretation should identify the input variables that most affect the output. A mathematical model can then be prepared that predicts outputs as a function of inputs. If results indicate some interaction between variables, a few more runs would be made to separate them.

- Verification of the tests. In this step, a few runs are made using the values of the variables determined in the experiment to verify that the results can be replicated. This is to gain assurance that the indicated relationship truly exists. This is a highly simplified description of how experiments are conducted. Someone knowledgeable in DOE fundamentals should be involved in every step.

METHODOLOGY

The following steps are important in using DOE.

1. Obtain management support for the implementation of an experiment and approval for the required resources.
2. Select a simple product and process to practice teamwork, methodology, and interpretation of results. This will also aid in educating management to its value and gaining its support.
3. Organize the experiment team with people possessing both technical expertise and operating knowledge of the product and process to be studied. It is also necessary for someone to be fully competent in the application and interpretation of the statistical aspects of constructing the experiment and assisting in interpreting results.
4. Have the team establish objectives, kinds of data and measurements, and method of operating.
5. Perform the process analysis using appropriate QC tools to select the input factors for study. Choose responses to be measured. Select the factor levels.
6. Formulate an experiment design and data sheets.
7. Manipulate the process. Run the experiment.
8. Analyze the results. Draw conclusions. Identify the controlling factors and their levels.
9. Make an experimental confirmation run and identify refinements.

Although the emphasis in the use of DOE has been on industrial processes, Koselka describes some other applications.[1] For example, a sneaker manufacturer that was planning an expensive, high-tech advertising display evaluated its plan against other lower-cost approaches using DOE. The result was a much less costly display that boosted sales by 35 percent. Another application was the successful improvement of Southwestern Bell service calls. DOE has application in all instances in which there are several variables that can affect the response.

Figure 15.3 is a simple, nonindustrial example that illustrates the method. It is an experiment to select the best combination of price, advertising, and layaway to maximize the sales of packages of golf balls.

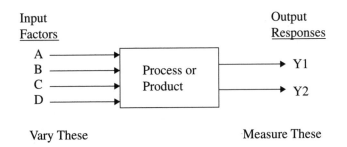

Figure 15.3 *Identify important input factors, vary them (different orders and combinations), and measure the effect on the process.*

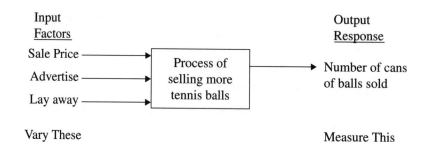

Figure 15.3 *Objective: Determine the combination of input factors that sells the most packages of golf balls.*

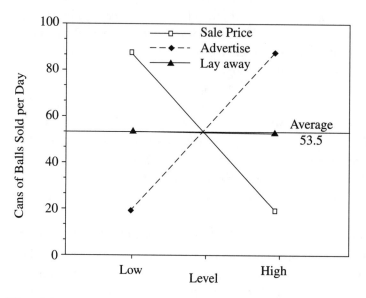

Figure 15.3 *Plotted Sales Results*

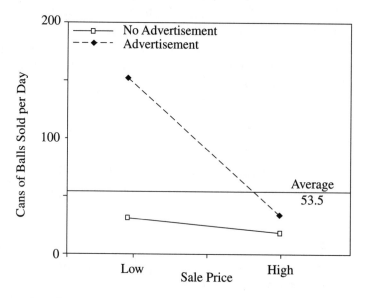

Figure 15.3 *continued*

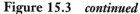

The Experiment Matrix (Aray) and Results

Price	Advertise	Lay Away	Sales
low	No	No	28
Regular	No	No	12
Low	Yes	No	152
Regular	Yes	No	24
Low	No	Yes	22
Regular	No	Yes	16
Low	Yes	Yes	148
Regular	Yes	Yes	26

Figure 15.3 *continued*

Conclusion:

1. To sell the most golf balls.
   • Offer a sale price
   • Advertise
2. This should result in an expected daily sale of about 150 cases of balls.
3. Lay away doesn't matter.

REFERENCES

1. R. Koselka. "The New Mantra MVT." *Forbes Magazine* (March 1996).

ADDITIONAL READINGS

Montgomery, D.C. *Design and Analysis of Experiments*, 4th ed. Milwaukee: ASQ Quality Press, 1997.

Pugh, G.A. *Industrial Experiments Without Statistical Pain.* Milwaukee: ASQC Quality Press, 1994.

Ross, P.J. *Taguchi Techniques for Quality Engineering*, 2nd ed. Milwaukee: ASQC Quality Press, 1996.

Appendix A

Example of the Application of QFD and Design of Experiments to a Product

QUALITY FUNCTION DEPLOYMENT

QFD is a way to connect customer requirements through many activities to production requirements.

Each of the connecting arrows in Figure A.1 represents a matrix that can be generated, but what other opportunities exist to make sure customer requirements are met more consistently? A QFD matrix (Figure A.2) can be used to provide four pieces of information:

1. What is important to the customer?
2. How is it provided?
3. The relationships between the whats and hows.
4. How much must be provided by the hows to satisfy customers?

Designed experiments provide information concerning the real relationships that exist in the matrices.

QFD for a transmission casting is shown simplistically by the overlapping matrices shown in Figure A.3. Matrix A.1 relates the voice of the customer (VOC) to the systems that provide those functions. Matrix A.2 relates the systems to the parts in the systems. Matrix A.3 relates the parts to the specifications for those parts. Matrix A.4 relates the specifications to the processes that generate those specifications. Matrix A.5 relates the processes to the production requirements to run the processes.

Source: P. J. Ross, President, Quality Services International, Inc., from his article entitled, "The Role of Taguchi Methods and Design of Experiments in QFD," ASQ *Quality Progress* (June 1988).

Quality Function Deployment

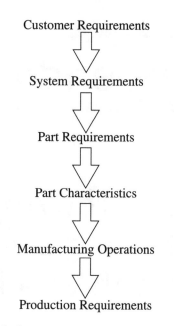

Customer Requirements

System Requirements

Part Requirements

Part Characteristics

Manufacturing Operations

Production Requirements

Figure A.1   *Quality function deployment.*

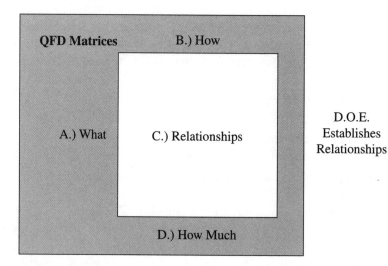

QFD Matrices   B.) How

A.) What   C.) Relationships

D.) How Much

D.O.E.
Establishes
Relationships

Figure A.2   *QFD matrices.*

Further development of matrices is possible into the production control methods, etc. The matrix process can start with a system or parts within a system, if desired—as long as the VOC is heard.

QUALITY FUNCTION DEPLOYMENT

QFD is a way to connect customer requirements through many activities to production requirements. Each of the connecting arrows in Figure 1 represents a matrix that can be generated, but what other opportunities exist to make sure customer requirements are met more consistently? A QFD matrix (Figure 2) can be used to provide four pieces of information.

1. What is important to the customer?
2. How is it provided?
3. The relationships between the whats and hows
4. How much must be provided by the hows to satisfy customers?

Designed experiments provide information concerning the real relationships that exist in the matrices.

QFD for a transmission casting is shown simplistically by the overlapping matrices shown in Figure 3. Matrix 1 relates the voice of the customer (VOC) to the systems that provide those functions. Matrix 2 relates the systems to the parts in the systems. Matrix 3 relates the parts to the specifications for those parts. Matrix 4 relates the specifications to the processes that generate those specifications. Matrix 5 relates the processes to the production requirements to run the processes.

Further development of matrices is possible into the production control methods, etc. The matrix process can start with a system or parts within a system, if desired—as long as the VOC is heard.

In reference to Figure A.3, does mold time, pour tempeature, cooling time, etc., really hear the VOC saying the transmission should last a long time?

SIMULTANEOUS ENGINEERING

QFD, for the first time, provides a means to operationalize simultaneous engineering (SE). The information in the various matrices requires that different groups of individuals reach consensus on the product, process, and production requirements necessary to effectively meet customer requirements (Figure A.4).

In the past, different organizations and different locations for people have been used to try to create SE, but usually without any means for accomplishing SE. The result is a less effective throw-it-over-the-wall approach.

CASTING PRODUCTION REQUIREMENTS

Consider a case study concerning a problem in production where a percentage of center support castings were cracked at the end of the casting process. About 10% of the castings had cracks that violated the wall thickness requirements per the center support drawing.

QFD for Transmission Casting

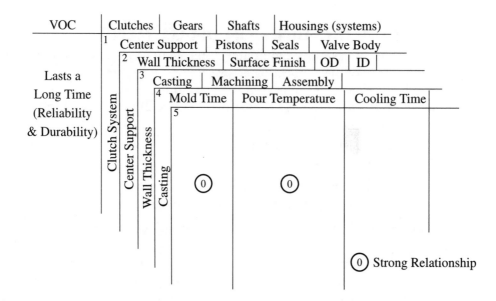

Figure A.3 *QFD for transmission casting.*

Concurrent (Simultaneous) Engineering

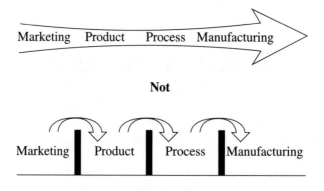

Figure A.4 *Concurrent (simultaneous) engineering.*

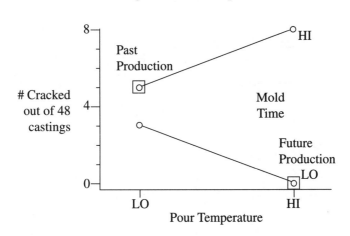

Figure A.5 *Center support casting production requirements.*

Of all the factors studied in a designed experiment, the two that really controlled the quality of the castings were time and temperature (Figure A.5). Engineering had recently run production at the conditions of high time and low temperature, based on their experience, to prevent cracks. However, the process obviously needs to be run at the condition of low time and higher temperature to avoid any cracking. The results of the experiment were confirmed over the next 1,5000 castings and provided a cost savings of over $15,000 per year in scrap and inspection avoidance. The designed experiment established the real relationships and strengths of relationships in the QFD matrices.

In many cases, Taguchi Methods are applied to a current production problem to improve quality when this could have been done much earlier in the design phase of the process (off-line QC).

QFD matrices for an engine cam follower (Figure A.6) are very similar to the ones in Figure A.3, but in this case the cam follower relates to more items in the VOC. Again, do the process parameters hear the VOC?

HEAT TREAT PRODUCTION REQUIREMENTS

A designed experiment was applied to the problem of meeting the height requirements for a cam follower. The results indicated that the amount of ammonia had a strong influence on controlling the change in height experienced during heat treat. The past production standard of 5 cubic feet caused a lot of batch-to-batch variation in height due to the precision of the ammonia measuring system (Figure A.7). When the process was adjusted to the 8.75 cubic feet value, the batch-to-batch variation was reduced greatly without incurring the cost of improving the ammonia measuring system. The cost of the additional ammonia was less than a penny per batch.

QFD for Engine Cam Follower

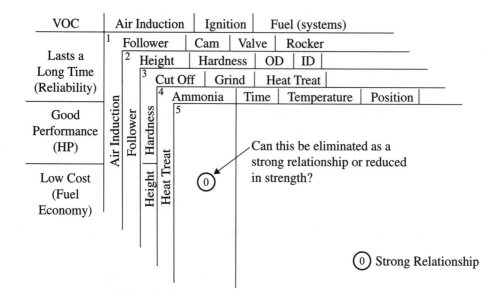

Figure A.6   *QFD for engine cam follower.*

**Follower Heat Treat
Production Requirements**

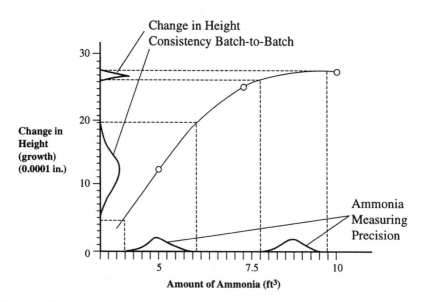

Figure A.7   *Follower heat treat production requirements.*

Genichi Taguchi calls this concept parameter design. The idea is to reduce variation by selecting appropriate levels of control factors without increasing cost or unnecessarily controlling any noise factors. Control factors are those factors that a manufacturer can set and customers can do little about. (A noise factor, on the other hand, is something a manufacturer cannot control or wishes not to control in a manufacturing or customer environment.) This experiment actually eliminated a critical process parameter from the QFD matrix.

The castin gexample and the engine example demonstrated how production requirements could relate back to product specifications. Other experiments could relate product specifications back to customer requirements or system requirements. Product experiments should precede process experiments to ferret out true critical characteristics; however, parameter design should be done whenever possible. In the engine example, reliability, horsepower, fuel economy, or air induction system requirements could relate to part specifications.

A part of the house of quality not discussed so far, the roof, shows which system requirements may affect one antoher during development. Some effort is required to understand what to include in the experiments and the compromises that may have to be made for optimum system performance.

COMPLEMENTARY TOOLS

In today's competitive environment, customers demand and can obtain high value-added products that are quite consistent in the way they perform. This sums up the DOE Taguchi approach to product and process development, which attempts to minimize losses (high value-added) by improving consistency of performance.

Quality function deployment also has become an accepted and powerful tactic for assuring that customer requirements are consistently met. The different relationships are consistently met. The different relationships of customer needs to systems, to parts, to part characteristics, to process, to production requirements, help transmit the customer's voice throughout the business.

These two quality tools of DOE and QFD are complementary. QFD can help identify key product or process concerns with respect to customer requirements. Designed experiments, can help identify what product or process relationships truly exist. Designed experiments not only identify which relationships exist, but also their relative strengths and the nature of the relationship. Taguchi concepts such as parameter design also tend to minimize the number of highly critical product or process parameters.

All of these activities should occur during the offline phase of a product or process life cycle. By simultaneously improving quality (improving consistency), lowering losses, and identifying key product and process characteristics before production begins, manufacturers will be able to enter their chosen market on a highly competitive basis from several different viewpoints of quality.

Phillip J. Ross is the President of Quality Services International, Inc. He holds a BME from General Motors Institute.

Appendix B

Benchmark Case Study: Housekeeping System Cycle Time Reduction at The Ritz-Carlton Hotel Company

Prepared with the cooperation of Judy N. Kirk, quality leader, with process analysis prepared by Alan F. Galanty, cycle time advisor, The Ritz-Carlton Hotel Company, Dearborn, Michigan

- Background
- Customer Requirements
- Organizations or Industries Benchmarked
- Best Practices Learned
- Actions Taken
- Summary

BACKGROUND

The Ritz-Carlton Hotel Company successfully operates in one of the most logistically complex service businesses. Targeting primarily industry executives, meeting and corporate travel planners, and affluent travelers, the Atlanta, Georgia-based company manages 30 luxury hotels while pursuing the distinction of being the best in each mar-

Source: R. C. Camp, "Business Process Benchmarking: Finding and Implementing Best Practices," Milwaukee: ASQC Quality Press, 1995.

ket. The hotel company builds it success on the strength of a comprehensive service quality initiative, which is integrated into its marketing and business objectives.

Winner of the 1992 Malcolm Baldrige National Quality Award, The Ritz-Carlton Hotel Company operates business and resort hotels in the United States, Europe, Hong Kong, Mexico, and Australia. It has 13 international sales offices and employs 13,500 people. Restaurants and banquets are also marketed heavily to local residents. The company claims distinctive facilities and environments, highly personalized anticipatory services, and exceptional food and beverages.

The Ritz-Carlton, Dearborn is close to downtown Detroit, Michigan, and the city's airport and business district. It houses 308 guest rooms, including 15 suites. The hotel features full service and a la carte dining and over 20,000 square feet of meeting space, including two ballrooms and several conference rooms. A fitness center is complete with indoor lap pool and whirlpool spa. Additional hotel amenities include private concierge service, 24-hour room service, valet, and personal guest profile capability.

Focus/Topic

Through focus groups and independent marketing surveys, The Ritz-Carlton Hotel Company identified several hotel processes that were highly important to customers. These processes, however, were also given low satisfaction ratings. Thus, the company set out to accomplish several tasks at the corporate level.

- Identify what was important to customers and how they rated those features.
- Complete a gap analysis.
- Identify the primary processes and if the company had existing work areas or processes that were aligned to meet those needs.

The company learned two things: (1) There were primary processes common to any hotel, such as housekeeping and front office registration; and (2) there were vital support processes, such as purchasing and human resources for the selection of new employees.

From this research the customers of The Ritz-Carlton Hotel Company identified 19 critical processes as vital to their continuing business decision to loyally patronize the company's properties. Each of The Ritz-Carlton hotels elected one of these processes to investigate in a one-year research study. Then each hotel picked process teams, identified study boundaries, and ran the research process with help from corporate headquarters in Atlanta. This process involved cross-functional teams using a total team approach and scientific methods.

One of the 19 processes that customers identified was a "clean, fresh, fully stocked guest room." The Ritz-Carlton in Dearborn, Michigan, took on the housekeeping system with the goal of creating an error-proof, reliable process that could be standardized within the company to ensure 100 percent customer satisfaction.

Objective/Purpose

Customers indicated that they wanted their hotel services better, faster, cheaper, and with greater reliability than before. It was the aim of the Dearborn process team to identify and reduce waste through process analysis by simplifying, eliminating, and combining steps within the housekeeping system. This was done to meet The Ritz-Carlton Hotel Company's 1996 quality goals of

1. Six sigma
2. 50 percent cycle time reduction
3. 100 percent customer retention

Team Operation

The housekeeping system studied had boundaries of guest arrival through guest departure. The director of housekeeping was the process owner. The team consisted of those individiauls active in the housekeeping system and impacted by any changes to it. Process team members represented the following organizations and individuals.

- Housekeeping, including room attendants, houseperson, and director
- Laundry, including laundry attendants
- Engineering, including preventive maintenance engineer/painter
- Rooms division, including the executive assistant manager of rooms
- Total quality management, including the cycle time advisor, the quality manager/historian, and the quality leader activing as facilitators

The roles of quality leader and cycle time advisor are present in each Ritz-Carlton property as an investment in the company's competitive future. The quality leader advises on the total team approach, team building, and problem-solving techniques. The cycle time advisor contributes scientific techniques of data collection and analysis and statistical process control. Both persons act as change agents to encourage and embrace continuous improvement.

The housekeeping process team met for two-hour weekly meetings beginning in May 1993. Team-building exercises were discussed and practiced at these meetings. A mission statement, from the guidance team of hotel senior leaders, served as the focus of the process team's progress (see Figure B.1). The team used consensus decision making and shared leadership as participative themes in the total team approach to cycle time reduction.

A nine-step quality improvement process benchmarked from Xerox Corporation gave structure to the process identification and analysis. Because of its emphasis on assembly, the Xerox Quality Tool Kit was readily applied by the Dearborn process team. Many hotel functions and processes involve assembling items.

The housekeeping process team will simplify, eliminate, and combine steps resulting in 50 percent housekeeping cycle time reduction and providing clean, fresh, fully stocked guest rooms "right the first time on time" efficiently meeting our guests' key requirements and ensuring 100 percent customer satisfaction.

Figure B.1 *Housekeeping process team mission statement.*
Used with permission of The Ritz-Carlton Hotel Company.

CUSTOMER REQUIREMENTS

By listening to the voice of its customers, The Ritz-Carlton, Dearborn process team learned what was wanted, needed, and expected in a guest room experience. It included the following characteristics.

- A clean, fresh, fully stocked room
- A guest room serviced right the first time
- Few, if any, interruptions
- Short interruptions when they do occur
- Consistent service provided for the stay over
- A room ready when the guest arrives
- A room cleaned at the guest's convenience
- Correct and timely honor bar billing (The honor bar consists of food and beverage items available a la carte in each guest room.)
- The assurance that guest's possessions are safe and secure
- Reduced housekeeping costs and labor

This last characteristics identified the need to eliminate waste. It was an internal customer requirement.

The process team's goal was to meet these external and internal customer needs with reliability, while reducing the overall housekeeping system cycle time by 50 percent. The customers' requirements and The Ritz-Carlton's measures of fulfilling those requirements are illustrated in the house of quality in Figure B.2. Reduced internal costs would increase profitability and market competitiveness for the hotel. The savings would ultimately be shared with the hotel's ladies and gentlemen who contributed to it.

Note that alignment with The Ritz-Carlton Hotel Company's Gold Standards ensures that employees are "ladies and gentlemen serving ladies and gentlemen." This is considered the behavioral standard.

ORGANIZATIONS OR INDUSTRIES BENCHMARKED

Current Process

Consecutive, task-by-task work by one room attendant was the time-honored method of cleaning a guest room. Random sample observations of 30 housekeeping room attendants produced the pie chart shown in Figure B.3. Analysis revealed that the bathroom-cleaning task was the most time-consuming of room-cleaning tasks and the obvious limiting factor.

The process team had already brainstormed the concept of simultaneous work; that is, multiple task completion by a number of room attendants in one guest room. Thus, the team-cleaning concept was born.

The process owner was fortunate to have seen a four-person cleaning team in action at a competitor's hotel in New York City. It referred the process owner to a sister facility on Maui, Hawaii, since this was the only hotel that used teams daily. While

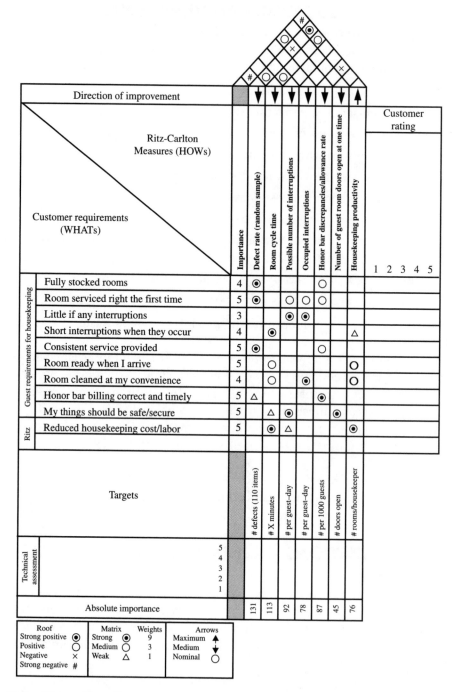

Figure B.2 *House of quality.*
Used with permission of The Ritz-Carlton Hotel Company.

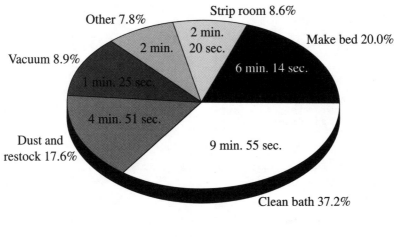

Average room cycle time 26 minutes, 45 seconds;
based on sample size of 30.

Figure B.3 *Five steps in cleaning a room.*

this experience served as an inspiration to the Dearborn team, investigating the competitor's team-cleaning process was neither a reciprocal benchmark nor a tutorial.

Process-to-Process Analysis

The greatest value of investigating the competitor's process was the practical application of team cleaning in daily practice. Operational questions were answered and from that reality check the housekeeping team-cleaning system was customized to meet customer needs at The Ritz-Carlton, Dearborn.

The Pugh concept selection chart of cleaning alternatives facilitated the team pilot process (see Figure B.4). Initially, four-person teams were piloted. After analysis and internal customer feedback, three-person teams were found to have the greatest effectiveness within the housekeeping parameters of The Ritz-Carlton, Dearborn.

Key Measures

Key measures used to collect the baseline data on the reliability of the housekeeping system changes included the following:

1. Defect rate per soom
2. Room cycle time
3. Possible interruption rate
4. Honor bar discrepancies and allowances
5. Housekeeping productivity (rooms cleaned per team)
6. Distance traveled

Measures \ Alternatives	1 person	4 person	3 person	2 person and honor bar attendant	Cartless plus 3 person
Cycle time	↑	+, +	+, +	+	+
Number of guest room doors open		−, −	+	S	+
Defects per room		+	+, +	+	+, +
Possible number of interruptions		+	+	S	+
Honor bar discrepancies and allowances	Baseline	+	+	S	+
Number of occupied interruptions		S	S	S	S
Productivity		+	+	+	+
Cost effectiveness		+	+	+	−, −
Reduce loneliness		+, +	+, +	+, +	+, +
Clear hallway		+	+	+	+, +
Time to implement		+	+	+	−, −
Probability for success (paradigm shift)	↓	−, −	−, −	−	−, −
Total		11 + 4 −	13 + 2 −	8 + 6 −	11 + 6 −

Figure B.4 *Pugh concept selection chart of cleaning alternatives.*

Baseline data collected through random sample techniques and plotted on statistical process control charts proved independent cleaning of a guest room resulted in the following:

1. 7.4 defects
2. A cycle time of 26.45 minutes to clean a room, plus 7 to 10 minutes to service the honor bar
3. Three standard interruptions of maid service, honor bar service, and turndown service
4. Chronic honor bar discrepancies
5. Productivity of 13 guest rooms per attendant
6. 525 feet, or about one-tenth of a mile traveled to clean a guest room.

Benchmarking Partners

Although it was an important discovery, finding the team-cleaning process at a domestic competitor's facility was unplanned. The Ritz-Carlton, Dearborn team did adopt some of the competitor's practices. No other external benchmarking partners were sought.

The Dearborn team sought an internal benchmarking partner at the sister property in Naples, Florida. The Naples team provided new practices to reduce the logo fading and matching on the company's towels.

The Dearborn team also examined one of its member's hospital laundry experiences and elected to modify part of that process to Ritz-Carlton standards. This new practice reduced the handling of linen and terry items during the transportation and distribution processes.

BEST PRACTICES LEARNED

Key Findings

Key in the housekeeping study was the customer-supplier relationships vital to productivity. Housekeeping is the laundry department's primary customer. The entire housekeeping operation can grind to a halt if the supply of clean terry and linen is limited or interrupted. A great deal of time was wasted if room attendants received an inadequate supply of terry and linen items and were forced to go in search of more during their shift. This created slowdowns and rework to reenter rooms to replace missing items. A common practice was hoarding of supplies and hiding them, thus wasting up to 45 minutes daily while collecting materials vital to guest room cleaning.

To combat these recurring problems, a process change spear-headed by the laundry department to listen to the voice of its internal customer occurred. It was determined that the process from soiled to clean terry and linen was needed within the same day. If distribution centers on each guest floor could be stocked by the turndown attendants before the end of their shift, then supplies would be available for the room attendants at the beginning of their shift. Thus, this process would save 30 to 45 minutes per person per day.

After careful analysis and process identification, the laundry pilots were implemented to have sufficient terry and linen processed by 10 P.M. daily to allow for the stocking activity. Reliability of this process has not reached 100 percent, yet significant progress has been made allowing for increased room attendant productivity.

The industry rule of three par of terry was disproved during this study. The normal practice is to have one par of terry in the guest room, one par available for use, and one par in process from soiled to clean. Usage figures showed that hotel guests dirtied only 50 percent of the nine terry items placed in a room. It was learned through guest usage patterns that the hotel could function on 1.5 par of terry on the weekdays and 2.0 on the weekends. The outcome of this discovery was an annual savings of $60,000 in terry purchases.

The greatest paradigm shift of this process study involved the team-cleaning concept. Independent work by 30 individuals was totally impacted by such a change. The normal human response of resistance to accepted and practiced habits was experienced. Behaviors, which had up to five years to develop, were markedly changed. Individual pacing of work, singular patterns of productivity, and personal preferences were all under study. Best practices were revealed through observation, discussion, cycle timings, and work flow diagrams. These superior practices, or "knacks" as Dr. Juran notes, were identified and documented to standardize current best practices for efficiency and reliability.

Potential Opportunity for Improvement

Team cleaning of guest rooms held both tangible and intangible benefits. Tangible benefits included the following:

1. Reduction in room cleaning cycle time by 65 percent of 8 minutes with the added task of servicing the honor bar
2. Reduction in defects per room by 42 percent to 3.7, which translated to a higher reliability in cleanliness factor
3. Reduction of standard guest room interruptions by 33 percent due to combining of honor bar tasks with room cleaning
4. Reduction in time guest would be disturbed if occupying the room at the time cleaning was provided.
5. Increase in the property and life safety for guests and staff due to fewer guest room doors being opened at any one time, as well as the presence of more than one room attendant within a room
6. Increase in productivity from 13 to 15 rooms per person and still increasing with resultant labor savings
7. Reduction in individual travel by 64 percent to 205 feet within a guest room

Intangible benefits of team cleaning included the following:

1. Reduction in loneliness from working independently
2. Increased teamwork through shared tasks and responsibilities
3. Increase in camaraderie and morale from working with others
4. Job enrichment through the team process, which provided coaching, feedback, and stimulation during repetitive housekeeping tasks
5. Increased communication among team members and between guests and team members
6. Increased effect of peer pressure to perform to standards, resulting essentially in self-directed work teams
7. Reduced monotony from switching roles throughout a shift
8. A stronger customer-supplier relationship between the housekeeping and laundry departments

Conclusion

The goal of reducing the housekeeping cycle time by 50 percent was realized and exceeded through this total team study. The external customers have expressed amazement while viewing the room-cleaning process and delight in finding their rooms completely cleaned in such an expeditious manner. A strong contributor to the success of the team-cleaning concept was involving people directly impacted by the housekeeping system and using their expertise to drive change. The benchmark was important to lend credibility to the team's possible solutions, as well as providing evidence of practicality to move forward in piloting teams.

The reduced process time delighted the hotel's customers in another important way. The front office staff benefited greatly from up-to-the-minute room availability. This was accomplished by team self-inspection and status updating directly tied to the hotel's room inventory computer. This practice allowed the front office receptionists to give customers the rooms they wanted. It also reduced the following:

- Customer queue time at the registration desk
- Delays at the front office because the right rooms were available when they were needed
- Defects and errors in out-of-inventory situations

Three important factors contributed to the success of this study.

1. Team meetings were held with the individuals and departments that were impacted by the study and its subsequent changes.
2. Daily lineups at the beginning of each shift served as a means of communication.
3. Staff members were involved and empowered to make changes and to pilot the same.

Two practices that did not work during this study were the following:

1. Small, incremental changes were met with resistance and a "what-next?" attitude. Combined, comprehensive changes were much more welcome by the staff.
2. Managers discussing the team's work and process changes was less effective than peer-to-peer coaching.

ACTIONS TAKEN

Implementation

The implementation of housekeeping teams to clean guest rooms was a task of great proportion as it was a major change in how work was done (see Figures B.5 and B.6). The biggest obstacle was the human response to change or the reengineering of a

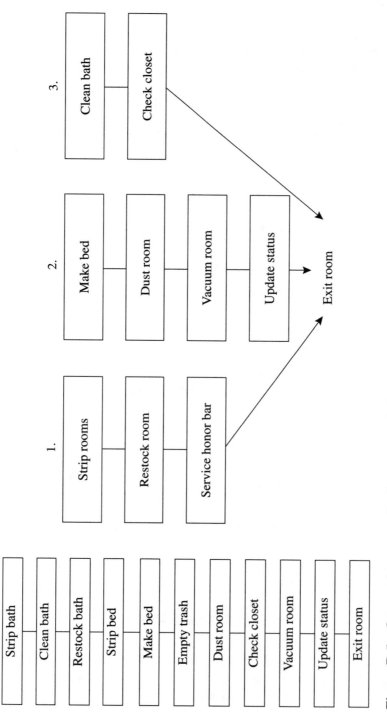

Figure B.5 *Consecutive versus simultaneous work flowchart.*

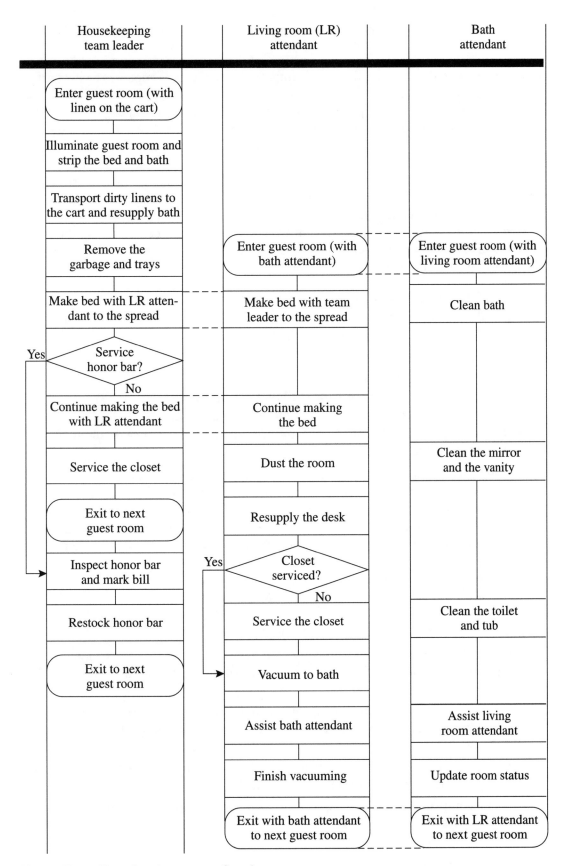

Figure B.6 *Housekeeping process flowchart.*

process. As noted, involving the people impacted by process change was a vital part of the study's overall success. Using a total team approach and scientific tools also markedly increased the acceptability and buy-in of the whole changes.

Large-scale change also took place in the laundry department as it is housekeeping's major supplier. Shift changes to accommodate terry and linen productivity, priority of wash loads, and modified handling of sorted, soiled pieces, all contributed to increase productivity to return cleaned supplies to customers. The room attendants contributed to these handling changes by separating linen and terry on the guest room floors. It was discovered that the room attendants were the only ones who combined terry and linen items throughout the entire soiled-to-clean process. Keeping the items separated throughout the cycle saved time-consuming sorting and reduced the possibility of injury in the laundry chute room.

Planned Changes/Next Steps

The final frontiers to tackle for total process reliability in producing a clean, fresh, fully stocked guest room include the following:

1. Linen distribution system
2. Honor bar servicing system
3. Continuous training process for the housekeeping staff
4. Even use of guest rooms through rotation selling
5. Scheduling of housekeeping teams to meet identified customer requirements for room cleaning

Both internal and external customers are affected by these processes. Their involvement in producing reliability will be tersted and measured for 100 percent satisfaction.

Customer-supplier relationships are crucial to the reliability of the housekeeping system. Error proofing these processes will ensure that the guests are served right the first time and that they are served on time. Clearly, the original goal of a 50 percent reduction in cycle time has been achieved and exceeded. For the future, the housekeeping system will continue to improve in cycle time and reliability with the participation of the ladies and gentlemen of The Ritz-Carlton, Dearborn.

SUMMARY

- The Ritz-Carlton Hotel Company operates 30 business and resort hotels throughtout the world. It has 13 international sales offices and employs 13,500 people.
- The Ritz-Carlton in Dearborn, Michigan, houses 308 guest rooms and features several dining options, over 20,000 square feet of meeting space, and a fitness center.
- The Ritz-Carlton Hotel Company identified several processes that customers judged with highly important, but low satisfaction, ratings.
- The company set forth the following tasks: identify what was important to customers and how they rated those features; complete a gap analysis; identify

the primary processes and if the company had existing work areas or processes that were aligned to meet those needs.

- The Ritz-Carlton in Dearborn, Michigan, investigated the housekeeping system. Its goal was to create an error-proof, reliable process that could be standardized within the company.

- The process team's goal was to identify and reduce waste through analysis by simplifying, eliminating, and combining steps within the housekeeping system. This was done to meet the company's quality goals of six sigma; 50 percent cycle time reduction; and 100 percent customer retention.

- The team consisted of those individuals active in the housekeeping system and impacted by any changes to it. This included housekeeping and laundry department representatives and engineering and TQM personnel.

- Team-building exercises were discussed and practiced at weekly meetings. The team used consensus decision making and shared leadership.

- Ten characteristics of a clean, fresh, fully stocked guest room were identified as internal and external customer requirements.

- Consecutive, task-by-task work by one room attendant was the current method of room cleaning.

- The team explored the concept of simultaneous work done by a number of room attendants.

- Team cleaning, as brainstormed, was observed at a competitor's facility and piloted at The Ritz-Carlton, Dearborn.

- Seven key measures were used to check the reliability of both the current and new housekeeping processes.

- As the housekeeping department's primary supplier, the laundry department examined and changed its daily processes to better meet its customer's needs.

- At least seven tangible and eight intangible benefits resulted from the team-cleaning concept.

- A strong contributor to the success of the team-cleaning concept was involving people directly impacted by the house-keeping system and using their expertise to drive change.

- Using a total team approach and scientific tools markedly increased the acceptability of all the housekeeping changes implemented.

- Five additional planned changes have been identified to further increase the reliability of the housekeeping system.

Appendix C

ASQ Glossary of Terms

ability test: an assessment device that measures a person's ability to learn or acquire skills (also referred to as an *aptitude test*).

acceptable quality level (AQL): when a continuing series of lots is considered, a quality level that, for the purposes of sampling inspection, is the limit of a satisfactory process average.

acceptance sampling: inspection of a sample from a lot to decide whether to accept or not accept that lot. There are two types: attributes sampling and variables sampling. In attributes sampling, the presence or absence of a characteristic is noted in each of the units inspected. In variables sampling, the numerical magnitude of a characteristic is measured and recorded for each inspected unit; this involves reference to a continuous scale of some kind.

acceptance sampling plan: a specific plan that indicates the sampling sizes and the associated acceptance or nonacceptance criteria to be used. In attributes sampling, for example, there are single, double, multiple, sequential, chain, and skip-lot sampling plans. In variables sampling, there are single, double, and sequential sampling plans. (For detailed descriptions of these plans, see the standard ANSI/ISO/ASQC A35342, *Statistics—Vocabulary and Symbols—Statistical Quality Control.*)

accreditation: certification by a duly recognized body of the facilities, capability, objectivity, competence, and integrity of an agency, service, or operational group or individual to provide the specific service or operation needed. For example, the Registrar Accreditation Board accredits those organizations that register companies to the ISO 9000 series standards.

accuracy: a characteristic of measurement which addresses how close an observed value is to the true value. It answers the question, "Is it right?"

ACSI: The American Customer Satisfaction Index, released for the first time in October 1994, is a new economic indicator, a cross-industry measure of the satisfaction of U.S. household customers with the quality of the goods and services available to them—both those goods and services produced within the United States and those provided as imports from foreign firms that have substantial market shares or dollar sales. The ACSI is co-sponsored by the University of Michigan Business School and ASQC.

affinity diagram: a management and planning tool used to organize ideas into natural groupings in a way that stimulates new, creative ideas.

analysis: the first phase in the design of instruction in which data are gathered to identify gaps between actual and desired organizational performance.

analysis of means (ANOM): a statistical procedure for troubleshooting industrial processes and analyzing the results of experimental designs with factors at fixed levels. It provides a graphical display of data. Ellis R. Ott developed the procedure in 1967 because he obsened that nonstatisticians had difficulty understanding analysis of variance. Analysis of means is easier for quality practitioners to use because it is an extension of the control chart. In 1973, Edward G. Schilling further extended the concept, enabling analysis of means to be used with nonnormal distributions and attributes data where the normal approximation to the binomial distribution does not apply. This is referred to as analysis of means for treatment effects.

analysis of variance (ANOVA): a basic statistical technique for analyzing experimental data. It subdivides the total variation of a data set into meaningful component parts associated with specific sources of variation in order to test a hypothesis on the parameters of the model or to estimate variance components. There are three models: fixed, random, and mixed.

ANSI: American National Standards Institute

AOQ: average outgoing quality

AOQL: average outgoing quality limit

appraisal costs: costs incurred to determine the degree of conformance to quality requirements.

AQL: acceptable quality level

AQP: Association for Quality and Participation

arrow diagram: a management and planning tool used to develop the best possible schedule and appropriate controls to accomplish the schedule; the critical path method and the program evaluation review technique make use of arrow diagrams.

ASME: American Society of Mechanical Engineers

ASQ: a society of individual and organizational members dedicated to the ongoing development, advancement, and promotion of quality concepts, principles, and technologies. The Society serves more than 130,000 individuals and 1,000 corporate members in the United States and 63 other countries.

ASTD: American Society for Training and Development

ASTM: American Society for Testing and Materials

attribute data: go/no-go information. The control charts based on attribute data include percent chart, number of affected units chart, count chart, count-per-unit chart, quality score chart, and demerit chart.

availability: the ability of a product to be in a state to perform its designated function under stated conditions at a given time. Availability can be expressed by the ratio:

$$\frac{\text{uptime}}{\text{uptime} + \text{downtime}}$$

uptime being when the product is operative (in active use and in standby state) and downtime being when the product is inoperative (while under repair, awaiting spare parts, and so on).

average chart: a control chart in which the subgroup average, $\bar{X}$, is used to evaluate the stability of the process level.

average outgoing quality (AOQ): the expected average quality level of outgoing product for a given value of incoming product quality.

average outgoing quality limit (AOQL): the maximum average outgoing quality over all possible levels of incoming quality for a given acceptance sampling plan and disposal specification.

award: something given in recognition of performance or quality.

benchmarking: an improvement process in which a company measures its performance against that of best-in-class companies, determines how those companies achieved their performance levels, and uses the information to improve its own performance. The subjects that can be benchmarked include strategies, operations, processes, and procedures.

bias: a characteristic of measurement that refers to a systematic difference.

big Q, little Q: a term used to contrast the difference between managing for quality in all business processes and products (big Q) and managing for quality in a limited capacity—traditionally in only factory products and processes (little q).

blemish: an imperfection that is severe enough to be noticed but should not cause any real impairment with respect to intended normal or reasonably foreseeable use (see also "defect," "imperfection," and "nonconformity").

block diagram: a diagram that shows the operation, interrelationships, and interdependencies of components in a system. Boxes, or blocks (hence the name), represent the components; connecting lines between the blocks represent interfaces. There are two types of block diagrams: a functional block diagram, which shows a system's subsystems and lower-level products, their interrelationships, and interfaces with other systems; and a reliability block diagram, which is similar to the functional block diagram except that it is modified to emphasize those aspects influencing reliability.

brainstorming: a problem-solving tool that teams use to generate as many ideas as possible related to a particular subject. Team members begin by offering all their ideas; the ideas are not discussed or reviewed until after the brainstorming session.

breakthrough: a method of solving chronic probelms, which results from the effective execution of a strategy designed to reach the next level of quality. Such change often requires a paradigm shift within the organization.

BSI: British Standards Institute

business partnering: the creation of cooperative business alliances between constituencies within an organization or between an organization and its customers. Partnering occurs through a pooling of resources in a trusting atmosphere focused on continuous, mutual improvement (also see "customer supplier partnership").

business processes: processes that focus on what the organization does as a business and how they go about doing it. A business has functional processes (generating output within a single department) and cross-functional processes (generating output across several functions or departments).

c chart: count chart (also see "attribute data").

calibration: the comparison of a measurement instrument or system of unverified accuracy to a measurement instrument or system of a known accuracy to detect any variation from the required performance specification.

capability ratio (Cp): is equal to the specification tolerance width divided by the process capability.

cascading training: training that is implemented in an organization from the top down.

cause-and-effect diagram: a tool for analyzing process dispersion. It is also referred to as the Ishikawa diagram, because Kaoru Ishikawa developed it, and the fishbone diagram, because the complete diagram resembles a fish skeleton. The diagram illustrates the main causes and subcauses leading to an effect (symptom). The cause-and-effect diagram is one of the seven tools of quality.

champion: an individual who has accountability and reponsibility for many processes or who is involved in making strategic-level decisions for the organization. The champion ensures ongoing dedication of project resources and monitors strategic alignment (also referred to as a sponsor).

change agent: the person who takes the lead in transforming a company into a quality organization by providing guidance during the planning phase, facilitating implementation, and supporting those who pioneer the changes.

check sheet: a simple data-recording device. The check sheet is custom-designed by the user, which allows him or her to readily interpret the results. The check sheet is one of the seven tools of quality. Check sheets are often confused with data sheets and checklists (see individual entries).

checklist: a tool used to ensure that all important steps or actions in an operation have been taken. Checklists contain items that are important or relevant to an issue or situation. Checklists are often confused with check sheets and data sheets (see individual entries).

chronic problem: a long-standing adverse situation which can be remedied by changing the status quo. For example, actions such as revising an unrealistic manufacturing process or addressing customer defections can change the status quo and remedy the situation.

CMI: certified mechanical inspector (ASQ)

coaching: a continuous improvement technique by which people receive one-to-one learning through demonstration and practice and which is characterized by immediate feedback and corection.

commercial/industrial market: refers to business market customers who are described by variables such as location, SIC code, buyer industry, technological sophistication, purchasing process, size, ownership, and financial strength.

common causes of variation: causes that are inherent in any process all the time. A process that has only common causes of variation is said to be stable or predictable.

company culture: a system of values, beliefs, and behaviors inherent in a company. To optimize business performance, top management must define and create the necessary culture.

competence: refers to a person's ability to learn and perform a particular activity. Competence generally consists of skill, knowledge, aptitude, and temperament components.

concurrent engineering: a process in which an organization designs a product or service using input and evaluations from business units and functions early in the process, anticipating problems, and balancing the needs of all parties. The emphasis is on upstream prevention vs. downstream correction and maintaining customer requirements.

conformance: an affirmative indication or judgment that a product or service has met the requirements of a relevant specification, contract, or regulation.

conformance quality: occurs when a company focuses on conforming to requirements, doing things right the first time, and reducing scrap and rework.

consensus building: a decision-making approach in which a facilitator makes a decision only after ensuring that all team members support the decision.

constancy of purpose: occurs when goals and objectives are properly aligned to the organizational vision and mission.

consulting: a decision-making approach in which a facilitator talks to others and considers their input before making a decision.

consumer market customers: end users of a product or service.

consumer's risk: for a sampling plan, refers to the probability of acceptance of a lot, the quality of which has a designated numerical value representing a level that is seldom desirable. Usually the designated value will be the limiting quality level.

continuous probability distribution: means that the greatest number of observations fall in the center with fewer observations falling on either side of the average, forming a normal bell-shaped curve.

continuous process improvement: includes the actions taken throughout an organization to increase the effectiveness and efficiency of activities and processes in order to provide added benefits to the customer and organization. It is considered a subset of total quality management and operates according to the premise that organizations can always make improvements. Continuous improvement can also be equated with reducing process variation.

control chart: a basic tool which consists of a chart with upper and lower control limits on which values of some statistical measure for a series of samples or subgroups are plotted. It frequently shows a central line to help detect a trend of plotted values toward either control unit. It is used to monitor and analyze variation from a process to see whether the process is in statistical control.

corrective action: the implementation of solutions resulting in the reduction or elimination of an identified problem.

correlation: refers to the measure of the relationaship between two sets of numbers or variables.

correlation coefficient: describes the magnitude and direction of the relationship between two variables.

cost of poor quality: the costs associated with providing poor-quality products or services. There are four categories of costs: internal failure costs (costs associated with defects found before the customer receives the product or service); external failure costs (costs associated with defects found after the customer receives the product or service); appraisal costs (costs incurred to determine the degree of conformance to quality requirements); and prevention costs (costs incurred to keep failure and appraisal costs to a minimum).

cost of quality (COQ): a term coined by Philip Crosby referring to the cost of poor quality.

count chart: a control chart for evaluating the stability of a process in terms of the count of events of a given classification occurring in a sample.

count-per-unit chart: a control chart for evaluating the stability of a process in terms of the average count of events of a given classification per unit occurring in a sample.

C$_p$: a widely used process capability index. It is expressed as

$$C_p = \frac{\text{upper control limit} - \text{lower control limit}}{6\sigma}$$

C$_{pk}$: a widely used process capability index. It is expressed as

$$C_{pk} = \text{the lesser of } \frac{\text{USL} - \mu}{3\sigma} \text{ or } \frac{\mu - \text{USL}}{3\sigma}$$

CQA: certified quality auditor (ASQ)

CQE: certified quality engineer (ASQ)

CQI: continuous quality improvement (ASQ)

CQT: certified quality technician (ASQ)

CRE: certified reliability engineer (ASQ)

CSQE: certified software quality engineer (ASQ)

critical path: refers to the sequence of tasks that takes the longest time and determines a project's completion date.

Critical Path Method (CPM): an activity-oriented project management technique which uses arrow-diagramming techniques to demonstrate both the time and cost required to complete a project. It provides one time estimate—normal time.

Crosby, Philip: the founder and chairman of the board of Career IV, an executive management consulting firm. Crosby also founded Philip Crosby Associates, Inc. and the Quality College. He has written many books, including *Quality Is Free*, *Quality Without Tears*, *Let's Talk Quality*, and *Leading: The Art of Becoming an Executive*. Crosby, who originated the zero defects concept, is an ASQ senior member and past president.

cross-functional team: a group organized by management and drawn from a variety of functinal areas whose responsibility is to identify, analyze, and solve chronic problems that are beyond the scope of a quality circle's effort.

cumulative sum control chart: a control chart on which the plotted value is the cumulative sum of deviations of successive samples from a target value. The ordinate of each plotted point represents the algebraic sum of the previous ordinate and the most recent deviations from the target.

customer: see "external customer" and "internal customer"

customer delight: the result achieved when customer requirements are exceeded in ways the customer finds valuable.

customer satisfaction: the result of delivering a product or service that meets customer requirements, needs, and expectations.

customer service: refers to quality activities after the sale is made.

customer-supplier chain: a series of inputs, added value, and outputs which occur as employees are both customers and suppliers to one another.

customer-supplier partnership: a long-term relationship between a buyer and supplier characterized by teamwork and mutual confidence. The supplier is considered an extension of the buyer's organization. The partnership is based on several commitments. The buyer provides long-term contracts and uses fewer suppliers. The supplier implements quality assurance processes so that incoming inspection can be minimized. The supplier also helps the buyer reduce costs and improve product and process designs.

customer value: the market-perceived quality adjusted for the relative price of a product.

cycle time: refers to the time that it takes to complete a process from beginning to end and is a critical MBNQA criterion.

cycle time reduction: to reduce the time that it takes, from start to finish, to complete a particular business process.

data: facts presented in descriptive, numeric, or graphic form.

d chart: demerit chart

decision matrix: a matrix used by teams to evaluate problems or possible solutions. After a matrix is drawn to evaluate possible solutions, for example, the team lists them in the far-left vertical column. Next, the team selects criteria to rate the possible solutions, writing them across the top row. Third, each possible solution is rated on a scale of 1 to 5 for each criterion and the rating recorded in the corresponding grid. Finally, the ratings of all the criteria for each possible solution are added to determine its total score. The total score is then used to help decide which solution deserves the most attention.

defect: a product's or service's nonfulfillment of an intended requirement or reasonable expectation for use, including safety considerations. There are four classes of defects: Class 1, Very Serious, leads directly to severe injury or catastrophic economic loss; Class 2, Serious, leads directly to significant injury or significant economic loss; Class 3, Major, is related to major problems with respect to intended normal or reasonably foreseeable use; and Class 4, Minor, is related to minor problems with respect to intended normal or reasonably foreseeable use (see also "blemish," "imperfection," and "nonconformity").

delegation: a decision-making approach in which a facilitator shifts the responsibility for making a decision to someone else.

demerit chart: a control chart for evaluating a process in terms of a demerit (or quality score), i.e., a weighted sum of counts of various classified nonconformities.

Deming Cycle: see "plan-do-check-act cycle"

Deming Prize: award given annually to organizations that, according to the award guidelines, have successfully applied companywide quality control based on statistical quality control and will keep up with it in the future. Although the award is named in honor of W. Edwards Deming, its criteria are not specifically related to Deming's teachings. There are three separate divisions for the award: the Deming Application Prize, the Deming Prize for Individuals, and the Deming Prize for Overseas Companies. The award process is overseen by the Deming Prize Committee of the Union of Japanese Scientists and Engineers in Tokyo.

Deming, W. Edwards (deceased): a prominent consultant, teacher, and author on the subject of quality. After he had shared his expertise in statistical quality control to help the U.S. war effort during World War II, the War Department sent Deming to Japan in 1946 to help that nation recover from its wartime losses. Deming has published more than 200 works, including the well-known books *Quality, Productivity, and Competitive Position* and *Out of the Crisis*. Deming, who developed the 14 points for managing, is an ASQC Honorary member.

demographics: variables among buyers in the consumer market, which include geographic location, age, sex, marital status, family size, social class, education, nationality, occupation, and income.

dependability: the degree to which a product is operable and capable of performing its required function at any randomly chosen time during its specified operating time, provided that the product is available at the start of that period. (Nonoperation-related influences are not included.) Dependability can be expressed by the ratio

$$\frac{\text{time available}}{\text{time available} + \text{time required}}$$

design: the second phase in the design of instruction in which decisions are made regarding course content, delivery methods, measurement, evaluation, and implementation. The outcome of this phase is a training plan.

design of experiments (DOE): a branch of applied statistics dealing with planning, conducting, analyzing, and interpreting controlled tests to evaluate the factors that control the value of a parameter or group of parameters. It is often used in conjuction with Quality Function Deployment (QFD).

designing in quality vs. inspecting in quality: see "prevention vs. detection"

desired quality: refers to the additional features and benefits a customer discovers when using a product or service which lead to increased customer satisfaction. If desired quality is missing, a customer may become dissatisfied.

diagnostic journey and remedial journey: a two-phase investigation used by teams to solve chronic quality problems. In the first phase, the diagnostic journey, the team journeys from the symptom of a JOURNEY chronic problem to its cause. In the second phase, the remedial journey, the team journeys from the cause to its remedy.

discrete probability distribution: means that the measured process variable takes on a finite or limited number of values; no other possible values exist.

distribution: describes the amount of potential variation in outputs of a process; it is usually described in terms of its shape, average, and standard deviation.

Dodge-Romig sampling plans: plans for acceptance sampling developed by Harold F. Dodge and Harry G. Romig. Four sets of tables were published in 1940: single-sampling lot tolerance tables, double-sampling lot tolerance tables, single-sampling average outgoing quality limit tables, and double-sampling average outgoing quality limit tables.

education: refers to the knowledge employees need to learn to perform a future job or accept increased job responsibilities (also see "training").

80-20: a term referring to the Pareto principle, which was first defined by J. M. Juran in 1950. The principle suggests that most effects come from relatively few causes, that is, 80% of the effects come from 20% of the possible causes.

employee involvement: a practice within an organization whereby employees regularly participate in making decisions on how their work areas operate, including making suggestions for improvement, planning, goal setting, and monitoring performance.

empowerment: a condition whereby employees have the authority to make decisions and take action in their work areas without prior approval. For example, an operator can stop a production process upon detecting a problem or a customer service representative can send out a replacement product if a customer calls with a problem.

end users: external customers who purchase products/services for their own use or receive products/services as gifts; they are not employees of the organization supplying the product or service.

ethics: a code of conduct that is based on morals and defines what is fair for individuals and what is right for the public.

event: the starting or ending point for a group of tasks.

excited quality: the additional benefit a customer receives when a product or service goes beyond basic expectations. Excited quality "wows" the customer and separates the provider from the competition. If excited quality is missing, the customer will still be satisfied.

expected quality: also known as basic quality, is the minimum benefit a customer expects to receive from a product or service.

experimental design: a formal plan that details the specifics for conducting an experiment, such as which responses, factors, levels, blocks, treatments, and tools are to be used.

external customer: a person or organization who receives a product, a service, or information but is not part of the organization supplying it (see also "internal customer").

external failure costs: costs associated with defects found after the customer receives the product or service.

facilitator: a team member who is responsible for creating favorable conditions that will enable a team to reach its purpose or achieve its goals by bringing together the necessary tools, information, and resources to get the job done.

factor analysis: a statistical technique that examines the relationships between a single dependent variable and multiple independent variations. For example, it is used to determine which questions on a questionnaire are related to a specific question such as "Would you buy this product again?"

failure mode analysis (FMA): a procedure to determine which malfunction symptoms appear immediately before or after a failure of a critical parameter in a system. After all the possible causes are listed for each symptom, the product is designed to eliminate the problems.

failure mode effects analysis (FMEA): a procedure in which each potential failure mode in every sub-item of an item is analyzed to determine its effect on other sub-items and on the required function of the item.

failure mode effects and criticality analysis (FMECA): a procedure that is performed after a failure mode effects analysis to classify each potential failure effect according to its severity and probability of occurrence.

feedback: the return of information in interpersonal communication; it may be based on fact or feeling and helps the party who is receiving the information judge how well he/she is being understood by the other party.

feedback and feedforward: terms defined by Feigenbaum to differentiate past quality traditions from today's strategic approach. Feedback is more reactive and is centered around the progression of an unsatisfactory product. Feedforward is more proactive and focuses on developing a satisfactory product in the first place.

Feigenbaum, Armand V.: the founder and president of General Systems Co., an international engineering company that designs and implements total quality systems. Feigenbaum originated the concept of total quality control in his book, *Total Quality Control,* which was published in 1951. The book has been translated into many languages, including Japanese, Chinese, French, and Spanish. Feigenbaum is an ASQ Honorary member and served as ASQ president for two consecutive terms.

fishbone diagram: see "cause-and-effect diagram"

fitness for use: a term used to indicate that a product or service fits the customer's defined purpose for that product or service.

flowchart: a graphical representation of the steps in a process. Flowcharts are drawn to better understand processes. The flowchart is one of the seven tools of quality.

FMA: failure mode analysis

FMEA: failure mode effects analysis

FMECA: failure mode effects and criticality analysis

force field analysis: a technique for analyzing the forces that aid or hinder an organization in reaching an objective. An arrow pointing to an objective is drawn down the middle of a piece of paper. The factors that will aid the objective's achievement, called the driving forces, are listed on the left side of the arrow. The factors that will hinder its achievement, called the restraining forces, are listed on the right side of the arrow.

formal communcation: the officially sanctioned data within an organization, which includes publications, memoranda, training materials/events, public relations information, and company meetings.

14 points: W. Edwards Deming's 14 management practices to help companies increase their quality and productivity. The 14 points are listed in Appendix C.

funnel experiment: an experiment that demonstrates the effects of tampering. Marbles are dropped through a funnel in an attempt to hit a flat-surfaced target below. The experiment shows that adjusting a stable process to compensate for an undesirable result or an extraordinarily good result will produce output that is worse than if the process had been left alone.

gap analysis: a technique that compares a company's existing state to its desired state (as expressed by its long-term plans) and determines what needs to be done to remove or minimize the gap.

Gantt chart: a type of bar chart used in process planning and control to display planned work and finished work in relation to time.

gauge repeatability and reproducibility (GR&R): the evaluation of a gauging instrument's accuracy by determining whether the measurements taken with it are repeatable (i.e., there is close agreement among a number of consecutive measurements of the output for the same value of the input under the same operating conditions) and reproducible (i.e., there is close agreement among repeated measurements of the output for the same value of input made under the same operating conditions over a period of time).

geometric dimensioning and tolerancing (GDT): a method to minimize production costs by showing the dimension and tolerancing on a drawing while considering the functions or relationships of part features.

goal: a nonquantitative statement of general intent, aim, or desire; it is the end point toward which management directs its efforts and resources.

go/no-go: state of a unit or product. Two parameters are possible: go—conforms to specifications, and no-go—does not conform to specifications.

hierarchy structure: describes an organization that is organized around functional departments/product lines or around customers/customer segments and is charaterized by top-down management (also referred to as a *bureaucratic model* or *pyramid structure*).

high performance work: defined by the MBNQA criteria as work approaches systematically directed toward achieving ever higher levels of overall performance, including quality and productivity.

histogram: a graphic summary of variation in a set of data. The pictorial nature of the histogram lets people see patterns that are difficult to see in a simple table of numbers. The histogram is one of the seven tools of quality.

horizontal structure: describes an organization which is organized along a process or value-added chain, eliminating hierarchy and functional boundaries (also referred to as a *systems structure*).

hoshin planning: breakthrough planning. A Japanese strategic planning process in which a company develops up to four vision statements that indicate where the company should be in the next five years. Company goals and work plans are developed based on the vision statements. Periodic audits are then conducted to monitor progress.

House of Quality: a diagram (named for its house-shaped appearance) that clarifies the relationship between customer needs and product features. It helps correlate market or customer requirements and anlysis of competitive products with higher level technical and product charateristics, and it makes it possible to bring several factors into a single figure.

IEEE: Institute of Electrical and Electronics Engineers

imperfection: a quality characteristic's departure from its intended level or state without any association to conformance to specification requirements or to the usability of a product or service (see also "blemish," "defect," and "nonconformity").

in-control process: a process in which the statistical measure being evaluated is in a state of statistical control, i.e., the variations among the observed sampling results can be attributed to a constant system of chance causes (see also "out-of-control process").

informal communication: the unofficial communication which takes place in an organization as people talk freely and easily; it includes phone communication, e-mail, impromptu meetings, and personal conversations.

information: data transferred into an ordered format that makes it usable and allows one to draw conclusions.

inspection: measuring, examining, testing, and gauging one or more characteristics of a product or service and comparing the results with specified requirements to determine whether conformity is achieved for each characteristic.

intermediate customers: ditributors, dealers, or brokers who make products and services available to the end user by repairing, repackaging, reselling, or creating finished goods from components or subassemblies.

internal customer: the recipient, person or department, of another person's or department's output (product, service, or information) within an organization (see also "external customer").

internal failure costs: costs associated with defects found before the customer receives the product or service.

interrelationship digraph: a management and planning tool that displays the relationship between factors in a complex situation. It identifies meaningful categories from a mass of ideas and is useful when relationships are difficult to determine.

intervention: an action taken by a leader to resolve an underlying conflict within a team or work group.

intervention focus: refers to how an intervention is directed—toward a group or toward a specific individual.

intervention intensity: refers to the strength of the intervention by the intervening person; intensity is affected by words, voice inflection, and nonverbal behaviors.

IQA: Institute of Quality Assurance

Ishikawa diagram: see "cause-and-effect diagram"

Ishikawa, Kaoru (deceased): a pioneer in quality control activities in Japan. In 1943, he developed the cause-and-effect diagram. Ishikawa, an ASQ Honorary member, published many works, including *What Is Total Quality Control? The Japanese Way*, *Quality Control Circles at Work*, and *Guide to Quality Control*. He was a member of the quality control research group of the Union of Japanese Scientists and Engineers while also working as an assistant professor at the University of Tokyo.

ISO: International Organization for Standardization

ISO 9000 series standards: a set of five individual but related international standards on quality management and quality assurance developed to help companies effectively document the quality system elements to be implemented to maintain an efficient quality system. The standards, initially published in 1987, are not specific to any particular industry, product, or service. The standards were developed by the International Organization for Standardization (ISO), a specialized international agency for standardization composed of the national standards bodies of 91 countries.

job description: a narrative explanation of the work, the work process, the work setting, and the organizational culture.

job specification: a list of the important functional and quality attributes (knowledge, skills, aptitudes, and personal characteristics) needed to succeed in the job.

Juran, Joseph M.: the chairman emeritus of the Juran Institute and an ASQ Honorary member. Since 1924, Juran has pursued a varied career in management as an engineer, executive, government administrator, university professor, labor arbitrator, corporate director, and consultant. Specializing in managing for quality, he has authored hundreds of papers and 12 books, including *Juran's Quality Control Handbook*, *Quality Planning and Analysis* (with F. M. Gryna), and *Juran on Leadership for Quality*.

Juran Trilogy: *see:* "quality trilogy"

JUSE: Union of Japanese Scientists and Engineers

just-in-time manufacturing (JIT): an optimal material requirement planning system for a manufacturing process in which there is little or no manufacturing material inventory on hand at the manufacturing site and little or no incoming inspection.

kaizen: a Japanese term that means gradual unending improvement by doing little things better and setting and achieving increasingly higher standards. The term was made famous by Masaaki Imai in his book, *Kaizen: The Key to Japan's Competitive Success.*

Kano model: a representation of the three levels of customer satisfaction defined as dissatisfaction, neutrality, and delight.

ladder of inference: a mental model that explains how individuals have different interpretations about what happens in an organization. The model explains how people move beyond observable data and culturally understood meanings by adding their own meanings, assumptions, and theories.

leadership: an essential part of a quality improvement effort. Organization leaders must establish a vision, communicate that vision to those in the organization, and provide the tools, knowledge, and motivation necessary to accomplish the vision.

long-term goals: refers to goals that an organization hopes to achieve in the future, usually in three to five years. They are commonly referred to as strategic goals.

lot: a defined quantity of product accumulated under conditions that are considered uniform for sampling purposes.

lower control limit (LCL): control limit for points below the central line in a control chart.

macro processes: broad, far-ranging processes that often cross functional boundaries and are completed by more than one organization.

maintainability: the probability that a given maintenance action for an item under given usage conditions can be performed within a stated time interval when the maintenance is performed under stated conditions using stated procedures and resources. Maintainability has two categories: serviceability, the ease of conducting scheduled inspections and servicing, and repairability, the ease of restoring service after a failure.

Malcolm Baldrige National Quality Award (MBNQA): an award established by Congress in 1987 to raise awareness of quality management and to recognize U.S. companies that have implemented successful quality management systems. Two awards may be given annually in each of three categories: manufacturing company, service company, and small business. The award is named after the late Secretary of Commerce Malcolm Baldrige, a proponent of quality management. The U.S. Commerce Department's National Institute of Standards and Technology manages the award, and ASQ administers it. The major emphasis in determining success is achieving results.

management by policy: the organizational infrastructure that ensures the right things are done at the right time.

managerial grid: a management theory developed by Robert Blake and Jane Mouton, which maintains that a manager's management style is based on his or her mindset toward people; it focuses on attitudes rather than behavior. The theory uses a grid to measure concern with production and concern with people.

market-perceived quality: the customer's opinion of your products or services as compared to those of your competitors.

materials review board (MRB): a quality control committee or team, usually employed in manufacturing or other materials-processing installations, which possesses the responsibility and authority to deal with items or materials that do not conform to fitness-for-use specifications. An equivalent, error review board, is sometimes used in software development.

matrix chart: a management and planning tool that shows the relationships among various groups of data; it yields information about the relationships and the importance of task/method elements of the subjects.

matrix structure: describes an organization which is organized into a combination of functional and product departments; it brings together teams of people to work on projects and is driven by product scope.

maturity: the balance of courage and consideration that enables one to speak openly, give honest feedback, and demonstrate respect for the feelings of others.

mean: a measure of central tendency and is the arithmetic average of all measurements in a data set.

mean time between failures (MTBF): the average time interval between failures for repairable product for a defined unit of measure, for example, operating hours, cycles, miles.

measurement: refers to the reference standard or sample used for the comparison of properties.

median: the middle number or center value of a set of data when all the data are arranged in an increasing sequence.

micro processes: narrow processes made up of detailed steps and activities which could be accomplished by a single person.

mission statement: an explanation of purpose or reasons for existing as an organization; it provides the focus for the organization and defines its scope of business.

MIL-Q-9858A: a military standard that describes quality program requirements.

MIL-STD: military standard

MIL-STD-105E: a military standard that describes the sampling procedures and tables for inspection by attributes.

MIL-STD-45662A: a military standard that describes the requirements for creating and maintaining a calibration system for measurement and test equipment.

mode: the score that occurs most frequently in a data set.

multivariate control chart: a control chart for evaluating the stability or a process in terms of the levels of two or more variables or characteristics.

n: sample size (the number of units in a sample)

NDE: nondestructive evaluation (see "nondestructive testing and evaluation")

NIST: National Institute of Standards and Technology

nominal group technique: a technique similar to brainstorming, used by teams to generate ideas on a particular subject. Team members are asked to silently come up with as many ideas as possible, writing them down. Each member is then asked to share one idea, which is recorded. After all the ideas are recorded, they are discussed and prioritized by the group.

nonconformity: the nonfulfillment of a specified requirement (see also "blemish," "defect," and "imperfection").

nondestructive testing and evaluation (NDT): testing and evaluation methods that do not damage or destroy the product being tested.

non-value-added: refers to tasks or activities that can be eliminated with no deterioration in product or service functionality, performance, or quality in the eyes of the customer.

NQM: National Quality Month

number of affected units chart (np chart): a control chart for evaluating the stability of a process in terms of the total number of units in a sample in which an event of a given classification occurs.

objective: a quantitative statement of future expectations and an indication of when the expectations should be achieved; it flows from goals and clarifies what people must accomplish.

off-the-job training: training that takes place away from the actual work site.

operating characteristic curve (OC curve): a graph used to determine the probability of accepting lots as a function of the lots' or processes' quality level when using various sampling plans. There are three types: Type A curves, which give the probability of acceptance for an individual lot coming from finite production (will not continue in the future); Type B curves, which give the probability of acceptance for lots coming from a continuous process; and Type C curves, which, for a continuous sampling plan, give the long-run percentage of product accepted during the sampling phase.

optimization: refers to achieving planned process results that meet the needs of the customer and supplier alike and minimize their combined costs.

out-of-control process: a process in which the statistical measure being evaluated is not in a state of statistical control, i.e., the variations among the observed sampling results can be attributed to a constant system of chance causes (see also "in-control process").

out of spec: a term used to indicate that a unit does not meet a given specification.

p chart: percent chart

parallel structure: describes an organizational module in which groups, such as quality circles or a quality council, exist in the organization in addition to and simultaneously with the line organization (also referred to as *collateral structure*).

pareto chart: a basic tool used to graphically rank causes from most significant to least significant. It utilizes a vertical bar graph in which the bar height reflects the frequency or impact of causes.

PDCA cycle: plan-do-check-act cycle

percent chart: a control chart for evaluating the stability of a process in terms of the percent of the total number of units in a sample in which an event of a given classification occurs. The percent chart is also referred to as a proportion chart.

performance appraisal: a formal method of measuring employees' progress against performance standards and providing feedback to them.

performance management system: a system that supports and contributes to the creation of high performance work and work systems by translating behavioral priniciples into procedures.

performance plan: a performance management tool that describes desired performance and provides a way to assess the performance objectively.

performance test: an assessment device that requires candidates to complete an actual work task in a controlled situation.

personality test: an assessment device that measures a person's interaction skills and patterns of behavior.

plan-do-check-act cycle: a four-step process for quality improvement. In the first step (plan), a plan to effect improvement is developed. In the second step (do), the plan is carried out, preferably on a small scale. In the third step (check), the effects of the plan are observed. In the last step (act), the results are studied to determine what was learned and what can be predicted. The plan-do-check-act cycle is sometimes referred to as the Shewhart cycle because Walter A. Shewhart discussed the concept in his book *Statistical Method from the Viewpoint of Quality Control* and as the Deming cycle because W. Edwards Deming introduced the concept in Japan. The Japanese subsequently called it the Deming cycle.

point estimate: the single value used to estimate a population parameter. Point estimates are commonly referred to as the points at which the interval estimates are centered; these estimates give information about how much uncertainty is associated with the estimate.

poka-yoke: a term that means to foolproof the process by building safegaurds into the system that avoid or immediately find errors. It comes from *poka*, which means error, and *yokeru*, which means to avoid.

population: a group of people, objects, observations, or measurements about which one wishes to draw conclusions.

precision: a characteristic of measurement which addresses the consistency or repeatability of a measurement system when the identical item is measured a number of times.

prevention costs: costs incurred to keep internal and external failure costs and appraisal costs to a minimum.

prevention vs. detection: a term used to contrast two types of quality activities. Prevention refers to those activities designed to prevent nonconformances in products and services. Detection refers to those activities designed to detect nonconformances already in products and services. Another term used to describe this distinction is "designing in quality vs. inspecting in quality."

primary: process which refers to the basic steps or activites that will produce the output without the nice-to-haves.

probability: refers to the likelihood of occurrence.

probability distribution: a mathematical formula which relates the values of characteristics with their probability of occurrence in a population.

process: an activity or group of activities that takes an input, adds value to it, and provides an output to an internal or external customer.

process capability: a statistical measure of the inherent process variability for a given characteristic. The most widely accepted formula for process capability is 6σ.

process capability index: the value of the tolerance specified for the characteristic divided by the process capability. There are several types of process capability indexes, including the widely used C_{pk} and C_p.

process decision program chart (PDPC): a management and planning tool that identifies all events that can go wrong and the appropriate countermeasures for these events. It graphically represents all sequences that lead to a desirable effect.

process improvement: refers to the act of changing a process to reduce variability and cycle time and make the process more effective, efficient, and productive.

process improvement team (PIT): a natural work group or cross-functional team whose responsibility is to achieve needed improvements in existing processes. The life span of the team is based on the completion of the team purpose and specific goals.

process management: the collection of practices used to implement and process improve management and process effectiveness; it focuses on holding the gains achieved through process improvement and assuring process integrity.

process mapping: the flowcharting of a work process, in detail, including key measurements.

process owner: the manager or leader who is responsible for ensuring that the total process is effective and efficient.

producer's risk: for a sampling plan, refers to the probability of not accepting a lot, the quality of which has a designated numerical value representing a level that is generally desirable. Usually the designated value will be the acceptable quality level.

product orientation: refers to a tendency to see customers' needs in terms of a product they want to buy, not in terms of the services, value, or benefits the product will produce.

product or service liability: the obligation of a company to make restitution for loss related to personal injury, property damage, or other harm caused by its product or service.

professional development plan: a career development tool created for an individual employee. Working together, the employee and his/her supervisor create a plan which matches the individual's career needs and aspirations with organizational demands.

profound knowledge theory: as defined by W. Edwards Deming, states that learning cannot be based on experience only; it requires comparisons of results to a prediction, plan, or an expression of theory. Predicting why something happens is essential to understand results and to continually improve.

program evaluation and review technique (PERT): an event-oriented project management planning and measurement technique which utilizes an arrow diagram or road map to identify all major project events and demonstrates the amount of time needed to complete a project. It provides three time estimates: optimistic, most likely, and pessimistic.

project life cycle: refers to the four sequential phases of project management: conceptualization, planning, implementation, and completion.

project plan: the blueprint for process improvement and the first step in changing a process. It includes a step-by-step description of how the process works, including current inputs, transformations, and outputs.

psychographic customer characteristics: variables among buyers in the consumer market which address lifestyle issues and include consumer interests, activities, and opinions.

QA: quality assurance

QC: quality control

Q9000 series: refers to ANSI/ISO/ASQC Q9000 series standards, which is the Americanized version of the 1994 edition of the ISO 9000 series standards. The United States adopted the ISO 9000 series standards as the ANSI/ISO/ASQC Q9000 series.

QEIT: quality engineer in training (ASQ)

QIC: Quality Information Center of ASQ

QMJ: *Quality Management Journal* (ASQ)

QP: *Quality Progress* (ASQ)

quality: a subjective term for which each person has his or her own definition. In technical usage, quality can have two meanings: (1) the characteristics of a product or service that bear on its ability to satisfy stated or implied needs and (2) a product or service free of deficiencies.

quality advisor: the person who helps team members work together in quality processes and is a consultant to the team. The advisor is concerned about the process and how decisions are made rather than about which decisions are made.

quality assessment: the process of identifying business practices, attitudes, and activities that are enhancing or inhibiting the achievement of quality improvement in an organization.

quality assurance/quality control: two terms that have many interpretations because of the multiple definitions for the words "assurance" and "control." For example, "assurance" can mean the act of giving confidence, the state of being certain, or the act of making certain; "control" can mean an evaluation to indicate needed corrective responses, the act of guiding, or the state of a process in which the variability is attributable to a constant system of chance causes. (For a detailed discussion on the multiple definitions, see ANSI/ISO/ASQC A35342, *Statistics—Vocabulary and Symbols—Statistical Quality Control.*) One definition of quality assurance is: all the planned and systematic activities implemented within the quality system that can be demonstrated to provide confidence that a product or service will fulfill requirements for quality. One definition for quality control is: the operational techniques and activities used to fulfill requirements for quality. Often, however, "quality assurance" and "quality control" are used interchangeably, referring to the actions performed to ensure the quality of a product, service, or process.

quality audit: a systematic, independent examination and review to determine whether quality activities and related results comply with planned arrangements and whether these arrangements are implemented effectively and are suitable to achieve the objectives.

quality circles: quality improvement or self-improvement study groups composed of a small number of employees—10 or fewer—and their supervisor. Quality circles originated in Japan, where they are called quality control circles.

quality control (QC): see "quality assurance/quality control"

quality costs: see "cost of poor quality"

quality cost reports: a system of collecting quality costs that uses a spreadsheet to list the elements of quality costs against a spread of the departments, areas, or projects where the costs will occur and summarizes the data in exact accordance with plans for its use. The reports help organizations review prevention costs, appraisal costs, and internal and external failure costs.

quality culture: consists of employee opinions, beliefs, traditions, and practices concerning quality.

quality engineering: the analysis of a manufacturing system at all stages to maximize the quality of the process itself and the products it produces.

quality evidence audit: the final part of the data-gathering phase of a quality assessment in which data related to quality improvements is complied, divided into key areas, and rated. The objective is to collect easily quantifiable data that can be clarified by follow-up interviews with select personnel.

quality function: the entire collection of activites through which an organization achieves fitness-for-use, no matter where these activities are performed.

quality function deployment (QFD): a structured method in which customer requirements are translated into appropriate technical requirements for each stage of product development and production. The QFD process is often referred to as listening to the voice of the customer.

quality loss function: a parabolic approximation of the quality loss that occurs when a quality characteristic deviates from its target value. The quality loss function is expressed in monetary units: the cost of deviating from the target increases quadratically the farther the quality characteristic moves from the target. The formula used to compute the quality loss function depends on the type of quality characteristic being used. The quality loss function was first introduced in this form by Genichi Taguchi.

quality metrics: numerical measurements that give an organization the ability to set goals and evaluate actual performance vs. plan.

quality plan: the document setting out the specific quality practices, resources, and sequence of activities relevant to a particular product, project, or contract.

quality planning: the activity of establishing quality goals and developing the processes and products required.

quality principles: the rules or concepts that an organization believes in collectively. The principles have been formulated by senior management with input from others and are communicated and understood at every level of the organization.

quality score chart (Q chart): a control chart for evaluating the stability of a process in terms of a quality score. The quality score is the weighted sum of the count of events of various classifications where each classification is assigned a weight.

quality system: the organizatinal structure, procedures, processes, and resources needed to implement quality management.

quality trilogy: a three-pronged approach to managing for quality. The three legs are quality planning (developing the products and processes required to meet customer needs), quality control (meeting product and process goals), and quality improvement (achieving unprecedented levels of performance).

quincunx: a tool that creates frequency distributions. Beads tumble over numerous horizontal rows of pins, which force the beads to the right or left. After a random journey, the beads are dropped into vertical slots. After many beads are dropped, a frequency distribution results. In the classroom, quincunxes are often used to simulate a manufacturing process. The quincunx was invented by English scientist Francis Galton in the 1890s.

RAM: reliability/availability/maintainability (see individual entries).

random sampling: a sampling method in which every element in the population has an equal chance of being included.

range chart (*R* chart): a control chart in which the subgroup range, *R*, is used to evaluate the stability of the variability within a process.

ratio analysis: the process of relating isolated business numbers, such as sales, margins, expenses, and profits, to make them meaningful.

red bead experiment: an experiment developed by W. Edwards Deming to illustrate that it is impossible to put employees in rank order of performance for the coming year based on their performance during the past year because performance differences must be attributed to the system, not to employees. Four thousand red and white beads, 20% red, in a jar and six people are needed for the experiment. The participants' goal is to produce white beads, because the customer will not accept red beads. One person begins by stirring the beads and then, blindfolded, selects a sample of 50 beads. That person hands the jar to the next person, who repeats the process, and so on. When everyone has his or her sample, the number of red beads for each is counted. The limits of variation between employees that can be attributed to the system are calculated. Everyone will fall within the calculated limits of variation that could arise from the system. The calculations will show that there is no evidence one person will be a better performer than another in the future. The experiment shows that it would be a waste of management's time to try to find out why, say, John produced four red beads and Jane produced 15; instead, management should improve the system, making it possible for everyone to produce more white beads.

Registrar Accreditation Board (RAB): a board that evaluates the competency and reliability of registrars (organizations that assess and register companies to the appropriate ISO 9000 series standards). The Registrar Accreditation Board, formed in 1989 by ASQ, is governed by a board of directors from industry, academia, and quality management consulting firms.

registration to standards: a process in which an accredited, independent third-party organization conducts an on-site audit of a company's operations against the requirements of the standard to which the company wants to be registered. Upon successful completion of the audit, the company receives a certificate indicating that it has met the standard requirements.

regression analysis: a study used to understand the relationship between two or more variables. Regression analysis makes it possible to predict one variable from knowledge about another. The relationship can be mathematically determined and expressed as a correlation coefficient.

reinforcement: the process of ensuring that the right knowledge and skills are being used; it has been described as *catching people doing things right.*

reliability: refers to the ability of a feedback instrument to produces the same results over repeated administration. It is the ability of an instrument to measure consistently and with relateive absence of error. It is also the probability of a product performing its intended function under stated conditions for a given period of time (also see: "mean time between failures").

resistance to change: the unwillingness to change beliefs, habits, and ways of doing things.

return on equity (ROE): the net profit after taxes, divided by last year's tangible stockholders' equity, and then multiplied by 100 to provide a percentage (also referred to as *return on net worth*).

return on investment (ROI): an umbrella term for a variety of ratios measuring an organization's business performance and is calculated by dividing some measure of return by a measure of investment and then multiplying by 100 to provide a percentage. In its most basic form, ROI indicates what remains from all money taken in after all expenses are paid.

return on net assets (RONA): a measurement of the earning power of the firm's investment in assets, calculated by dividing net profit after taxes by last year's tangible total assets and then multiplying by 100 to provide a percentage.

right the first time: a term used to convey the concept that it is beneficial and more cost-effective to take the necessary steps up front to ensure a product or service meets its requirements than to provide a product or service that will need rework or not meet customers' needs. In other words, an organization should engage in defect prevention rather than defect detection.

robustness: the condition of a product or process design that remains relatively stable with a minimum of variation even though factors that influence operations or usage, such as environment and wear, are constantly changing.

root cause analysis: a quality tool used to distinguish the source of defects or problems. It is a structured approach that focuses on the decisive or original cause of a problem or condition.

run chart: a form of trend analysis that uses a graph to show a process measurement on a vertical access against time, with a reference line to show the average of the data. A trend is indicated when a series of collected data points head up or down.

sample: a finite number of items of a similar type taken from a population for the purpose of examination to determine if all members of the population would conform to quality requirements or specifications.

sample size: refers to the number of units in a sample randomly chosen from the popluation.

sample standard deviation chart (s chart): a control chart in which the subgroup standard deviation, s, is used to evaluate the stability of the variability within a process.

sampling: the process of drawing conclusions about the population based on a part of the population.

scatter diagram: a graphical technique to analyze the relationship between two variables. Two sets of data are plotted on a graph, with the y axis being used for the variable to be predicted and the x axis being used for the variable to make the prediction. The graph will show possible relationships (although two variables might appear to be related, they might not be: those who know most about the variables must make that evaluation). The scatter diagram is one of the seven tools of quality.

self-inspection: the process by which employees inspect their own work according to specified rules.

self-managed team: a team that requires little supervision and manages itself and the day-to-day work it does; self-directed teams are responsible for whole work processes and schedules with each individual performing multiple tasks.

seven tools of quality: tools that help organizations understand their processes in order to improve them. The tools are the cause-and-effect diagram, check sheet, control chart, flowchart, histogram, Pareto chart, and scatter diagram (see individual entries).

Shewhart cycle: see "plan-do-check-act cycle"

Shewhart, Walter A. (deceased): referred to as the father of statistical quality control because he brought together the discipline of statistics, engineering, and economics. He described the basic principles of this new discipline in his book *Economic Control of Quality of Manufactured Product*. Shewhart, ASQC's first Honorary member, was best known for creating the control chart. Shewhart worked for Western Electric and AT&T Bell Telephone Laboratories in addition to lecturing and consulting on quality control.

signal-to-noise ratio (S/N ratio): a mathematical equation that indicates the magnitude of an experimental effect above the effect of experimental error due to chance fluctuations.

situational leadership: a leadership theory which maintains that leadership style should change based on the person and the situation, with the leader displaying varying degrees of directive and supportive behavior.

six-sigma quality: a term used generally to indicate that a process is well controlled, i.e., process limits ±3 sigma from the centerline in a control chart and requirements/tolerance limits ±6 sigma from the centerline. The term was initiated by Motorola.

slack time: the time an activity can be delayed without delaying the entire project; it is determined by calculating the difference between the latest allowable date and the earliest expected date (see "PERT").

special causes: causes of variation that arise because of special circumstances. They are not an inherent part of a process. Special causes are also referred to as assignable causes (see also "common causes").

specification: the engineering requirement, used for judging the acceptibility of a particular product/service based on product characteristics, such as appearance, performance, and size. In statistical analysis, specifications refer to the document that prescribes the requirements with which the product or service has to perform.

sporadic problem: a sudden adverse change in the status quo which can be remedied by restoring the status quo. For example, actions such as changing a worn part or handling an irate customer can restore the status quo.

stages of team growth: refers to the four stages defined by Peter Scholtes: forming, storming, norming, and performing. The stages help team members accept the normal problems that occur on the path from forming a group to becoming a team.

stakeholders: people, departments, and organizations that have an investment or interest in the success or actions taken by the organization, but are not directly involved in the customer-supplier chain.

standard: a statement, specification, or quantity of material against which measured outputs from a process may be judged as acceptable or unacceptable.

standard deviation: a calculated measure of variability which shows how much the data is spread out around the mean.

statement of work (SOW): a description of the actual work to be accomplished. It is derived from the work breakdown structure and, when combined with the project specifications, becomes the basis for the contractual agreement on the project (also referred to as *scope of work*).

statistical process control (SPC): the application of statistical techniques to control a process. Often the term "statistical quality control" is used interchangeably with "statistical process control"

statistical quality control (SQC): the application of statistical techniques to control quality. Often the term "statistical process control" is used interchangeably with "statistical quality control" although statistical quality control includes acceptance sampling as well as statistical process control.

storyboarding: a technique that visually displays thoughts and ideas and groups them into categories, making all aspects of a process visible at once.

strategic fit review: a process by which senior managers assess the future of each project to a particular organization in terms of its ability to advance the mission and goals of that organization.

strategic planning: a method to set an organization's long-range goals and observations.

structural variation: variation caused by regular, systematic changes in output, such as seasonal patterns and long-term trends.

supplier: any other-company provider of goods and services, whose goods and services may be used at any stage in the production, design, delivery and use of a company's products and services. Suppliers include businesses, such as distributors, dealers, warranty repair services, transportation contractors, and franchises; and service suppliers, such as health care, training, and education. Internal suppliers provide materials or services to internal customers.

supplier audits: reviews that are planned and carried out to verify the adequacy and effectiveness of a supplier's quality program, drive improvement, and increased value.

supplier certification: the process of evaluating the performance of a supplier with the intent of authorizing the supplier to self-certify shipments if such authorization is justified.

supplier quality assurance: confidence that a supplier's product or service will fulfill its customers' needs. This confidence is achieved by creating a relationship between the customer and supplier that ensures the product will be fit for use with minimal corrective action and inspection. According to J. M. Juran, there are nine primary activities needed: (1) define product and program quality requirements, (2) evaluate alternative suppliers, (3) select suppliers, (4) conduct joint quality planning, (5) cooperate with the supplier during the execution of the contract, (6) obtain proof of conformance to requirements, (7) certify qualified suppliers, (8) conduct quality improvement programs as required, and (9) create and use supplier quality ratings.

SWOT analysis: an assessment of an organization's key strengths, weaknesses, opportunities, and threats. It considers factors such as the organization's industry, the competitive position, functional areas, and management.

system: a network of connecting processes which work together to accomplish the aim of the system.

systems approach to management: a management theory which views the organization as a unified, purposeful combination of interrelated parts; managers must look at the organization as a whole and understand that activity in one part of the organization affects all parts of the organization (also known as *systems thinking*).

tactical plans: short-term plans, usually of one- to two-year durations, that describe actions the organization will take to meet its strategic business plan.

tactics: the strategies and processes that help an organization meet its objectives.

Taguchi, Genichi: the executive director of the American Supplier Institute, the director of the Japan Industrial Technology Institute, and an honorary professor at Nanjing Institute of Technology in China. Taguchi is well-known for developing a methodology to improve quality and reduce costs, which, in the United States, is referred to as the Taguchi methods. He also developed the quality loss function.

Taguchi methods: the American Supplier Institute's trademarked term for the quality engineering methodology developed by Genichi Taguchi. In this engineering approach to quality control, Taguchi calls for off-line quality control, on-line quality control, and a system of experimental design to improve quality and reduce costs.

tampering: action taken to compensate for variation within the control limits of a stable system. Tampering increases rather than decreases variation, as evidenced in the funnel experiment.

team: a set of two or more people who are equally accountable for the accomplishment of a purpose and specific performance goals; it is also defined as a small number of people with complimentary skills who are committed to a common purpose.

team-based structure: describes an organizational structure in which team members are organized around performing a specific function of the business, such as handling customer complaints or assembling an engine.

theory of knowledge: a belief that management is about prediction, and people learn not only from experience, but also from theory. When people study a process and develop a theory, they can compare their predictions with their observations; profound learning results.

theory x and theory y: a managment theory developed by Douglas McGregor that maintains that there are two contrasting management styles, each of which is based on the manager's view of human nature. Theory X managers take a negative view of human nature and assume that most employees do not like work and try to avoid it. Theory Y managers take a positive view of human nature and believe that employees want to work, will seek and accept responsibility, and can offer creative solutions to organizational problems.

theory z: coined by William G. Ouchi, refers to a Japanese style of management that is characterized by long-term employment, slow promotions, considerable job rotation, consensus-style decision making, and concern for the employee as a whole.

360-degree feedback process: an evaluation method that provides feedback from the perspectives of self, peers, direct reports, customers, and suppliers.

top-management commitment: participation of the highest-level officials in their organization's quality improvement efforts. Their participation includes establishing and serving on a quality committee, establishing quality policies and goals, deploying those goals to lower levels of the organization, providing the resources and training that the lower levels need to achieve the goals, participating in quality improvement teams, reviewing progress organizationwide; recognizing those who have performed well, and revising the current reward system to reflect the importance of achieving the quality goals.

total quality management (TQM): a term initially coined by the Naval Air Systems Command to describe its Japanese-style management approach to quality improvement. Since then, total quality management (TQM) has taken on many meanings. Simply put, TQM is a management approach to long-term success through customer satisfaction. TQM is based on the participation of all members of an organization in improving processes, products, services, and the culture they work in. TQM benefits all organization members and society. The methods for implementing this approach are found in the teachings of such quality leaders as Philip B. Crosby, W. Edwards Deming, Armand V. Feigenbaum, Kaoru Ishikawa, and J. M. Juran.

traditional organizations: those organizations not driven by customers and quality policies. Also refers to organizations managed primarily through functional units.

training: refers to the skills that employees need to learn in order to perform or improve their performances of their current jobs or tasks.

tree diagram: a management and planning tool that shows the complete range of subtasks required to achieve an objective. A problem-solving method can be identified from this analysis.

trend analysis: refers to the charting of data over time to identify a tendency or direction.

type I error: an incorrect decision to reject something (such as a statistical hypothesis or a lot of products) when it is acceptable.

type II error: an incorrect decision to accept something when it is unacceptable.

u chart: count per unit chart

upper control limit (UCL): control limit for points above the central line in a control chart.

validity: refers to the ability of a feedback instrument to measure what it was intended to measure.

value-added: refers to tasks or activities that convert resources into products or services consistent with customer requirements. The customer can be internal or external to the organization.

values: statements that clarify the behaviors that the organization expects in order to move toward its vision and mission. Values reflect an organization's personality and culture.

variables data: measurement information. Control charts based on variables data include average ($\bar{X}$) chart, range (R) chart, and sample standard deviation (s) chart.

variable sampling plan: a plan in which a sample is taken and a measurement of a specified quality characteristic is made on each unit. The measurements are summarized into a simple statistic, and the observed value is compared with an allowable value defined in the plan.

variation: a change in data, a characteristic, or a function that is caused by one of four factors: special causes, common causes, tampering, or structural variation (see individual entries).

virtual super team (VST): a team that functions as a de facto small business and manages itself as a value center. It can be organized along business, product, process, or technology lines and requires excellent lateral teaming skills and constant reshaping.

vision: a statement that explains in measurable terms what the company wants to become and what it hopes to achieve.

vital few, useful many: a term used by J. M. Juran to describe his use of the Pareto principle, which he first defined in 1950. (The principal was used much earlier in economics and inventory control methodologies.) The principal suggests that most effects come from relatively few causes; that is, 80% of the effects come from 20% of the possible causes. The 20% of the possible causes are referred to as the "vital few"; the remaining causes are referred to as the "useful many." When Juran first defined this principle, he referred to the remaining causes as the "trivial many," but realizing that no problems are trivial in quality assurance, he changed it to "useful many."

voice of the customer: a company's efforts to provide products and services that truly reflect customer needs and expectations ("voice").

work breakdown structure (WBS): a project management technique by which a project is divided into tasks, subtasks, and units of work to be performed.

work group: a group composed of people from one functional area who work together on a daily basis and whose goal is to improve the processes of their function.

world-class quality: a term used to indicate a standard of excellence: best of the best.

$\bar{X}$ chart: average chart

zero defects: a performance standard developed by Philip B. Crosby to address a dual attitude in the workplace: people are willing to accept imperfection in some areas, while, in other areas, they expect the number of defects to be zero. This dual attitude had developed because of the conditioning that people are human and humans make mistakes. However, the zero defects methodology states that, if people commit themselves to watching details and avoiding errors, they can move closer to the goal of zero.

Appendix D

Deming's 14-Point Theory for Management

1. **Create constancy of purpose.**
   Create constancy of purpose toward improvement of the product and service with the aim to become competitive, stay in business, and provide jobs.
2. **Adopt the new philosophy.**
   Adopt the new philosophy. We are in a new economic age. Western management must awaken to the challenge, must learn their responsibilities, an must take on leadership for a change.
3. **Cease dependence on inspection.**
   Cease dependence on inspection to achieve quality. Eliminate the need for inspection on a mass basis by building quality into the product in the first place.
4. **End the practice of awarding business on the basis of price tag.**
   End the practice of awarding business on the basis of price tag. Instead, minimize the total cost. Move toward a single supplier for any one item, based on a long-term relationship of loyalty and trust.
5. **Improve constantly and forever.**
   Improve constantly and forever the system of production and service to improve quality and productivity; thus, constantly decrease costs.
6. **Institute training.**
   Institute training on the job.
7. **Institute leadership (see Point 12).**
   Institute leadership. The aim of leadership should be to help people and machines and gadgets do a better job. Leadership in management is in need of an overhaul, as well as leadership of production workers.

8. **Drive out fear.**
   Drive out fear, so everyone will work effectively for the company.
9. **Break down barriers.**
   Break down barriers between departments. People in research, design, sales, and production must work as a team to foresee problems of production and usage that may be encountered with the product and service.
10. **Eliminate slogans, exhortations, and targets for the work force.**
    Eliminate slogans, exhortations, and targets for the work force asking for zero defects and new levels of productivity.
11. **Eliminate work standards; eliminate management by objective.**
    a. Eliminate work standards (quotas) on the factory floor. Substitute leadership.
    b. Eliminate management by objective. Eliminate management by numbers, numerical goals. Substitute leadership.
12. **Remove barriers that rob employees of the right to pride of workmanship.**
    a. Remove barriers that rob the hourly worker of the right to pride of workmanship. The responsibility of supervisors must be changed from sheer numbers to quality.
    b. Remove barriers that rob people in management and engineering of their right to pride of workmanship. This means "inter alia," abolishment of the annual or merit rating, management by objective, or management by numbers.
13. **Institute a vigorous program of education.**
    Institute a vigorous program of education and self-improvement.
14. **Put everybody in the company to work to accomplish the transformation.**
    Put everybody in the company to work to accomplish the transformation. The transformation is everybody's job.

Source: Reprinted from *Out of the Crisis* by W. Edwards Deming by permission of MIT and The W. Edwards Deming Institute. Published by MIT, Center for Advanced Educational Services, Cambridge, MA 02139. Copyright 1986 by The W. Edwards Deming Institute.

Appendix E

Quality-Related World Wide Web Sites

There are more than 1,000 quality-related web sites worldwide. The following is a list of non-commerical sites that are useful in pursuing quality improvement information.

http://www.asq-qmd.org . . . . ASQ Quality Management Division
http://www.asq.org . . . . ASQ Headquarters
http://qualityprogress.asq.org . . . . Quality Progress Magazine
http://www.asq.org/rab/index.html . . . . Registration Accreditation Board
http://www.asq.org/about/divtech/qad/qad.html . . . . ASQ Quality Audit Division
http://www.quality.nist.gov . . . . National Quality Award Homepage
http://www.ansi.org . . . . American National Standards Institute
http://www.nssn.org . . . . National Standards System Network
http://www.iso.ch . . . . International Organization for Standardization
http://www.library.ucsb.edu/subj/standard.html . . . . Standards Resources on the Internet
http://www.apqc.org . . . . American Productivity & Quality Center
http://www.nhmccd.edu/aqp/index.htm . . . . Association for Quality & Participation
http://www-caes.mit.edu/products/deming/home.html .The Deming Home Page
http://www.deming.org . . . . The W. Edwards Deming Institute
http://www.wineasy/se/qmp . . . . The Quality Management Principle Site
http://akao.larc.nasa.gov/dfc/qtec.html . . . . NASA Quality Pages
http://iosun.lanl.gov:2001/qp/qp.html . . . . Los Alamos National Laboratory Quality &
Planning Program Office
http://www.acq.osd.mil/es/std/stdhome/html . . . . Defense Standardization Program
http://www.npr.gov . . . . National Performance Review
http://ts.nist.gov/ts/htdocs/210/216/giqlp.htm . . . . Government/Industry Quality Liaison Panel
http://www.cqhq-hqcb.org . . . . Health Care Quality Certification Board
http://www.nahq.org . . . . National Association for Healthcare Quality
http://www.sae.org . . . . Society of Automotive Enginners
http://www.asnt.org . . . . American Society for Nondestructive Testing
http://www.aiag.org . . . . Automotive Industry Action Group

Many of the listed web sistes have links to other quality-related sites that can provide you with valuable information. If the information you need cannot be found on the above sites, try:

http://www.quality.org/qc ....Quality Resources Online
or
http://www.nicom.com/qadude/qualitylinks.html ....World of Quality Index

Index